Masterpieces from the
Peggy Guggenheim Collection

Masterpieces from the
Peggy Guggenheim Collection

GUGGENHEIM MUSEUM

© The Solomon R. Guggenheim Foundation,
New York, 1993
All rights reserved
ISBN 0–89207–112–5
Printed in Italy

Published by the Guggenheim Museum
1071 Fifth Avenue
New York, New York 10128

Design by Michelle Martino

All works of art reproduced in color were
photographed by David Heald

FOREWORD

The selection of works illustrated in this guide to the Peggy Guggenheim Collection has been based on several related considerations. The number of masterpieces in the collection's relatively small holdings is as high as in many a larger museum of Modern art. Furthermore, these outstanding works exemplify some of the major art movements of the first half of the twentieth century. The selection of works and the order in which they appear have been determined by both quality and the historical progress of the avant-garde, from Cubism to European abstraction in its various manifestations, Surrealism, and American Abstract Expressionism. Indeed, Peggy Guggenheim herself viewed the collection—foreseen from its inception as a museum of Modern art—as a presentation of Modernism's history. This notion of the museum collection as an encyclopedia of masterpieces, representing in its scope and depth the historical passage of a cultural period, has driven the collecting practices of most contemporary institutions. Yet clearly no museum can pretend to completeness. More interesting perhaps is the individuality of the collection and those elements specific to its historical development. In his essay for this publication, Philip Rylands describes the extraordinary role Peggy Guggenheim assumed as an art collector, and the decisive influences that determined her impressive personal collection. The presence of certain art works in this handbook—the paintings by Tancredi and Edmondo Bacci, for example, or the numerous examples of the work of Max Ernst and Jackson Pollock—reflect biographical and historical situations that informed Peggy's choices.

This publication relies for most of its text on entries by Lucy Flint and Elizabeth C. Childs that appeared in the 1983 and subsequent editions of *Handbook: The Peggy Guggenheim Collection*. The 1983 catalogue was the first to be published on the Peggy Guggenheim Collection under the administration of the Solomon R. Guggenheim Foundation, and it benefited from research undertaken by Angelica Zander Rudenstine for her award-winning catalogue raisonné of the collection, *Peggy Guggenheim Collection, Venice: The Solomon R. Guggenheim Foundation* (1985). We would like therefore to acknowledge the contributions of these authors, which in the case of Dr. Rudenstine's are monumental.

Many Guggenheim staff members lent their expertise to this project. The quality of the superb color images is the work of Photographer David Heald. Collections Curator Lisa Dennison assisted in the difficult selection of works, while Juliet Nations-Powell, Collections Curatorial Assistant, contributed valuable research. The efforts of Anthony Calnek, Managing Editor; Laura Morris, Assistant Editor; Beth Levy, Production Editor; and Jennifer Knox, Editorial Assistant, were essential to the production of this catalogue. We also wish to recognize the work of Philip Rylands, Deputy Director, Peggy Guggenheim Collection, who contributed enormously to the development of this project, and the able staff who manage the Venice museum.

The works of art illustrated herein all belonged to Peggy Guggenheim; it is therefore to her, and to the artists who created them, that this book is dedicated.

Thomas Krens

Director, The Solomon R. Guggenheim Foundation

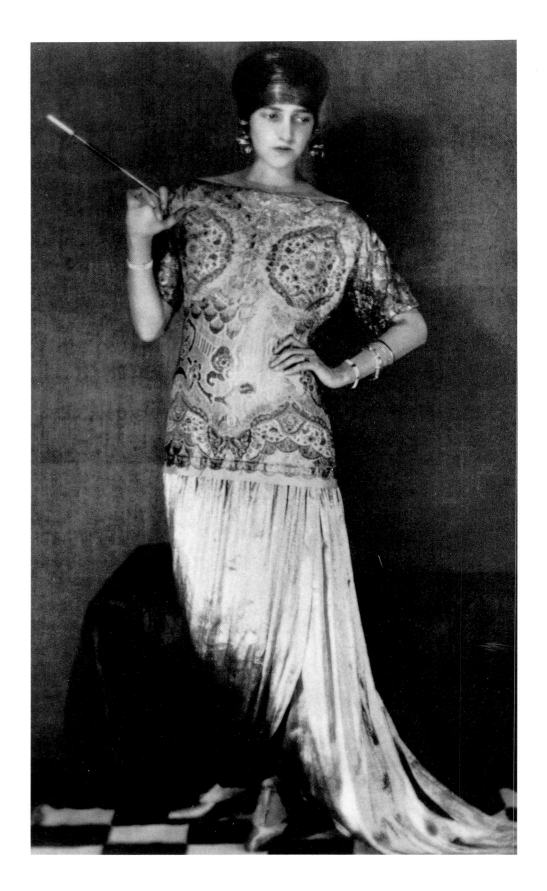

Peggy Guggenheim in a gold lamé dress with Oriental top by Paul Poiret and a headdress by Vera Stravinsky, photographed in Paris around 1924 by Man Ray. This image was published in 1925 in a Swedish magazine article about Paris socialites.

THE STORY OF A MUSEUM-COLLECTION

Philip Rylands

Peggy Guggenheim used to say that it was her duty to protect the art of her own time. She dedicated half of her life to this mission, as well as to the creation of the museum in Venice that still carries her name.

The Guggenheims

The Guggenheims originated in German-speaking Switzerland. An impoverished Simon Guggenheim, Peggy's great-grandfather, emigrated to Philadelphia in 1847. Beginning as peddlers, but soon producing stove polish and coffee essence, Simon and his son Meyer prospered. It was Meyer who was the architect of the family fortune. By 1880 he was a millionaire, thanks to his manufacturing and importation businesses, but the Guggenheims' really immense wealth came from metals. The fortune dated from Meyer's 1879 purchase of an interest in lead and silver mines in Leadville, Colorado. In 1900 the Guggenheims took control of the American Smelting and Refining Company, a legend in the history of American corporate capitalism. Beginning in 1907, in partnership with J. P. Morgan and Jacob Schiff, the Guggenheims forged a railroad through the tundra to mine Kennecott, a mountain in Alaska made up of about three-quarters pure copper. In 1910 the Guggenheims bought the Chuquicamata mine in Chile, which would yield 300 million tons of copper. By the beginning of World War I, the Guggenheims were reported to own between 75 and 80 percent of the world's silver, copper, and lead.

Born in 1898, Peggy Guggenheim was the second daughter of Benjamin Guggenheim, Meyer's sixth child, but her share in the family fortune was to be a modest one. Benjamin, the handsomest of Meyer's sons, was something of a playboy. He petulantly left the family business in 1901. Therefore, when he drowned on the *Titanic* in April 1912 (his dignified, even heroic behavior forms part of the *Titanic* legend), Peggy and her mother, Florette Seligman, found themselves mere spectators as the vast riches of the Guggenheims grew and grew.[1]

Hence, Peggy never had unlimited funds. During the spring of 1939, when she was planning her museum in London, Peggy recalled, "I tried to think of ways to cut down my own personal expenses, in order to have sufficient money for the project. . . . Actually I did not have nearly enough money for this venture as I had commitments of about ten thousand dollars a year to various old friends and artists whom I had been supporting for years. I could not suddenly let them down for the museum. . . . Every penny that I could raise was to be used for the museum."[2] Peggy's commitment to art required some of the qualities handed down by her grandfather Meyer—determination and imagination. She called upon those qualities as she set out to create a museum of contemporary art.

Guggenheim Jeune

Peggy's career in Modern art began in January 1938, when she opened the Guggenheim Jeune gallery in London. Her friend Samuel Beckett insisted that she show contemporary art because it was "a living thing." Marcel Duchamp taught her, as she put it, "the difference between Abstract and Surrealist art," and introduced her to the artists.[3] Although she professed ignorance about art, it is clear that she enjoyed an important advantage: since her arrival in Europe in 1921 she had lived among intellectuals and artists in England and France. Her first husband, Laurence Vail, whom she married in 1922, was a Dada sculptor and collage artist; more important, he introduced her to that world.

The first show at Guggenheim Jeune was a presentation of Jean Cocteau's drawings and furniture for his play *The Knights of the Round Table*. The British press mistakenly described the opening as a Surrealist event. Furthermore, Peggy had to do battle with British customs, which objected to the nudity in one of Cocteau's works. Peggy found herself the focus of shocked attention and controversy.

That exhibition was followed, at Duchamp's suggestion, by the first showing in England of the art of Vasily Kandinsky. The work attracted considerable interest; for example, art schools in Gloucester and Bristol asked to borrow the paintings for exhibitions. Peggy bought a painting for herself, *Dominant Curve*, a magnificent work of 1936 that now belongs to the Solomon R. Guggenheim Museum.

Peggy could not have predicted that contemporary sculptures by Jean Arp, Constantin Brancusi, Antoine Pevsner, and others would be blocked in customs on the way from Paris for a show opening in April at her gallery. The director of the Tate Gallery, James B. Manson, declined to certify the sculptures as art. The faculty of Chelsea Polytechnic, which included Henry Moore and Graham

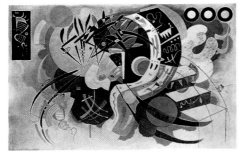

Vasily Kandinsky, *Dominant Curve (Courbe dominante)*, April 1936. Oil on canvas, 129.4 x 194.2 cm. Solomon R. Guggenheim Museum, 45.989.

Sutherland, wrote complaints to *The Daily Telegraph*; others accused Manson of Fascism (this incident took place only months before the Nazis' auctions of "degenerate art" in Germany), and the case was taken up in the House of Commons. But Peggy was to win, and thus, in a way directly parallel to the notorious trial in New York in 1928 over whether Brancusi's *Bird in Space* constituted a work of art, she had a hand in changing regulations and attitudes toward avant-garde art.

Meanwhile Duchamp had introduced Peggy to Arp, and for sheer pleasure she bought from him a small, polished-brass sculpture, *Head and Shell*, which remains in the Peggy Guggenheim Collection, the earliest of her purchases to have survived her compulsive gifts. In July 1938 she gave Yves Tanguy an exhibition, her one financial success and the debut of Surrealism in her art career. She bought *The Sun in Its Jewel Case* (cat. no. 62) from her own show. Such purchases—sometimes made anonymously from her own gallery to gratify disappointed exhibitors—preceded Peggy's conscious decision to form an art collection.

By March 1939 Peggy was tiring of her gallery. She had lost, she counted, £600, and resolved instead to open a museum of contemporary art in London. In a recent biography of Herbert Read this was referred to as her "whim of iron."[4] That crucial moment points to something fundamental about Peggy's collection, for although she had bought some works as a consequence of Guggenheim Jeune, her collection was conceived as a museum.

In view of the importance of her decision it is interesting to speculate how she came to make it. Peggy herself was matter-of-fact: "I felt that if I was losing that money I might as well lose a lot more and do something worthwhile."[5] An incident that occurred twelve months earlier may have been in the back of her mind. At Kandinsky's suggestion, Peggy had offered to sell one of his paintings, *Red Spot 2*, to her uncle Solomon. She received a stinging reply from Hilla Rebay, Solomon's artistic adviser, chastising her for dealing in art under the name Guggenheim. Rebay also wrote, "If you are interested in non-objective art you can well afford to buy it and start a collection. . . . You can leave a fine collection to your country if you know how to chose [sic]."[6]

Peggy had met Read at that time; she supplied him with materials for an article on Kandinsky for *The Listener*. At some point Read showed Peggy an unpublished essay he had written in 1937, "Proposals for a Scottish

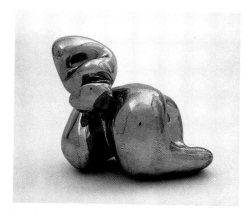

Jean Arp, *Head and Shell* (*Tête et coquille*), ca. 1933. Bronze, 19.7 cm high. Peggy Guggenheim Collection, 76.2553 PG54.

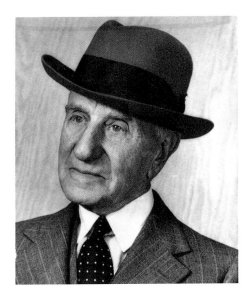

Peggy's uncle, Solomon R. Guggenheim.

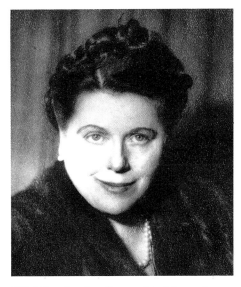

Hilla Rebay, founding director of the Solomon R. Guggenheim Museum.

Philanthropist," in which he envisioned a combined Bauhaus and Kunsthalle in Edinburgh. In 1935 he had been involved in a plan by Ben Nicholson to create a Museum of Living Art. When, therefore, Peggy proposed that he leave *The Burlington Magazine*, of which he was editor, to become director of her future museum, she clearly struck a chord, appealing to Read's idealistic belief that art was an antidote to war, a palliative or healer. Finally, it is worth remembering that the Museum of Modern Art in New York came about in 1929 through the alliance of three heiresses and Alfred H. Barr, Jr.; it is possible that Read and Peggy, separately, thought of themselves as followers of that precedent.

Read was the best choice that Peggy could have made. A firm friend of Naum Gabo, Barbara Hepworth, Ben Nicholson, Roland Penrose, and the Surrealists (he wrote a catalogue essay for their 1936 London exhibition), Read was a nonpartisan critic. His books, such as *Art Now* and *The Meaning of Art*, both published in the early 1930s, did much to open English eyes to contemporary European art, and they continue to be widely read.

The fact that Peggy, encouraged by Read and Duchamp, collected Cubist, abstract, and Surrealist art with equal determination is one of the remarkable features of her collection: it endows it with a comprehensiveness, an encompassing quality, that no other collection of the time has. We owe this above all to Peggy's capacity to surround herself with extraordinarily privileged and well-informed advisers. To Duchamp and Read should be added Nellie van Doesburg (widow of Theo van Doesburg) as well as a remarkable young man by the name of Howard Putzel. Putzel was a dealer from California with a gift for perceiving quality and innovation in contemporary art. In the early 1930s he had promoted European art at his West Coast gallery. In 1938 he moved to Europe and befriended Peggy.

The London museum was, however, ill-fated. Read wrote to Kenneth Clark and Penrose asking them to join Peggy and him as trustees. They planned to open the museum in Clark's house on Portland Place. But World War II intervened, and in any case Peggy did not feel ready. She amicably dissolved her contract with Read, and the funds that had been put aside for operating the museum were diverted to the purchasing of art.

With a list drawn up by Read for what would have been the inaugural exhibition of the London museum—a list revised by Duchamp, Nellie van Doesburg, Putzel, and Peggy herself—Peggy brought together, between 1939 and

1942, while in London, Paris, and New York, over 170 works of Modern European art. These were included in her first catalogue, published in 1942, to which André Breton contributed extensive research and an introduction. Most of those works are still in the Peggy Guggenheim Collection.

Art of This Century

In July 1941 Peggy fled Nazi-occupied France and returned to her native New York together with Max Ernst, who was to become her second husband, albeit briefly, a few months later. In October 1942 she opened a museum-gallery at 30 West Fifty-seventh Street in New York City and called it Art of This Century. The opening party was the occasion for a symbolic gesture: Peggy wore one earring created by Alexander Calder and one by Tanguy to demonstrate her impartiality between abstraction and Surrealism. This combining of the disparate trends was also manifest in the design of the gallery itself and in the installation of her collection.

Peggy had entrusted the project to Frederick Kiesler, the Austrian-American architect and sculptor. Kiesler, drawing on ideas that had been germinating since 1924, set out to unify the work of art with its spatial environment and to eliminate the barrier between the world of the object and that of the viewer (embodied most obviously in the picture frame, which he and Peggy banned from the installation). His solution was startling and quickly made Art of This Century the most exciting venue in New York for seeing contemporary art. The Cubist and abstract art was displayed in a blue-floored room with undulating blue canvas covering its walls. Paintings were hung on triangular suspension columns. The floating and transparent effect approximated the pictorial space we associate with Cubist and abstract painting. In the next gallery Surrealist art works hung on jointed wooden spokes, extruding from curved wood walls. A wire recording of the roar of an express train added an element of terror, while the lighting system, which turned on and off at regular intervals in the tunnel-like space, was intended to give the sensation of the pulse of one's own blood. Biomorphic wooden furniture, designed and even constructed by Kiesler, doubled as both chairs and bases for art in these galleries.

A third gallery was designed to display Peggy's paintings by Paul Klee, one work by Breton, and Duchamp's *Box in a Valise*. Seven paintings by Klee were

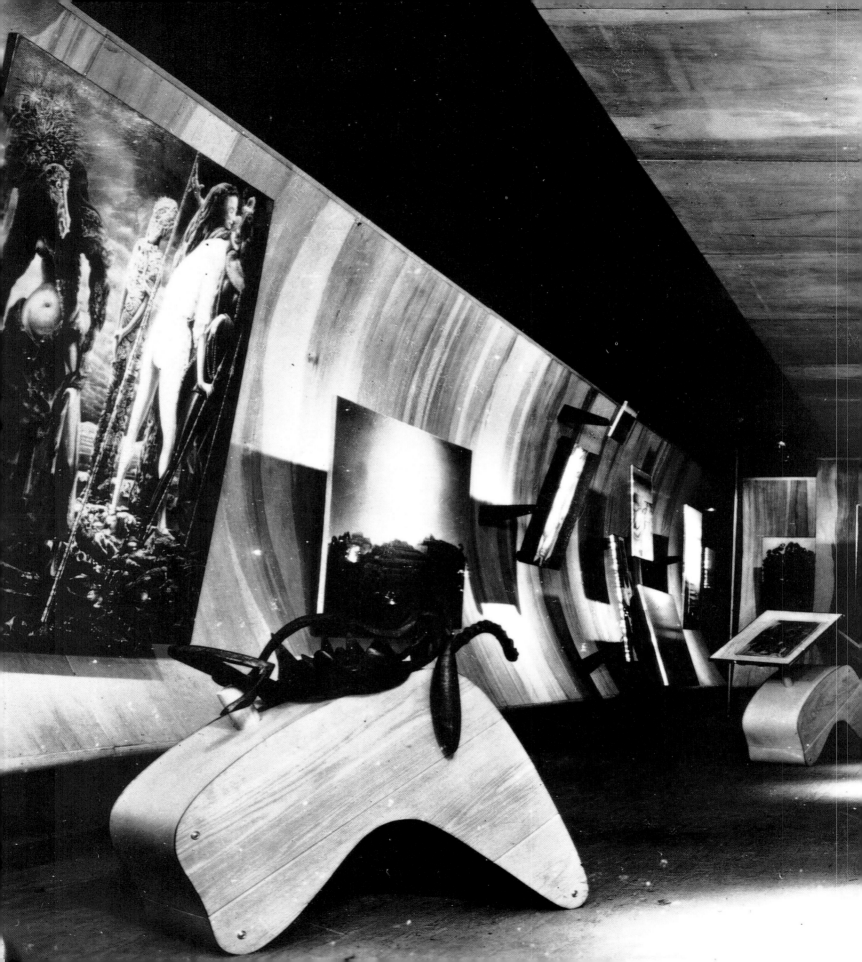

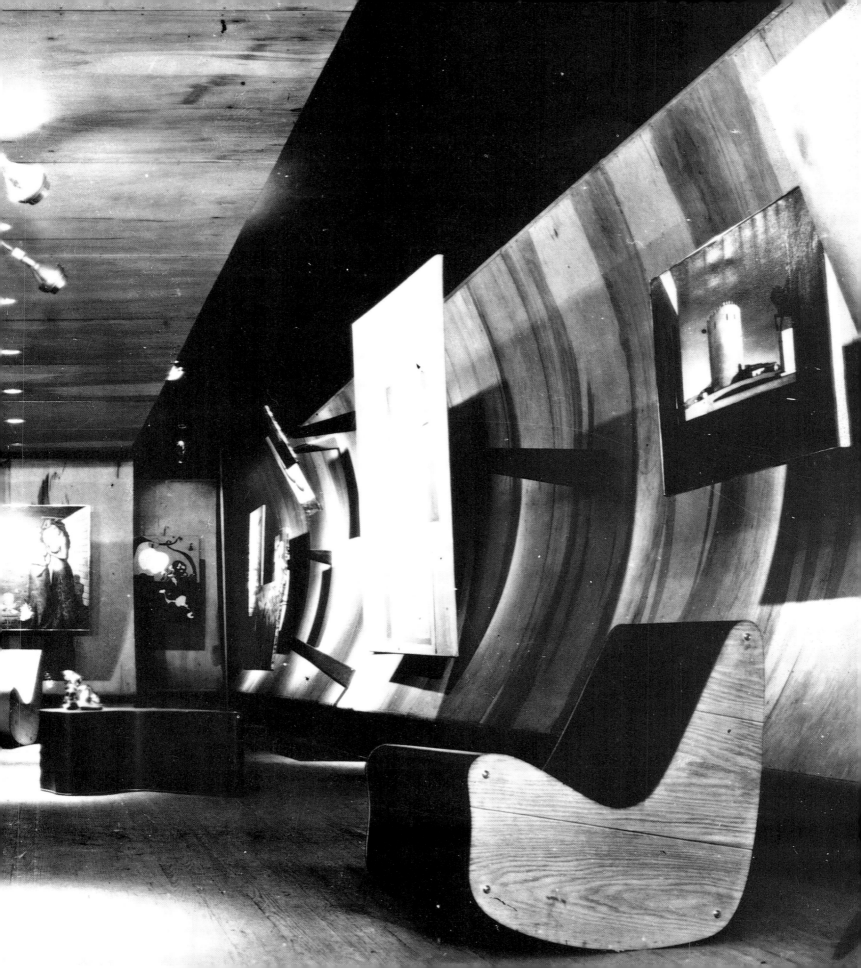

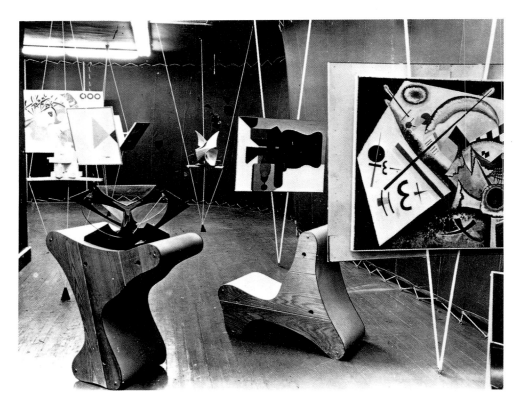

(Preceding two pages) Installation view of Surrealist art in Art of This Century, photographed by Berenice Abbott.

(Right) Installation view of Cubist and abstract art in Art of This Century, Peggy Guggenheim's New York gallery designed by Frederick Kiesler, photographed around 1942 by Berenice Abbott. In the background toward the left is Kandinsky's *Dominant Curve* (1936).

placed on a revolving wheel, which was set in motion when a visitor passed in front of an electric eye. The visitor looked through a peephole to view the *Valise*, which contained Duchamp's *oeuvre complète* in miniature, and turned the large, spidery wheel to bring each of its images into view. Peggy was the unwitting purveyor of a premonition of Duchamp's last work, *Etants donnés* (now in the collection of the Philadelphia Museum of Art), which places the viewer in a similarly voyeuristic posture. Peggy wrote, "The press named this part of the gallery Coney Island."[7] Temporary exhibitions of work by the European avant-garde and young Americans took place in another gallery.

Jackson Pollock

The thirty-two-year-old Jackson Pollock was introduced to Peggy in the spring of 1943 by Putzel, although it may have been Piet Mondrian who convinced her of Pollock's exceptional talent. In July 1943 Peggy began helping Pollock with monthly payments, enabling him to dedicate himself solely to painting. (She was to continue doing so until 1948.) Peggy's influence on Pollock's life was manifold. Before her support he had rarely exhibited, let alone sold any paintings. She spurred him to new challenges—beginning with collage and going on to *Mural* of

December 1943, his largest work, which she commissioned for her house (now in the collection of the Museum of Art of the University of Iowa). In November 1943 she gave Pollock his first solo exhibition, which included *The Moon Woman* (cat. no. 73), an early painting still in the Peggy Guggenheim Collection. James Johnson Sweeney wrote an enthusiastic preface to the catalogue of the show and Clement Greenberg immediately began placing him in the historical context of American art. Barr later bought from Peggy *The She-Wolf* for the Museum of Modern Art; it was the first Pollock to enter a public collection. Furthermore, the presence of Peggy's paintings at Art of This Century was in itself a stimulus, the Picassos and Mirós directly influencing Pollock's production.

Guided by Putzel, Peggy gave exhibitions to several other emerging American artists: William Baziotes, David Hare, Robert Motherwell, Mark Rothko, and Clyfford Still, for example. Americans were able to see work by the European avant-garde in Peggy's gallery and sometimes to meet the artists themselves at Peggy's New York house. In this way Peggy nurtured Abstract Expressionism and forged links between European art, whether Surrealist or abstract, and the new generation of Americans. The impact of Art of This Century and Peggy Guggenheim on the New York scene was such that her collection takes on the character of a historical document. It can be seen as a piece of history—both as a record of events in New York between 1942 and 1947 and as a force acting to influence them.[8]

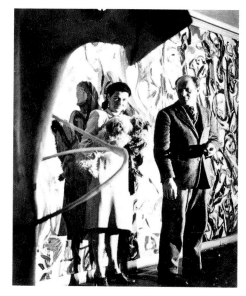

Peggy Guggenheim and Jackson Pollock, standing in front of the mural that Peggy commissioned in 1943 for her New York apartment. Photo by Mirko Lion, courtesy Eugene V. Thaw Archive.

Venice

In 1947 Peggy resolved to return to Europe. She convinced Betty Parsons to take on Pollock at her gallery, and went to Venice in search of a house. On the invitation of Rodolfo Pallucchini she displayed her collection at the 1948 Venice Biennale. In this way the works of artists such as Arshile Gorky, Pollock, and Rothko were exhibited for the first time in Europe.[9] The presence of Cubist, abstract, and Surrealist art made the Greek Pavilion, where her collection was installed, the most coherent survey of Modernism to have been presented anywhere in Italy to date. Peggy was flattered by the attention she was receiving. In 1941 she had left Europe anonymously as a private and arguably eccentric person. By 1947 she had become a celebrity.

In 1949 Peggy bought the unfinished Palazzo Venier dei Leoni: a long, wide

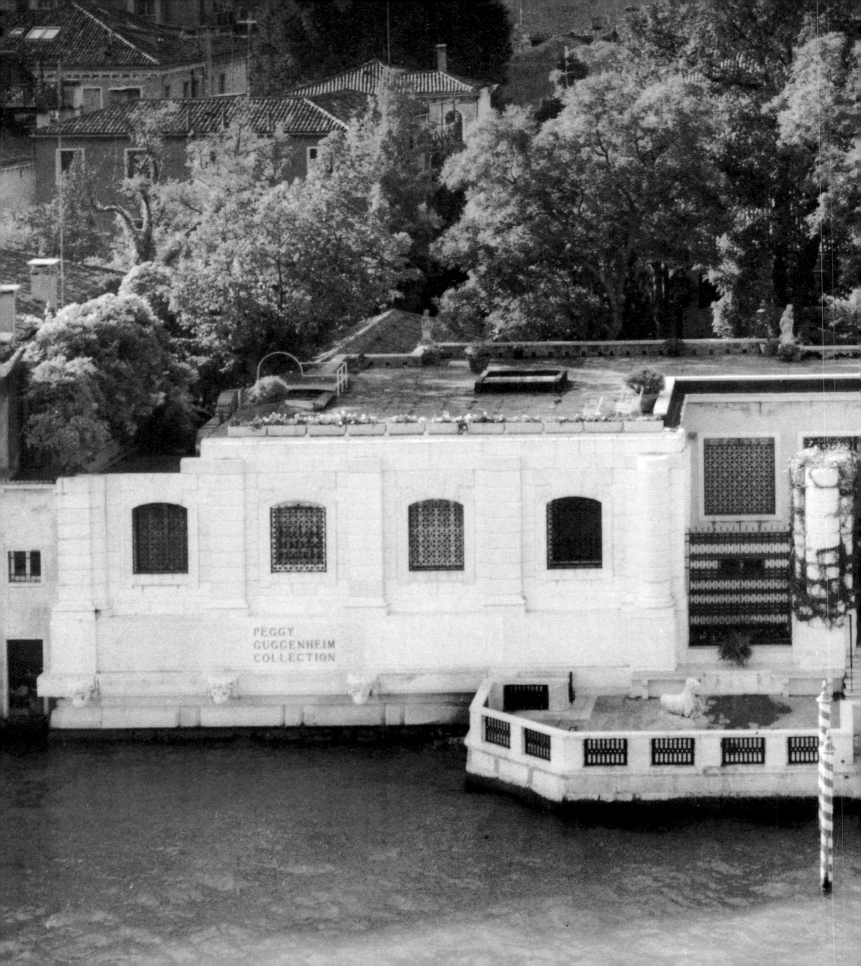

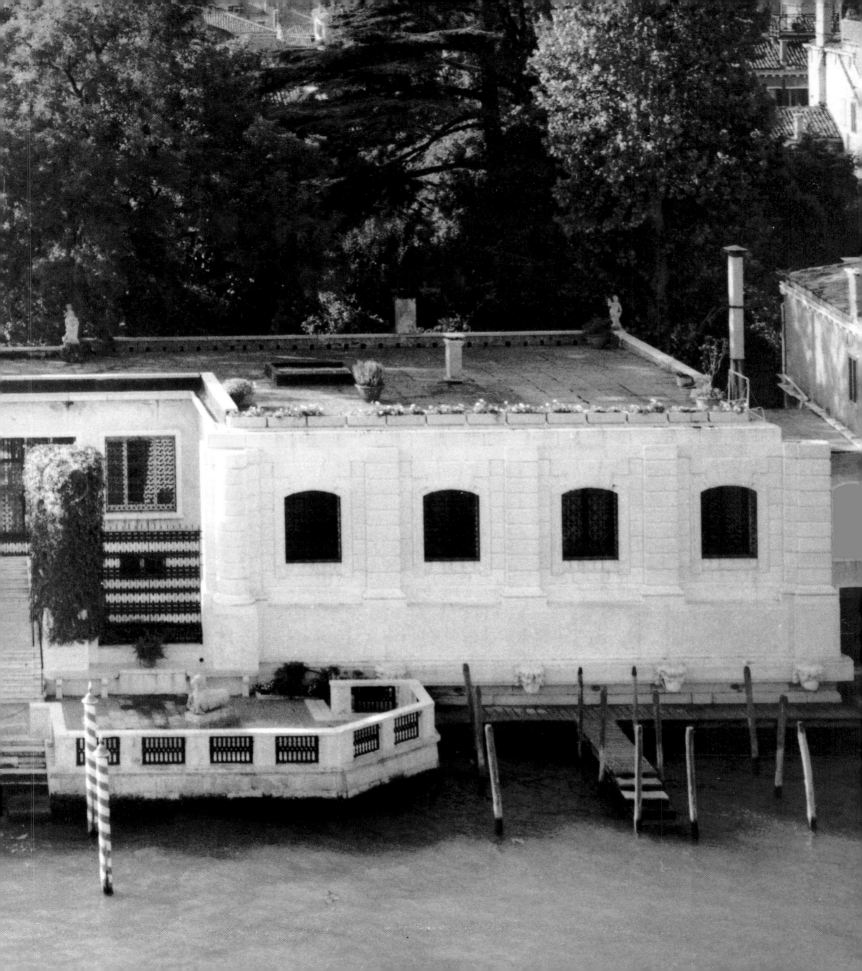

building with only a basement and ground floor, on the Grand Canal near the Salute. Begun in the mid-eighteenth century by architect Lorenzo Boschetti, it was left unfinished probably because of litigation with a neighboring family, whose Gothic palace suffered structural damage during building at the Palazzo Venier.[10] The nickname *dei Leoni* refers to the outsize stone lion heads on the façade, and gave rise to the legend that a lion was once kept in the garden. The building may have been made habitable only in this century. In the 1910s and 1920s Marchesa Casati, muse of Gabriele D'Annunzio and hostess to the Ballets Russes, threw parties in the palazzo. Peggy bought it from the heirs of Doris Viscountess Castlerosse, who lived there in the late 1930s.

After the Venice Biennale, Peggy was invited to travel her collection to the Palazzo Strozzi in Florence and the Palazzo Reale in Milan. In 1950 she showed her entire collection of eighteen paintings by Pollock (as well as two others that she had already given to the Stedelijk Museum, Amsterdam) at the Museo Correr, Venice. This coincided with Pollock's debut in the U.S. Pavilion at the Venice Biennale, but only three works by him were shown there—preeminence was accorded instead to an older artist, John Marin. As in 1948 Peggy proved herself to be a generation ahead of the Biennale.

She wrote that seeing Pollock's paintings through the windows of the Museo Correr from Piazza San Marco confirmed to her the greatness of his work. She later came to regret her numerous donations to art museums around the world, which she had made to promote the appreciation of Pollock's work and that of other Abstract Expressionists whose work she had collected.[11]

Peggy was to live the rest of her life in Venice, where she finally realized her ambition to open a museum of contemporary art. She continued to buy art from time to time; the postwar European art in her collection testifies to this. Her patronage of artists focused on two young Venetian abstract painters, Tancredi and Edmondo Bacci. By the early 1960s, however, her distaste for Pop art, as well as the steeply rising prices of contemporary art, brought her collecting to an end. She became interested above all in the presentation of the major movements so majestically represented in her collection—Cubism, European abstraction, Surrealism, and early Abstract Expressionism—and she became anxious to find a way to guarantee the future of the museum she had created.

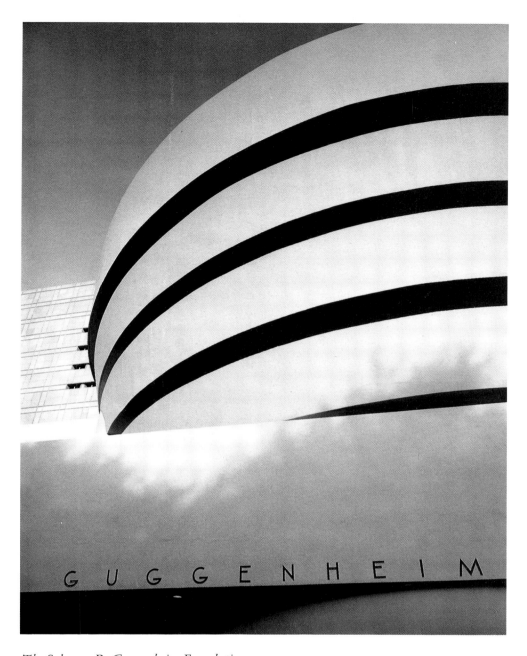

The Solomon R. Guggenheim Foundation

Peggy enthusiastically lent her collection to other museums, among them the Stedelijk Museum, Amsterdam (1950), the Kunsthaus Zürich (1951), the Tate Gallery, London (1964), the Moderna Museet, Stockholm, and the Louisiana Museum, Humlebaek, Denmark (both 1966), and the Civica Galleria d'Arte Moderna, Turin (1967). In the catalogue of her collection when it was shown at the Orangerie in Paris in 1974, Peggy wrote of her pleasure at seeing her paintings and sculptures installed in a museum environment.

Peggy Guggenheim, in her Venice home, ca. 1970.
Photo by Roloff Beny.

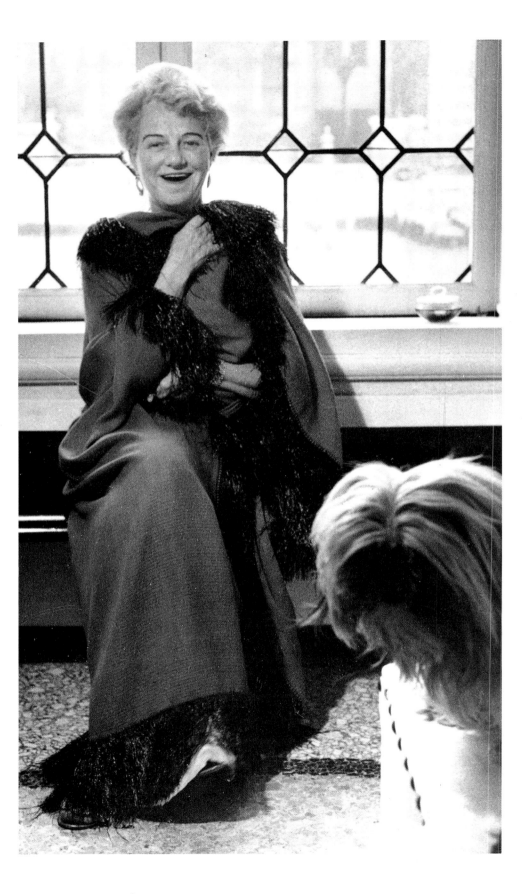

In 1969 the Solomon R. Guggenheim Museum invited Peggy to exhibit her collection in New York, and it was on this occasion that she resolved to donate her palazzo and art collection to the Solomon R. Guggenheim Foundation. She wrote, "I was like someone who was longing to be proposed to by someone who was longing to marry her."[12] She asked only that the collection remain in Venice and continue to be opened to the public during the summers. Although the gift was accomplished during Peggy Guggenheim's lifetime, it was not until her death at the end of 1979 that the foundation established by her uncle took on the management and full responsibility for the collection.[13]

The Solomon R. Guggenheim Foundation dates from 1937, and in 1939 Solomon's museum, directed by Hilla Rebay, opened in New York as the Museum of Non-Objective Painting. Solomon died in 1949, and the museum was renamed in his memory in 1952. Frank Lloyd Wright's famous spiral structure on Fifth Avenue opened in 1959, and the Solomon R. Guggenheim Museum has been housed there ever since. The foundation now operates two museums in Manhattan (the Solomon R. Guggenheim Museum and the Guggenheim Museum SoHo) and the Peggy Guggenheim Collection in Venice. Although the Guggenheim collections were formed independently, they nevertheless contain many comparable works by the same key figures of twentieth-century art. Together the Guggenheim collections form one of the most important holdings of Modern art in the world.

NOTES

1. For information about the Guggenheim family see John H. Davis, *The Guggenheims (1848–1988): An American Epic* (New York: Shapolsky Publishers Inc., 1988).

2. Peggy Guggenheim, *Out of This Century: Confessions of an Art Addict* (New York: Universe Books, 1979, and London: André Deutsch, 1979, reprinted 1992), pp. 196–97.

3. Guggenheim, *Out of This Century*, p. 161.

4. James King, *The Last Modern: A Life of Herbert Read* (London: Weidenfeld and Nicolson, 1990), p. 178.

5. Guggenheim, *Out of This Century*, p. 196.

6. Ibid., p. 171.

7. Ibid., p. 275.

8. The importance and history of Art of This Century is most fully explored in an unpublished Ph.D. dissertation by Melvin P. Lader, "Peggy Guggenheim's Art of This Century: The Surrealist Milieu and the American Avant-Garde, 1942–1947," University of Delaware, 1981.

9. Single works by some of these artists were included in the 1948 Biennale's U.S. Pavilion, the opening of which was delayed until one month after the installation containing Peggy's collection.

10. The mystery of why Palazzo Venier dei Leoni was left unfinished is explored in Paul H. D. Kaplan, Harry B. Titus, Jr., and Barbara J. Williams, *Palazzo Venier and Casa Artom: A Brief History of a Venetian Site* (Winston-Salem, North Carolina: Wake Forest University, 1984). The Palazzo Venier named in that book is the unfortunate Gothic palace next door, which was torn down and replaced by the present building, the former U.S. Consulate.

11. Some of Peggy's gifts to other museums were documented in the exhibition *Peggy Guggenheim's Other Legacy*, held at the Solomon R. Guggenheim Museum and then at the Peggy Guggenheim Collection in 1987 and 1988. The catalogue includes essays by Melvin P. Lader, "Peggy Guggenheim's 'Art of This Century,'" and by Fred Licht, "Peggy Guggenheim's Donations."

12. Guggenheim, *Out of This Century*, p. 371.

13. Prior to Peggy's death, the Solomon R. Guggenheim Foundation sponsored a catalogue raisonné. Published in 1985, it is the standard scholarly work about the collection: Angelica Zander Rudenstine, *Peggy Guggenheim Collection, Venice: The Solomon R. Guggenheim Foundation* (New York: Harry N. Abrams, 1985). It also includes extensive documentation of Peggy's galleries, Guggenheim Jeune and Art of This Century.

Please note that in the catalogue entries
the following abbreviations are used:

Authors
E.C.C.   Elizabeth C. Childs
L.F.   Lucy Flint

Publications
Rudenstine
Angelica Zander Rudenstine, *Peggy Guggenheim*
Collection, Venice: The Solomon R. Guggenheim
Foundation, New York, 1985

These entries were originally published in *Handbook:*
The Peggy Guggenheim Collection, New York, 1983, and
Handbook: Peggy Guggenheim Collection, New York,
1986. However, some titles of works and technical
information have been revised.

Dimensions are given in centimeters; height precedes
width, followed by depth when relevant.

CATALOGUE

PABLO PICASSO

The Poet (Le Poète), August 1911

Oil on linen canvas, 131.2 x 89.5 cm
76.2553 PG 1

Like *The Accordionist* in the collection of the Solomon R. Guggenheim Museum, *The Poet* was painted during the summer of 1911, when Pablo Picasso was working in close association with Georges Braque in the French Pyrenees town of Céret. Similar in style and composition to Braque's contemporaneous *Man with a Guitar* (Collection The Museum of Modern Art, New York), this canvas epitomizes the moment in the development of Analytic Cubism when the degree of abstraction was so extreme that objects in the painting are almost unrecognizable.

As the title indicates, it is the human form that has been visually dissected and reconstructed as an architecture of rectilinear and curvilinear elements. Despite the elusiveness of the visual clues, the viewer can detect a densely articulated central pyramidal figure fused coloristically and texturally with the less detailed ground. The small circle at the upper center of the canvas penetrated by the acme of a triangular plane becomes an eye when associated with the longer, broader plane of a possible nose and the crescents of a probable mustache. Once this recognition occurs, a complete image can be reconstituted by the inference of chin, pipe, neck, attenuated torso, elbows, and chair arms.

Picasso presents multiple views of each object, as if he had moved around it, and synthesizes them into a single compound image. The fragmentation of the image encourages a reading of abstract rather than representational form. The imagined volumes of figure and object dissolve into non-objective organizations of line, plane, light, and color. Interpenetrating facets of forms floating in a shallow, indeterminate space are defined and shaded by luminous, hatched, almost Neo-Impressionist brushstrokes. The continuity of certain lines through these facets creates an illusion of a system of larger planes that also float in this indefinite space yet are securely anchored within an architectonic structure. The chromatic sobriety characteristic of works by Picasso and Braque of this period corresponds with the cerebral nature of the issues they address. (L. F.)

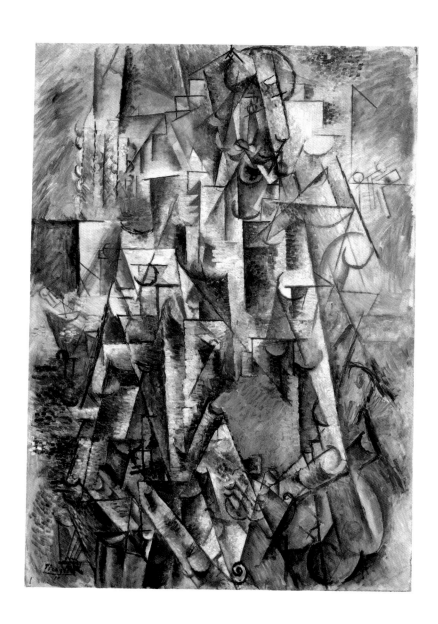

PABLO PICASSO

Pipe, Glass, Bottle of Vieux Marc (*Pipe, verre, bouteille de Vieux Marc*), spring 1914

Paper collage, charcoal, india ink, printer's ink, graphite, and gouache on canvas, 73.2 x 59.4 cm
76.2553 PG 2

After fragmenting representational form almost to the point of extinction in 1911 (see cat. no. 1), the following year Pablo Picasso and Georges Braque reintroduced more legible imagery, usually derived from the environment of studio or café. Without abandoning all devices of Analytic Cubism, they developed a new idiom, referred to as Synthetic Cubism, in which they built their compositions with broader, flatter, and chromatically more varied planes. In the summer of 1912 Braque produced the first papier collé, in which cut paper is glued to the support and used as a compositional element. In the present example Picasso's pasted papers include printed material—a piece of wallpaper and the January 1, 1914, issue of *Lacerba*, a Futurist magazine founded in Florence in 1913. These elements mimic their functions in the external world and therefore introduce a new level of reality into the picture. The printed papers appear to be integrated into the pictorial space rather than lying flat on the surface. A transparent plane outlined in chalk appears to penetrate the newspaper and the guitar seems to cast a shadow on it; the actual physical presence of the wallpaper is similarly contradicted by the addition of drawing.

The treatment of other collaged papers multiplies meaning. In the case of the pipe or table leg, the cutout itself defines the contour of the object and is modeled accordingly with chalk. Penciled indications of other objects, such as the guitar or glass, ignore the shape of the pasted paper, which acts as both a support and a compositional element. The opacity of the collage materials is refuted and the transparency of the object depicted is upheld when Picasso discloses parts of the guitar behind the glass. On the other hand, a piece of *Lacerba* remains visible through the guitar, which in reality is opaque. Not only does each object have a multiple nature, but its relations in space to other objects are changeable and contradictory. The table assuredly occupies a space between the wall and the picture plane; its collaged corner overlaps a portion of wallpaper and its visible leg obscures part of a baseboard molding. Yet the depth of this space is indeterminate, as the tabletop has reared up so that it is parallel to the picture plane. The respective situations in space of the still-life subjects are equally equivocal—the silhouette of the bottle of Vieux Marc simultaneously obscures and is obscured by the guitar. (L. F.)

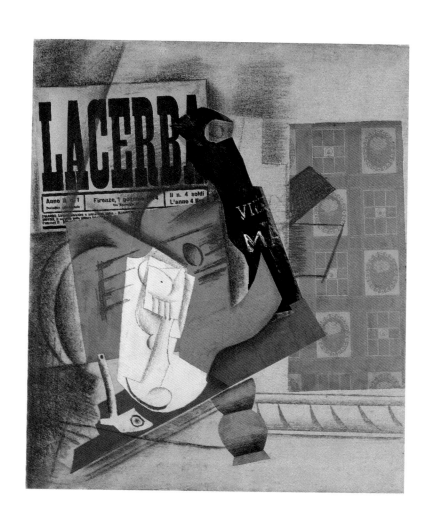

PABLO PICASSO

The Studio (L'Atelier), 1928

Oil and black crayon on canvas, 161.6 x 129.9 cm
76.2553 PG 3

From 1927 to 1929 Pablo Picasso elaborated a complex discourse on the activity of the artist through the theme of the studio. Among the variations in the series, the closest to the present example is *The Studio* of 1927–28 (Collection The Museum of Modern Art, New York; repr. Rudenstine, p. 620, fig. c). Both works share the vivid palette of Synthetic Cubism, limited to draw attention to a conspicuous and authoritative execution in planar areas. This painterliness contrasts with the geometrized, wirelike contours that define the figures in the manner of Picasso's contemporaneous wire sculpture.

The figures in the Guggenheim *The Studio* can be identified as a sculptured bust (at the left) and a full-length painted portrait (to the right). By depicting artistic representations of humans in a highly schematized form, Picasso places the figures at several removes from the world of living beings. He relies on the viewer's willingness to believe in the reality of depicted objects, however abstract, and to imagine a human exchange or relationship between the male and female forms. Like the artist in the Museum of Modern Art version, the bust has three eyes; this may reflect Picasso's personal identification with the work of art.

Picasso's development of the theme of the artist's perception of himself and his subjects can be traced from his etching of 1927 *Painter with a Model Knitting*, in which a realistically drawn artist paints a fantastic and abstract portrait of a very ordinary woman. The artist becomes an abstract sign in *The Studio* at the Museum of Modern Art and disappears, or is at least submerged, in *The Studio* in the Peggy Guggenheim Collection. He reappears in *Painter and Model*, also of 1928 (Collection The Museum of Modern Art, New York), as a figure that is even more difficult to detect, yet nonetheless is engaged in painting a relatively realistic profile. The theme of the interaction of reality and illusion explored here was a central concern for Picasso throughout his life. (L. F.)

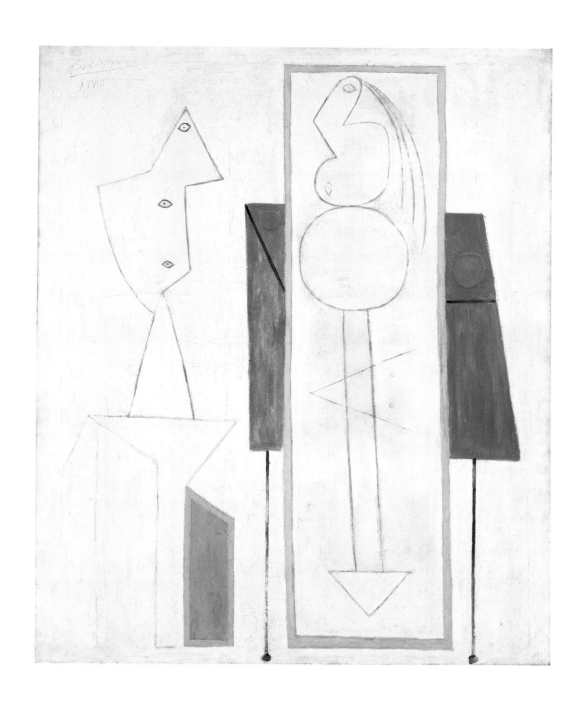

PABLO PICASSO

On the Beach (*La Baignade*), February 12, 1937
Oil, conté crayon, and chalk on canvas, 129.1 x 194 cm
76.2553 PG 5

During the early months of 1937 Pablo Picasso was responding powerfully to the Spanish Civil War with the preparatory drawings for *Guernica* (Collection Museo Nacional del Prado, Madrid) and with etchings such as *The Dream and Lie of Franco*, an example of which is in the Peggy Guggenheim Collection. However, in this period he also executed a group of works that do not betray this preoccupation with political events. The subject of *On the Beach*, also known as *Girls with a Toy Boat*, specifically recalls Picasso's *Three Bathers* of 1920 (Collection Stephen Hahn, New York). Painted at Le Tremblay-sur-Mauldre near Versailles, *On the Beach* is one of several paintings in which he returns to the ossified, volumetric forms in beach environments that appeared in his works of the late 1920s and early 1930s. *On the Beach* can be compared with Henri Matisse's *Le Luxe, II*, ca. 1907–08 (Collection Statens Museum for Kunst, Copenhagen), in its simplified, planar style and in the poses of the foreground figures. It is plausible that the arcadian themes of his friendly rival Matisse would appeal to Picasso as an alternative to the violent images of war he was conceiving at the time.

At least two preparatory drawings have been identified for this work. In one (Collection Musée Picasso, Paris; repr. Rudenstine, p. 625), the male figure looming on the horizon has a sinister appearance. In the other drawing (present whereabouts unknown),[1] as in the finished version, his mien is softened and neutralized to correspond with the features of the two female figures. The sense of impotent voyeurism conveyed as he gazes at the fertile, exaggeratedly sexual "girls" calls to mind the myth of Diana caught unawares at her bath. (L. F.)

1. Reproduced in C. Zervos, *Pablo Picasso*, Paris, 1957, vol. 8, no. 343.

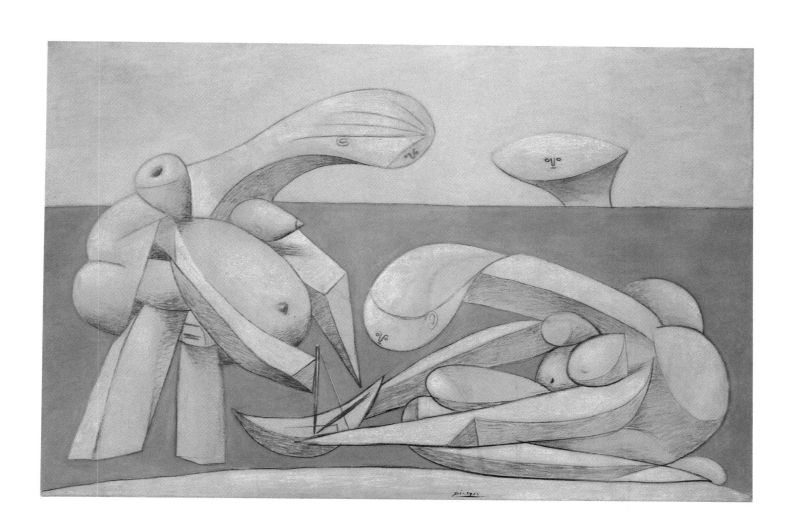

GEORGES BRAQUE

The Clarinet (*La Clarinette*), summer–fall 1912

Oil with sand on oval canvas, 91.4 x 64.5 cm
76.2553 PG 7

The Clarinet was probably executed in the late summer of 1912, during the waning moments of Analytic Cubism. Characteristic of this period are the oval format, which frees the canvas from the stringencies of corners, the appearance of letters within the image, and the use of imitation wood grain as trompe l'oeil (a technique Georges Braque introduced into the Cubist repertory). The image is paler and less strongly articulated than that of Pablo Picasso's *The Poet* of the previous summer (cat. no. 1); the structure of planes is more compact and produces a shallower picture space. The planes, because they are more consistently parallel to the picture plane than before, suggest the flat surfaces of papier collé. Braque's incorporation of sand into certain areas of his pigment, an innovation of this transitional period, enhances the differentiation of surfaces created by the variations of brushstrokes and increases the subtleties of coloration. The use of sand accords with Braque's conviction that tactile qualities define space. Despite this emphasis on materiality the image remains evanescent. The paradoxical combination of tangible presence and elusive, palpitating abstraction is embodied in the contrasting handling of clarinet and guitar: the clarinet is shown almost complete, the guitar is fragmented into pieces that emerge here and there throughout the composition. (L. F.)

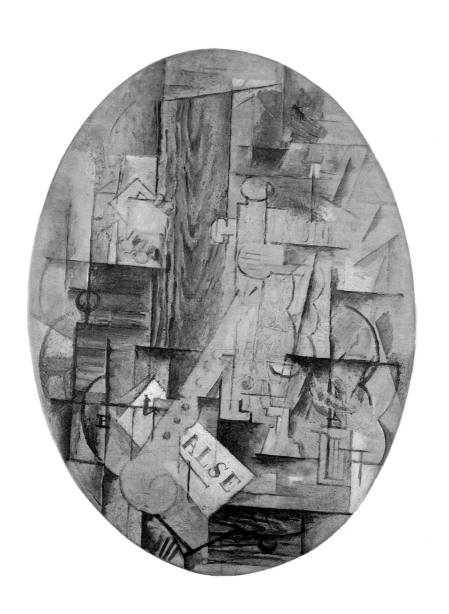

GEORGES BRAQUE

The Bowl of Grapes (*Le Compotier de raisins*), 1926
Oil with pebbles and sand on canvas, 100 x 80.8 cm
76.2553 PG 8

After his return from military service in 1917 Georges Braque, working independently of Pablo Picasso, developed the subjects and style of his prewar period. His use of collage in the teens provided formal innovations in paintings of the twenties. In still lifes such as the present example, he constructed objects with broad, frontal planes that remain discrete and are often vividly colored or decoratively patterned.

In subject matter, *The Bowl of Grapes* belongs to Braque's gueridon (round pedestal table) and mantelpiece series of about 1918 to 1929. It displays a rigorous and complex organization of shape and line combined with the sensuous appeal of rich color (three greens contrasted with chalky white and tan) and a masterful handling of paint. The structuring grid is softened by broad curves and clusters of circular forms, and in peripheral areas enriched by the textural variation provided by the addition of sand to pigment.

Formal rather than illusionistic needs govern the treatment of objects. The white drapery does not cascade down from the tabletop in foreshortened, shadowed folds, but rigidly asserts itself parallel to the picture plane. The distinction between lit and shadowed sides of the pitcher is artificially sharp. Reminiscent of Paul Cézanne's still lifes are the heavy contours and voluminous presence of the objects, the tilted planes, inconsistent perspective, and discontinuous background lines. (L. F.)

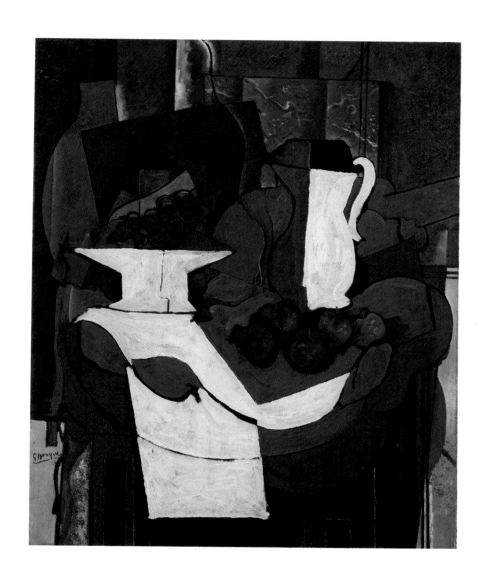

JUAN GRIS

Bottle of Rum and Newspaper (*Bouteille de rhum et journal*), June 1914

Paper collage, gouache, conté crayon, and pencil on newspaper, mounted on canvas, 54.8 x 46.2 cm
76.2553 PG 11

In 1913 Juan Gris began using the technique of papier collé developed by Georges Braque and Pablo Picasso, with whom he had been working in close contact since 1911. By 1914 Gris's handling of the technique was personal and sophisticated, as evidenced by works such as *Bottle of Rum and Newspaper*, executed in Paris shortly before he left for Collioure at the end of June. Here the pasted elements overlap and intermesh with one another in relationships calculated with mathematical rigor. These collaged papers cover the entire surface of the canvas, simultaneously forming an abstract composition and serving as a multilayered support for naturalistic details.

The dynamism of the picture derives from the tension between horizontals, verticals, and thrusting diagonals. Gris presents the table as if it were viewed from several vantage points at once, demonstrating that a diagonal can be understood as a horizontal perceived from an oblique angle, and also suggesting the movement of the observer or artist around objects. The telescoping of a number of viewpoints in a single image produces the illusion of a spatial dislocation of the objects themselves. Dissected parts of the bottle of rum, recognizable by correspondence of shape or by labeling, float beside, below, or above the drawing of the complete bottle. These paper cutouts, at once more tangible and more fragmented than the shadowy outline, confuse one's perceptions of the bottle's presence.

Gris confounds expectations of the nature of materials. He usually depicts the glass objects as transparent and the others as opaque but does not hesitate to betray this faithfulness to the properties of objects when formal demands intercede. (L. F.)

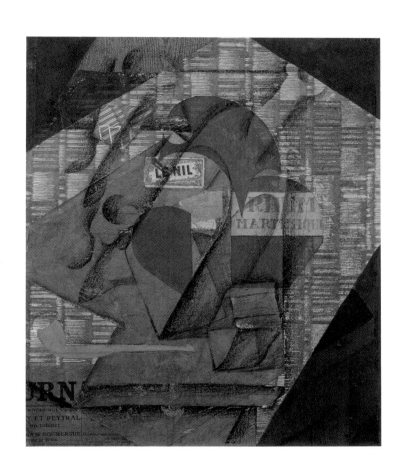

JEAN METZINGER

At the Cycle-Race Track (Au Vélodrome), ca. 1914 (?)

Oil and collage on canvas, 130.4 x 97.1 cm
76.2553 PG 18

Jean Metzinger, a sensitive and intelligent theoretician of Cubism, sought to communicate the principles of this movement through his paintings as well as his writings. Devices of Cubism and Futurism appear in *At the Cycle-Race Track*, though they are superimposed on an image that is essentially naturalistic. Cubist elements include printed-paper collage, the incorporation of a granular surface, and the use of transparent planes to define space. The choice of a subject in motion, the suggestion of velocity, and the fusing of forms find parallels in Futurist painting. Though these devices are handled with some awkwardness and the influence of Impressionism persists, particularly in the use of dots of color to represent the crowd in the background, this work represents Metzinger's attempt to come to terms with a new pictorial language. (L. F.)

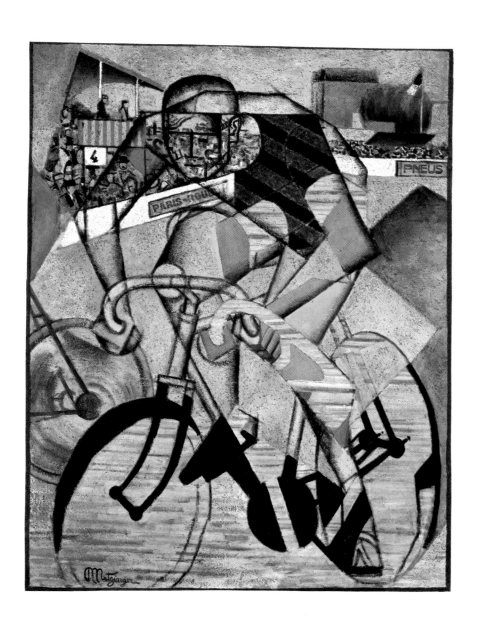

ALBERT GLEIZES

Woman with Animals (Madame Raymond Duchamp-Villon) (La Dame aux bêtes {Madame Raymond Duchamp-Villon}), completed by February 1914

Oil on canvas, 196.4 x 114.1 cm
76.2553 PG 17

As in a number of his other paintings of this period, Albert Gleizes depicts a domestic interior scene in a self-consciously "modern" style. Here the seated woman is the wife of Raymond Duchamp-Villon, the sculptor who took part in the discussions of the Cubist group at Puteaux during the early teens. She is portrayed as the epitome of bourgeois complacency, in a large armchair, with her dog and two cats, sensible tie shoe, wedding band, and string of beads. Typically Cubist elements are the fusion of figure and ground, the frontal, centralized pose, the multiple views of the sitter's face, the choppy brushstrokes defining and shading planes, and the patterning of areas to resemble collage. Futurist devices are the repetition of form to describe movement (the dog's wagging tail) and planar intersections and force lines meant to express notions of the dynamic interpenetration of matter and atmosphere. (L. F.)

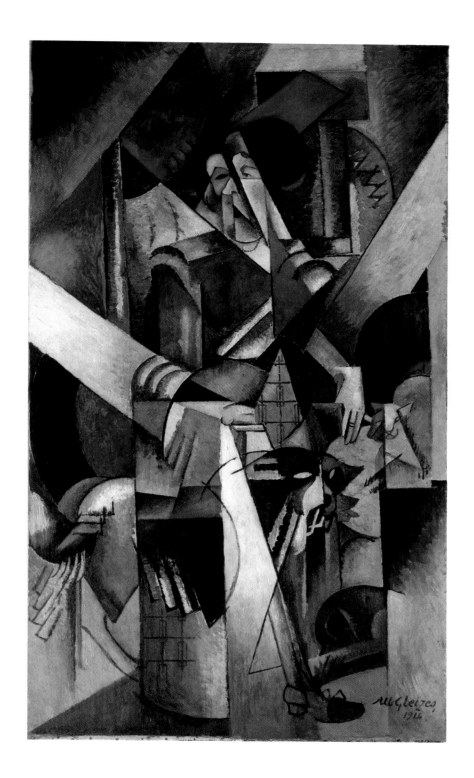

FERNAND LÉGER

Men in the City (Les Hommes dans la ville), 1919

Oil on canvas, 145.7 x 113.5 cm
76.2553 PG 21

Fernand Léger temporarily abandoned representational depiction in his *Contrast of Forms* series of 1913–14, begun a few months after he completed *Nude Model in the Studio* (Collection Solomon R. Guggenheim Museum, New York). When he returned from the front in 1917 and resumed painting, he reintroduced recognizable imagery in his work. Responsive to the technological advances and assertive advertising that followed World War I, he embarked on his "mechanical" period with works such as *Men in the City* and the related *The City* of 1919–29 (Collection Philadelphia Museum of Art).

In the urban themes of this period the human figure becomes as de-individualized and mechanized as the environment it occupies. Léger is able to express the rhythmic energy of contemporary life by finding its pictorial equivalent. Form, color, and shape are considered primarily for their plastic values and are given equal emphasis. They confront one another in a multitude of relations, creating single images that capture simultaneous sensations. Confusion of parts does not result, because Léger distributes planes evenly and builds his compositions with blocky areas of flat, easily read, unmixed color and clear and incisive outline. He conveys a sense of depth through overlapping planes and changes in scale rather than with modeling. Léger's simple, varied, and clear pictorial elements, like ideal machines, efficiently produce effects of maximum power. (L. F.)

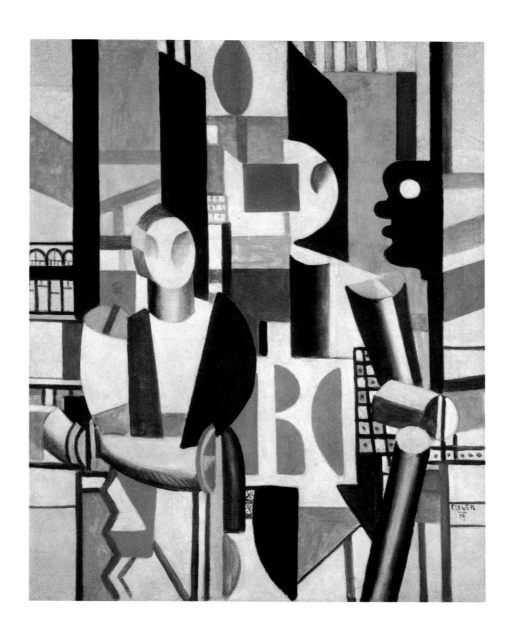

LOUIS MARCOUSSIS

The Regular (L'Habitué), 1920

Oil with sand and pebbles on canvas, 161.9 x 97 cm
76.2553 PG 22

In this Synthetic Cubist work of 1920 Louis Marcoussis presents a hieratic figure immobilized by habit, so much a part of his environment that he is barely distinguishable from it. Familiar Cubist motifs and effects are integrated in a strong, complex composition in which abstract and representational elements are harmonized. Sand, stippled paint, and imitation wood grain lend texture to the broad, angular planes that organize the picture space. The large proportions of the canvas increase the impact of the architectonic structure of planes. Blocks of color echo and respond to one another to establish balanced relationships over the entire surface.

The limits of abstraction are tested in the treatment of the figure, which would not be recognizable without the humanizing details indicating face and head—the schematic eyes, nose, mustache, furrowed brow, cigar, and hat. The right hand is merely a strip of modulated cylinders, the left only slightly more articulated with fingernails. The only naturalistically described objects are the dominoes on the table, which, unlike the human form, would be unidentifiable if they were distorted. Like letters, they are signs with unchangeable meanings that can be combined in various ways to produce larger meanings. Similarly, parts of a Cubist picture have an intrinsic, independent significance that is expanded and complicated when they are related within an ordered composition. (L. F.)

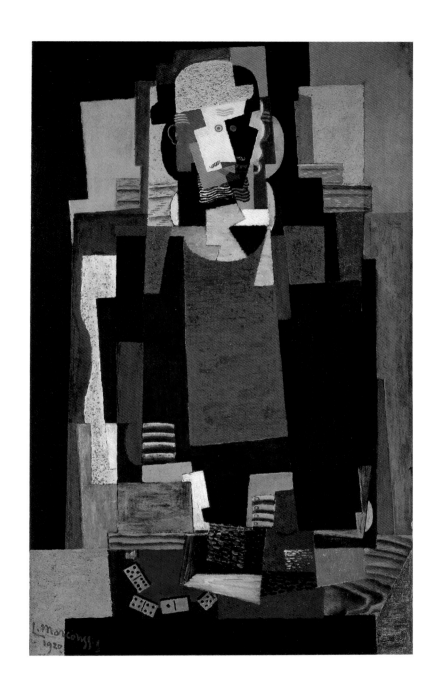

HENRI LAURENS

Head of a Young Girl (Tête de jeune fillette), 1920 (cast 1959)

Terra-cotta, 34.2 x 16.5 cm
76.2553 PG 27

Henri Laurens, who associated closely with the avant-garde painters of his native Paris, worked in a Cubist idiom from 1915. In about 1920 he turned from the production of bas-reliefs and frontalized constructions to the execution of more classically ordered, freestanding sculptures. *Head of a Young Girl* may have appeared originally as a drawing (see, for example, *Head* of 1917, Collection Mr. and Mrs. Irving W. Rabb, Cambridge, Massachusetts). However, in this bust Laurens expresses Cubist painting principles in essentially sculptural terms. The tilted surfaces and geometric volumes of the sculpture interpenetrate to constitute a compact whole. Circling the piece, the viewer perceives dramatically different aspects of the head, which provide a variety of visual experiences unexpected in a form so schematically reduced.

The structuring planes of one side of the head are broad and unadorned; its edges and planar junctures form strong, uninterrupted curves and straight lines. The other side is articulated with detail; its jagged, hewn contour describing hair contrasts rhythmically with the sweeping curve of the opposite cheek. Laurens slices into the polyhedron that determines the facial planes to describe nose, upper lip, and chin at one stroke. The subtle modeling, particularly of the almond eye and simplified mouth, produces nuanced relations of light and shadow. Despite the geometric clarity of structure, the delicacy of the young girl's features and her self-contained pose create a gentle, meditative quality. (L. F.)

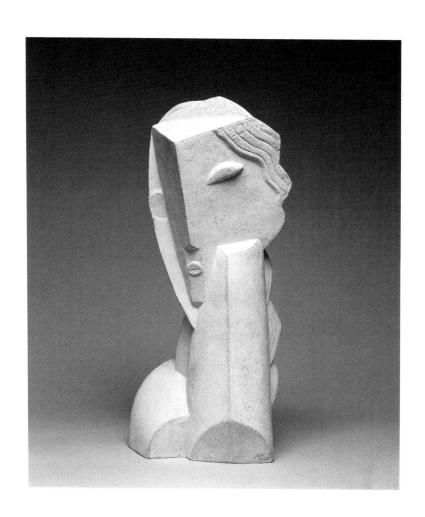

JACQUES LIPCHITZ

Seated Pierrot (Pierrot assis), 1922

Lead, 33.5 cm high, including base
76.2553 PG 28

In 1916 Jacques Lipchitz became a close friend of Juan Gris, who inspired him to paint his only completed Cubist oil the following year. Gris, in turn, made a foray into sculpture with his poly-chromed plaster *Harlequin*, 1917 (Collection Philadelphia Museum of Art), executed with the technical guidance of Lipchitz. *Seated Pierrot* is stylistically close to the Gris sculpture in its squat, massive proportions and the synthesis of angular and curvilinear elements.

By applying an ambiguous formal vocabulary in *Seated Pierrot*, Lipchitz has been able to fuse two recurrent Cubist themes—the commedia dell'arte figure of Pierrot and the still life. The figure's head and neck echo the similarly bifurcated shape of bottle neck and lip in certain of his bas-reliefs. The circular eyes recall the stylized mouth of a bottle; the encircling arms form a recessed oval like that of a compotier; and the configuration of legs and feet resembles the distorted glasses of Cubist painting. These volumes interpenetrate in apparent contradiction to the solidity of the sculptural form. The Cubist exchange of solid for void is wittily effected in the positive-negative handling of the two eyes. Lipchitz's concern with the effects of light is evident in the contrast between broad, deeply shadowed areas and dappled planes animated by surface texture. (L. F.)

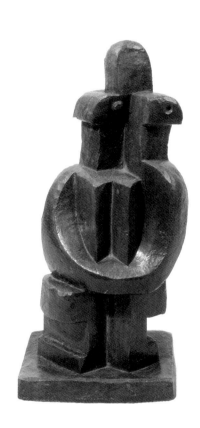

14

ALEXANDER ARCHIPENKO

Boxing (La Boxe), 1935

Terra-cotta, 76.6 cm high
76.2553 PG 26

Two plaster versions of this work were made from the same mold in 1913–14 (see Rudenstine, p. 55). One of these, known as *Struggle*, is in the collection of the Solomon R. Guggenheim Museum, New York; the second was given by the artist's widow to the Saarland Museum, Saarbrücken (Rudenstine, p. 56, fn. 6). The Peggy Guggenheim terra-cotta, though very similar to the original plasters, is slightly larger and was executed many years later.

Alexander Archipenko disavowed the influence of Cubism on his geometric simplification of form. However, one of his most important contributions to Modern sculpture, the breaking up of monolithic form with open spaces, finds its counterpart in the Cubist exchange of solid and void. He also shares with the Cubists an interest in the analysis of space and the interpenetration of planes within it.

The artist explains the choice of subject for this work in a poetic inscription at its base: "'LA BOXE'—C'est la musique monumental [sic] des volumes d'éspace [sic] et de la matière. . . ." (Boxing—the monumental music of volumes of space and of material). The thrusting figures of the two contenders are joined inextricably in opposition, forming an aggressively charged sculptural whole. Apart from the work of the Italian Futurists, few sculptures of this period combine radical essentialization of form with virile, assertive dynamism in the manner of *Boxing*. Another is Raymond Duchamp-Villon's *The Horse* (cat. no. 15), executed some months after the original version of the Archipenko was completed. (L. F.)

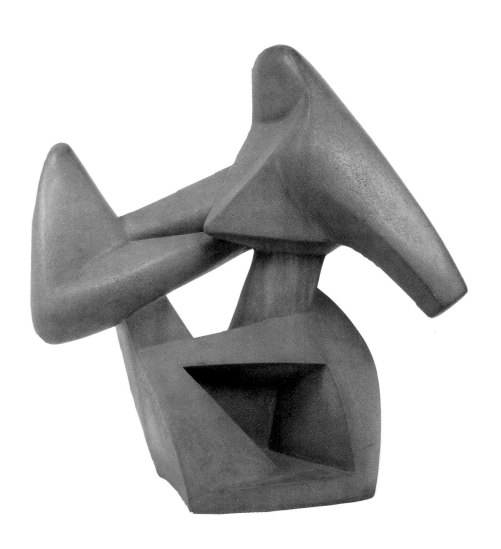

15

RAYMOND DUCHAMP-VILLON

The Horse (*Le Cheval*), 1914 (cast ca. 1930)

Bronze, 43.6 x 41 cm
76.2553 PG 24

Raymond Duchamp-Villon began work on the plaster original of *The Horse*, a composite image of an animal and machine, in 1914, finishing it on leaves from military duty in the fall. It was preceded by numerous sketches and by several other versions initiated in 1913. The original conception did not include the machine and was relatively naturalistic, as is evident in the early states of the small *Horse and Rider* of 1914. Duchamp-Villon then developed an increasingly dynamic, smooth-surfaced, and geometric synthesis of horse and machine. The Peggy Guggenheim version is highly abstract and parts of the horse's physiognomy are replaced by machine elements. Nonetheless, echoes of the original pose remain. As in the second state of *Horse and Rider* (Collection Judith Riklis, New York), the animal appears to be gathering its hooves, summoning strength to jump. Duchamp-Villon closely observed the dynamics of the movement of horses during his experience in the cavalry; he also studied the subject in the late nineteenth-century photographic experiments of Eadweard Muybridge and Etienne-Jules Marey.

With a handful of other sculptors, such as Alexander Archipenko, Umberto Boccioni, and Constantin Brancusi, Duchamp-Villon overturned conventional representation of form to suggest instead its inner forces. He associated these forces with the energy of the machine. The visual movement of the pistons, wheels, and shafts of this sculpture turns a creature of nature into a poised mechanical dynamo. The fusion of the horse, traditional symbol of power, and the machine that was replacing it reflects the emerging awareness of the new technological age.

The entire series was cast in bronze after the artist's death.[1] (L. F.)

1. For a discussion of the casting of various versions of *The Horse*, see Rudenstine, pp. 271–76.

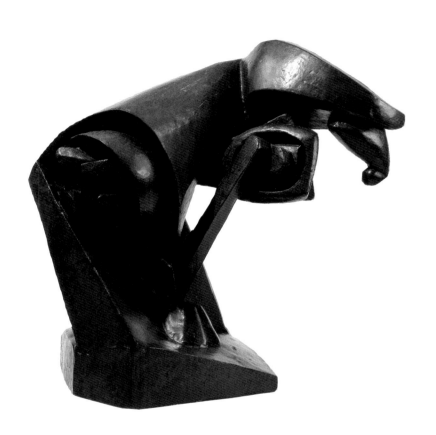

16

MARCEL DUCHAMP

Nude (Study), Sad Young Man on a Train (Nu {esquisse}, jeune homme triste dans un train), 1911–12

Oil on cardboard, 100 x 73 cm
76.2553 PG 9

This painting, which Marcel Duchamp identified as a self-portrait, was probably begun during December of 1911 in Neuilly, while he was exploring ideas for the controversial *Nude Descending a Staircase, No. 2* of 1912 (Collection Philadelphia Museum of Art; see Rudenstine, pp. 265–66). In *Nude (Study), Sad Young Man on a Train* his transitory though acute interest in Cubism is manifested in the subdued palette, emphasis on the flat surface of the picture plane, and in the subordination of representational fidelity to the demands of the abstract composition.

Duchamp's primary concern in this painting is the depiction of two movements, that of the train in which we observe the young man smoking and that of the lurching figure itself. The forward motion of the train is suggested by the multiplication of the lines and volumes of the figure, a semi-transparent form through which we can see windows, themselves transparent and presumably presenting a blurred, "moving" landscape. The independent sideways motion of the figure is represented by a directionally contrary series of repetitions. These two series of replications suggest the multiple images of chronophotography, which Duchamp acknowledged as an influence, and the related ideas of the Italian Futurists, of which he was at least aware by this time. Here he uses the device not only to illustrate movement, but also to integrate the young man with his murky surroundings, which with his swaying, drooping pose contribute to the air of melancholy. Shortly after the execution of this and similar works, Duchamp lost interest in Cubism and developed his eccentric vocabulary of mechanomorphic elements that foreshadowed aspects of Dada. (L. F.)

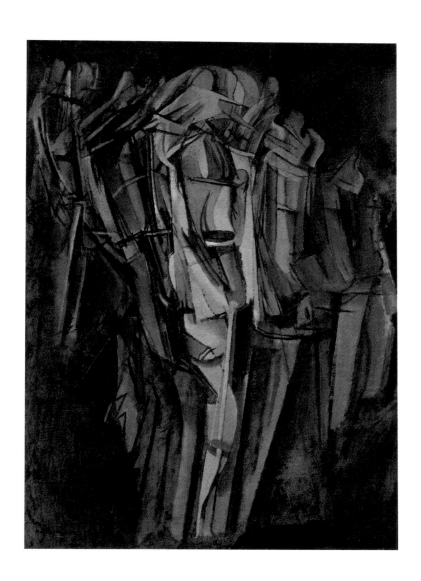

17

GIACOMO BALLA

Abstract Speed + Sound (Velocità astratta + rumore), 1913–14

Oil on board, 54.5 x 76.5 cm, including artist's painted frame
76.2553 PG 31

In late 1912 to early 1913 Giacomo Balla turned from a depiction of the splintering of light to the exploration of movement and, more specifically, the speed of racing automobiles. This led to an important series of studies in 1913–14. The choice of automobile as symbol of abstract speed recalls Filippo Tommaso Marinetti's notorious statement in his first Futurist manifesto, published on February 20, 1909, in *Le Figaro* in Paris, only a decade after the first Italian car was manufactured: "The world's splendor has been enriched by a new beauty: the beauty of speed . . . A roaring automobile . . . that seems to run on shrapnel, is more beautiful than the Victory of Samothrace."

It has been proposed that *Abstract Speed + Sound* was the central section of a narrative triptych suggesting the alteration of landscape by the passage of a car through the atmosphere.[1] The related *Abstract Speed* (present whereabouts unknown; formerly Collection Dr. W. Loeffler, Zurich) and *Abstract Speed—The Car Has Passed* (Collection Tate Gallery, London) would have been the flanking panels. Indications of sky and a single landscape are present in the three paintings; the interpretation of fragmented evocations of the car's speed varies from panel to panel. The Peggy Guggenheim work is distinguished by crisscross motifs, representing sound, and a multiplication of the number of lines and planes.

The original frames of all three panels were painted with continuations of the forms and colors of the compositions, implying the overflow of the paintings' reality into the spectator's own space. Many other studies and variations by Balla on the theme of a moving automobile in the same landscape exist. (L. F.)

1. V. Dortch Dorazio, *Giacomo Balla: An Album of His Life and Work*, New York, 1969, figs. 2–4. See also Rudenstine, 1985, pp. 92–93, in which all three panels are reproduced.

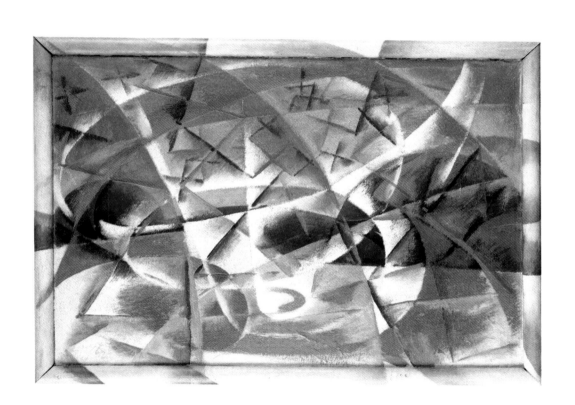

18

UMBERTO BOCCIONI

Dynamism of a Speeding Horse + Houses (*Dinamismo di un cavallo in corsa + case*), 1914–15

Gouache, oil, paper collage, wood, cardboard, copper, and coated iron, 112.9 x 115 cm
76.2553 PG 30

Umberto Boccioni turned to sculpture in 1912 after publishing his manifesto on the subject on April 11 of that year. The Futurist aesthetic platform as articulated in this document advocates the use of various materials in a single work, the rejection of closed form, and the suggestion of the interpenetration of form and the environment through the device of intersecting planes. In *Dynamism of a Speeding Horse + Houses* Boccioni assembled wood, cardboard, and metal, with painted areas showing a Futurist handling of planes influenced by the Cubism of Pablo Picasso and Georges Braque. Ironically, his intention of preserving "unique forms" caught in space and time is mocked by the perishability of his materials—the work has been considerably restored and continues to present conservation problems (see Rudenstine, pp. 99–106).

Boccioni, like Raymond Duchamp-Villon (see cat. no. 15), made studies of horses from nature before developing the motif into a nonspecific symbol of the modern age. This fully evolved symbol appears in Boccioni's painting *The City Rises* of 1910 (Collection The Museum of Modern Art, New York). In *Dynamism of a Speeding Horse + Houses* he used the horse to demonstrate his observation that the nature of vision produces the illusion of a fusing of forms. When the distance between a galloping horse and a stationary house is visually imperceptible, horse and house appear to merge into a single changing form. Sculptures such as the present example are concerned with the apparent compression of space as an object traverses it, and with the nature of the object's redefinition by that space.

In 1913 and 1914 Boccioni made many drawings and watercolors related to the present work that explore the relationship between a galloping horse and a group of houses in close proximity; these are now in the Civica Raccolta Bertarelli in Milan. In some of these studies the speed of the horse's motion serves to dissolve the legs below the muscles of the shanks. Boccioni's original conception of the sculpture gave forceful expression to this concept. (L. F.)

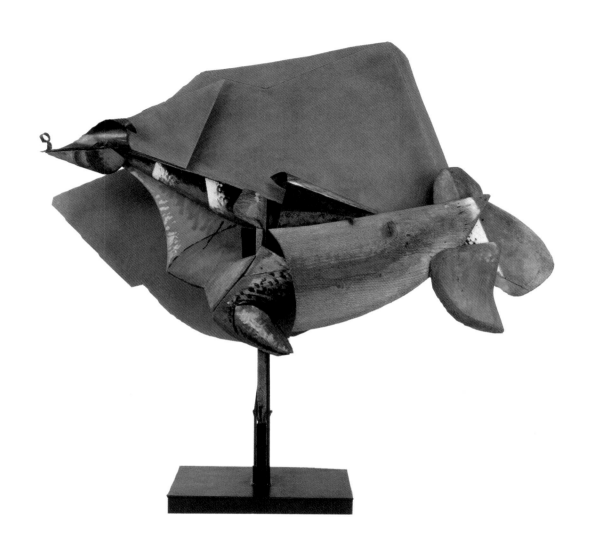

19

GINO SEVERINI

Sea = Dancer (Mare = Ballerina), January 1914

Oil on canvas, 105.3 x 85.9 cm, including artist's painted frame
76.2553 PG 32

Toward the end of 1913, after he left Paris for Pienza and Rome, Gino Severini traveled to coastal Anzio for reasons of health. It was after arriving there that he executed *Sea = Dancer*. This painting, in which the sea and a figure are equated, illustrates his notions of "plastic analogies" as outlined in a manifesto he prepared for his solo exhibition at the Marlborough Gallery in London in 1913. According to Severini, the environment is optically determined and hence fluid, and the human figure is merely a part, albeit an inseparable part, of that metamorphic reality. In this canvas and others the cadences of the swirling motion of the dance and the dancer's costume are compared with those of the sea's movement. The large curling planes are stippled with brilliant staccato dabs of paint that cause all surfaces to vibrate as if with light. As in many other Futurist paintings (see cat. no. 17), the image spills over onto the frame. The divisionist brushstroke derives from Giacomo Balla and ultimately from the Neo-Impressionists, particularly Georges Seurat. Works such as *Sea = Dancer* may have a specific source in Seurat's *Le Chahut* of 1889–90 (Collection Rijksmuseum Kröller-Müller, Otterlo).[1]

The play of cylindrical and flat planes in this painting brings to mind the contemporaneous Cubism of Fernand Léger, though the color is closer to the prismatic hues of Robert Delaunay. However, the absence of outline and the dissolution of volume distinguish Severini's work. During this period Severini's analogies of forms divest objects of their usual identities; later in 1914 he would produce entirely non-objective compositions. (L. F.)

1. A. Barr, *Cubism and Abstract Art*, exh. cat., New York, 1936, p. 58.

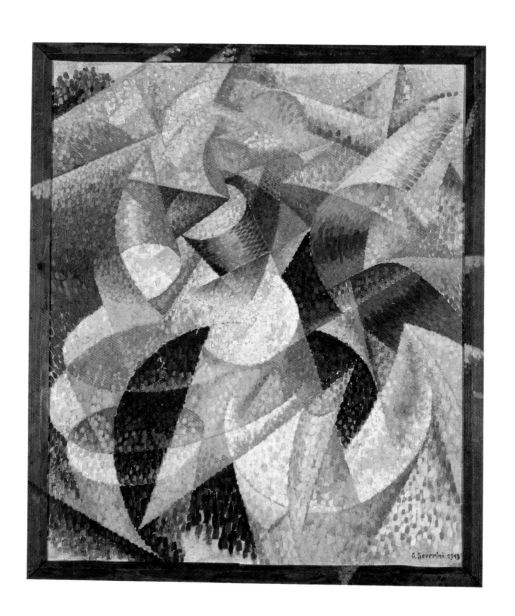

20

ROBERT DELAUNAY

Windows Open Simultaneously 1st Part, 3rd Motif (Fenêtres ouvertes simultanément 1ère partie, 3e motif), 1912

Oil on oval canvas, 57 x 123 cm
76.2553 PG 36

Though Robert Delaunay had virtually discarded representational imagery by the spring of 1912 when he embarked on the *Windows* theme, vestigial objects endure in this series. Here, as in *Simultaneous Windows 2nd Motif, 1st Part* (Collection Solomon R. Guggenheim Museum, New York) of the same moment, the centralized ghost of a green Eiffel Tower alludes to his enthusiasm for modern life.

Analytic Cubism inspired Delaunay's fragmentation of form, oval format, and organization of the picture's space as a grid supporting intersecting planes. However, unlike the monochromatic, tactile planes of Cubism, those of Delaunay are not defined by line and modeling, but by the application of diaphanous, prismatic color. Delaunay wrote in 1913: "Line is limitation. Color gives depth—not perspectival, not successive, but simultaneous depth—as well as form and movement."[1] As in visual perception of the real world, perception of Delaunay's painting is initially fragmentary, the eye continually moving from one form to others related by hue, value, tone, shape, or direction. As focus shifts, expands, jumps, and contracts in unending rhythms, one senses the fixed borders of the canvas and the tight interlocking of its contents. Because identification of representational forms is not necessary while the eye moves restlessly, judgments about the relative importance of parts are not made and all elements can be perceived as equally significant. The harmony of the pictorial reality provides an analogy to the concealed harmony of the world. At the left of the canvas Delaunay suggests glass, which, like his chromatic planes, is at once transparent, reflective, insubstantial, and solid. Glass may allude as well to the metaphor of art as a window on reality. (L. F.)

1. Quoted in D. Cooper, *The Cubist Epoch*, London, 1971, p. 84.

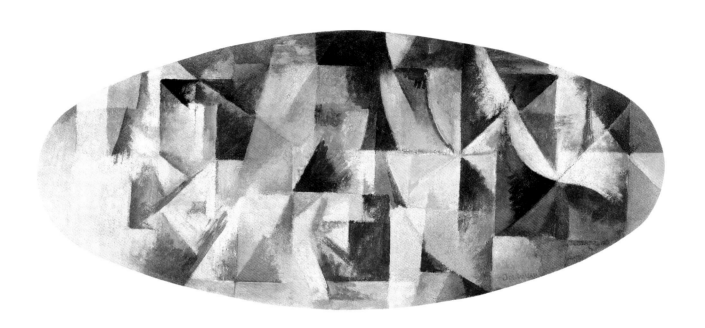

21

FRANTIŠEK KUPKA

Study for *Amorpha, Warm Chromatic* (*Amorpha, Chromatique chaude*) and for *Fugue in Two Colors* (*Fugue à deux couleurs*), ca. 1910–11

Pastel on paper, 46.8 x 48.3 cm
76.2553 PG 13

Two of František Kupka's earliest purely abstract compositions are *Amorpha, Warm Chromatic* of 1911–12 (Private Collection) and *Amorpha, Fugue in Two Colors* of 1911–12 (Collection Národní Galerie, Prague). The present pastel study reveals an early stage in the formal evolution of both of these paintings (Rudenstine, p. 436). In 1911 Kupka strove to eliminate objective subject matter from his paintings. His development toward abstraction is evident in his work of 1909 to 1911 in his interpretations of motion and of the light and color of Gothic stained-glass windows. The Peggy Guggenheim pastel relates to a series of studies that followed a naturalistic painting of 1908–09 of his stepdaughter Andrée playing naked with a red and blue ball in the garden of their home (Collection Musée National d'Art Moderne, Centre Georges Pompidou, Paris; see Rudenstine, p. 436). More than fifty studies led Kupka from conventional representation of this subject to the abstract formulations of the paintings of 1912. In a note on one of the pencil drawings of *Little Girl with Ball* (Collection The Museum of Modern Art, New York), Kupka details his frustrations: "Here I am only dissecting surfaces. The atmospheric copenetration is yet to be found. As long as there is a distinction in color between ground and flesh, I will fall back into the postcard photograph" (repr. and trans. Rudenstine, p. 436, fig. b).

In the Peggy Guggenheim study, Kupka articulated the girl's motion by depicting the continuous penetration of the atmosphere by the ball. A curving brown body shape guides the ball through the blue path of its trajectory. This action occurs on a light green background plane, which suggests the three-dimensional space of the garden. Such residue of naturalistic color is abandoned in culminating versions of the study, such as *Amorpha, Fugue in Two Colors*, which are conceived in blue, red, black, and white. Kupka discerned a musical parallel to these abstract forms in the rhythmic patterns of the fugue, "where the sounds evolve like veritable physical entities, intertwine, come and go."[1] Kupka's paintings of this period are not simple or formulaic abstractions from ultimate "sources" in nature, but are rather pictorial syntheses of the artist's formal ideas. (E. C. C.)

1. Quoted in M. Rowell, *František Kupka, 1871–1957: A Retrospective*, exh. cat., New York, 1975, p. 184.

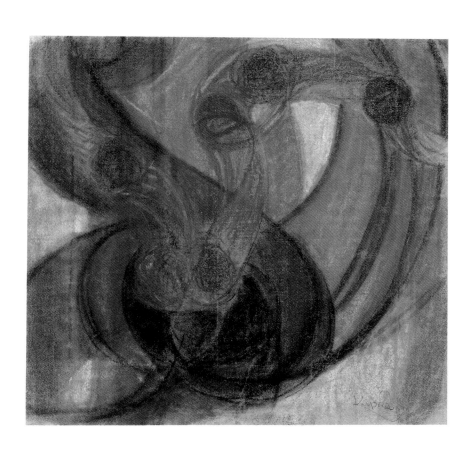

22

CONSTANTIN BRANCUSI

Maiastra, 1912 (?)

Polished brass, 73.1 cm high, including base
76.2553 PG 50

According to Constantin Brancusi's own testimony, his preoccupation with the image of the bird as a plastic form began as early as 1910. With the theme of the *Maiastra* in the early teens he initiated a series of about thirty sculptures of birds.

The word *maïastra* means "master" or "chief" in Brancusi's native Romanian, but the title refers specifically to a magically beneficent, dazzlingly plumed bird in Romanian folklore. Brancusi's mystical inclinations and his deeply rooted interest in peasant superstition make the motif an apt one. The golden plumage of the *Maiastra* is expressed in the reflective surface of the bronze; the bird's restorative song seems to issue from within the monumental puffed chest, through the arched neck, out of the open beak. The heraldic, geometric aspect of the figure contrasts with details such as the inconsistent size of the eyes, the distortion of the beak aperture, and the cocking of the head slightly to one side. The elevation of the bird on a saw-tooth base lends it the illusion of perching. The subtle tapering of form, the relationship of curved to hard-edge surfaces, and the changes of axis tune the sculpture so finely that the slightest alteration from version to version reflects a crucial decision in Brancusi's development of the theme.

Seven other versions of *Maiastra* have been identified and located: three are marble and four bronze. The Peggy Guggenheim example apparently was cast from a reworked plaster (now lost but visible in a 1955 photograph of Brancusi's studio).[1] This was probably also the source for the almost identical cast in the collection of the Des Moines Art Center. (L. F.)

1. Reproduced in A. Spear, *Brancusi's Birds*, New York, 1969, p. 55.

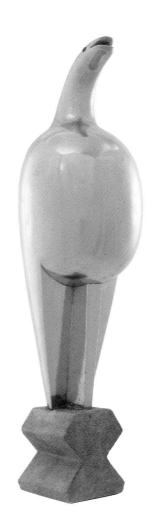

23

CONSTANTIN BRANCUSI

Bird in Space (*L'Oiseau dans l'espace*), 1932–40

Polished brass, 151.7 cm high, including base
76.2553 PG 51

The development of the bird theme in Constantin Brancusi's oeuvre can be traced from its appearance in the *Maiastra* sculptures (see cat. no. 22), through the *Golden Bird* group, and, finally, to the *Bird in Space* series. Sixteen examples of the *Bird in Space* sequence, dating from 1923 to 1940, have been identified. The streamlined form of the present *Bird in Space*, stripped of individualizing features, communicates the notion of flight itself rather than describing the appearance of a particular bird. A vestige of the open beak of the *Maiastra* is retained in the beveled top of the tapering form, a slanted edge accelerating the upward movement of the whole.

This bronze, closely related to a marble version completed in 1931 (Collection Kunsthaus Zürich), could have been cast as early as 1932 and finished in 1940 (see Rudenstine, pp. 124–25). Though the shaft of the first *Bird in Space* (Private Collection, New York) was mounted on a discrete conical support, the support of the present example is incorporated as an organically irregular stem, providing an earthbound anchor for the sleek, soaring form.

As was customary in Brancusi's work, the bronze is smoothed and polished to the point where the materiality of the sculpture is dissolved in its reflective luminosity. Brancusi's spiritual aspirations, his longing for transcendence of the material world and its constraints, are verbalized in his description of *Bird in Space* as a "project before being enlarged to fill the vault of the sky."[1] (L. F.)

1. Quoted in S. Geist, *Brancusi: A Study of the Sculpture*, New York, 1968, pp. 113–14.

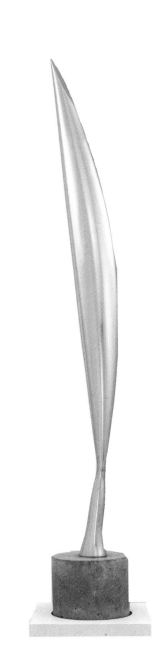

24

VASILY KANDINSKY

Landscape with Red Spots, No. 2 (Landschaft mit roten Flecken, No. 2), 1913

Oil on canvas, 117.5 x 140 cm
76.2553 PG 33

From 1908 Vasily Kandinsky often stayed in the town of Murnau in upper Bavaria, where his companion Gabriele Münter bought a house in 1909. The landscapes inspired by these Alpine surroundings developed from the flattened, densely colored views of 1908 to the luminous, antimaterial dream visions of 1913, such as this canvas and the closely related *Landscape with Red Spots, No. 1* (Collection Museum Folkwang, Essen).

The motif of the church in a landscape recurs often in Kandinsky's paintings of 1908–13. In examples of 1908–09 the particular design of the Murnau church makes identification possible, though the local topography may not be accurately reflected. By 1911 there is little specifying detail and the tower, which serves to divide the composition, has taken on a generalized, columnar appearance. In *Landscape with Red Spots, No. 2* the tower is replaced by a mysterious elongated vertical form that seems to continue beyond the canvas edge into another realm. Like the nineteenth-century German Romantic painters, Kandinsky presents the landscape as an exalted, spiritualized vision. He achieves the sublimity of the image by freeing color from its descriptive function to reveal its latent expressive content. The chromatic emphasis is on the primary colors, applied thinly over a white ground. The focal point, the red spot that inspires the picture's title, bears out Kandinsky's appraisal of red as an expanding color that pulses forward toward the viewer, in contrast to cooler colors, particularly blue, that recede. Kandinsky indicates the naturalistic content of subject matter with abbreviated signs, emphasizing the purely pictorial aspects of color and form, and thus is able to dematerialize the objective world. (L. F.)

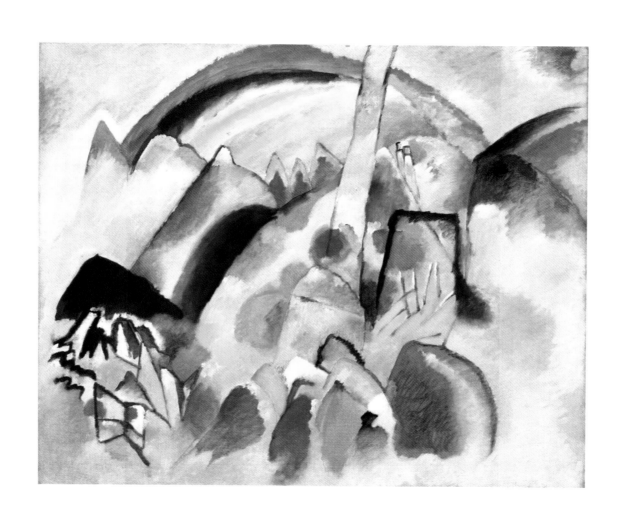

25

VASILY KANDINSKY

White Cross (*Weisses Kreuz*), January–June 1922

Oil on canvas, 100.5 x 110.6 cm
76.2553 PG 34

Vasily Kandinsky referred to the early 1920s as his "cool period." From this time geometric shapes became increasingly prevalent in his work, often floating in front of or within a broad plane, as in *White Cross*. Here straight lines and circles offset looser, organic forms and irregularly geometric shapes. A corresponding variation of brushstroke produces highly active passages contrasting with less inflected areas. Some shapes may have their distant origins in a naturalistic vocabulary of forms. Thus, the fishlike crescent and the lancing black diagonal that crosses it, which appear also in the related *Red Oval* of 1920 (Collection Solomon R. Guggenheim Museum, New York), may recall the boat with oars in earlier works. However, the motifs are stripped of their representational meaning and do not contribute to an interpretation of the whole in terms of realistic content.

The title isolates a detail of the composition, the white cross at upper right, a formal consequence of the checkerboard pattern (a recurrent motif in works of this period). In this instance negative space is treated as positive form. Once the cross of the title is seen, one begins to perceive throughout the work a proliferation of others, varying in degrees of explicitness. Though Kandinsky, like Kazimir Malevich, uses it as an abstract element, the cross is an evocative, symbolic form.

The viewer's compulsion to read imagery literally is used to unexpected ends by Kandinsky, who includes two signs resembling the numeral 3 upended and affixed to directional arrows. The variations in direction of the resulting forms suggest the rotation of the entire canvas. The antigravitational feeling of floating forms and the placement of elements on a planar support against an indefinite background in *White Cross* reveal affinities with Malevich's Suprematist works (see cat. no. 27). (L. F.)

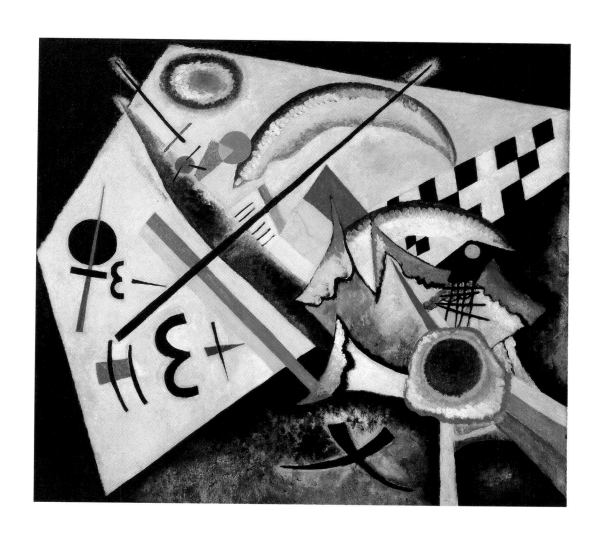

26

VASILY KANDINSKY

Upward (Empor), October 1929

Oil on cardboard, 70 x 49 cm
76.2553 PG 35

Geometric shapes and sections of circles combine in *Upward* in a structure suspended in a field of rich turquoise and green. A partial circle rests delicately on a pointed base. Another fragment of a circle glides along its vertical diameter, reaching beyond the circumference of the first form to penetrate the space above it. Vasily Kandinsky achieves an effect of energy rising upward, while anchoring the forms together by balancing them on either side of a continuous vertical line. In a closely related work of the same period, *Depressed* (Collection Galleria Marescalchi, Bologna), Kandinsky distributes motifs of partial circles horizontally. Here he represses the sense of energy found in *Upward* both through his composition and a subdued palette.

A linear design in the upper right corner of the present canvas echoes the vertical thrust of the central motif. This configuration resembles the letter E, as does the black cutout shape at the base of the central motif. Another E shape is legible in the upper right corner of a related drawing (Collection Musée National d'Art Moderne, Centre Georges Pompidou, Paris; repr. Rudenstine, p. 421). These forms may at once be independent designs and playful references to the first letter of *Empor*, the German title of the painting.

The related drawing reveals that the small black circle and the horizontal bars of the central motif, which have the physiognomic character of eye and mouth, were not part of Kandinsky's original design concept and evolved as he worked on the painting. As he wrote in 1929, the year he painted *Upward*, "I do not choose form consciously; it chooses itself within me."[1] The physiognomic character of *Upward* indicates Kandinsky's association at the Dessau Bauhaus with fellow Blaue Vier artists Paul Klee and Alexej Jawlensky. Jawlensky showed sixteen abstract heads, a motif that appeared in his work as early as 1918, in an exhibition of the Blaue Vier at the Galerie Ferdinand Möller in Berlin in October 1929. Shown during the month when *Upward* was completed, these paintings offered Kandinsky the model of large, abstract faces composed of geometric planes of non-naturalistic color and accented by bar-shaped features. However, Kandinsky's working method more closely resembled that of Klee, who began with intuitively chosen forms that gradually suggested counterparts in the natural world, than that of Jawlensky, who began with the model and moved toward abstraction. In particular, the whimsy of the hovering black eye in *Upward* and the incorporation of a letter as a pictogram with a possible reference to the title of the painting suggest the reverberations of Klee's art. (E. C. C.)

1. Quoted in *Kandinsky: Complete Writings on Art*, ed. K. C. Lindsay and P. Vergo, Boston, 1982, vol. 2, p. 740.

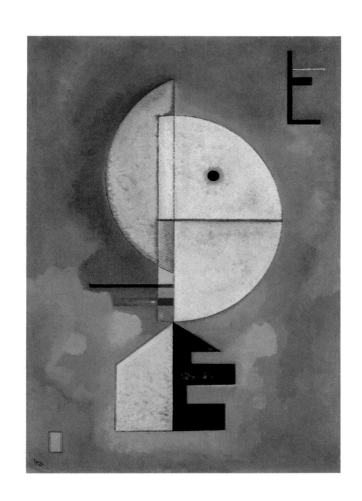

27

KAZIMIR MALEVICH

Untitled, ca. 1916

Oil on canvas, 53 x 53 cm
76.2553 PG 42

Kazimir Malevich proposed the reductive, abstract style of Suprematism as an alternative to earlier art forms, which he considered inappropriate to his own time. He observed that the proportions of forms in art of the past corresponded with those of objects in nature, which are determined by their function. In opposition to this he proposed a self-referential art in which proportion, scale, color, and disposition obey intrinsic, nonutilitarian laws. Malevich considered his non-objective forms to be reproductions of purely affective sensations that bore no relation to external phenomena. He rejected conventions of gravity, clear orientation, horizon line, and perspective systems.

Malevich's units are developed from the straight line and its two-dimensional extension, the plane, and are constituted of contrasting areas of unmodeled color, distinguished by various textural effects. The diagonal orientation of geometric forms creates rhythms on the surface of the canvas. The overlapping of elements and their varying scale relationships within a white ground provide a sense of indefinitely extensive space. Though the organization of the pictorial forms does not correspond with that of traditional subjects, there are various internal regulatory principles. In the present work a magnetic attraction and repulsion seem to dictate the slow rotational movement of parts. (L. F.)

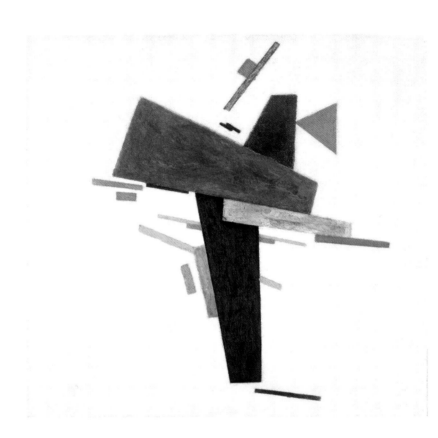

28

EL LISSITZKY

Untitled, ca. 1919–20

Oil on canvas, 79.6 x 49.6 cm
76.2553 PG 43

This painting reveals the principles of Suprematism that El Lissitzky absorbed under the influence of Kazimir Malevich in 1919–20. Trained as an engineer and possessing a more pragmatic temperament than that of his mentor, Lissitzky soon became one of the leading exponents of Constructivism. In the 1920s, while living in Germany, he became an important influence on both the Dutch De Stijl group and the artists of the German Bauhaus.

Like Malevich, Lissitzky believed in a new art that rejected traditional pictorial structure, centralized compositional organization, mimesis, and perspectival consistency. In this work the ladder of vividly colored forms seems to be floating through indeterminate space. Spatial relationships are complicated by the veil of white color that divides these forms from the major gray diagonal. The linkage of elements is not attributable to a mysterious magnetic pull, as in Malevich's untitled painting (cat. no. 27), but is indicated in a literal way by the device of a connecting threadlike line. The winding line changes color as it passes through the various rectangles that may serve as metaphors for different cosmic planes. (L. F.)

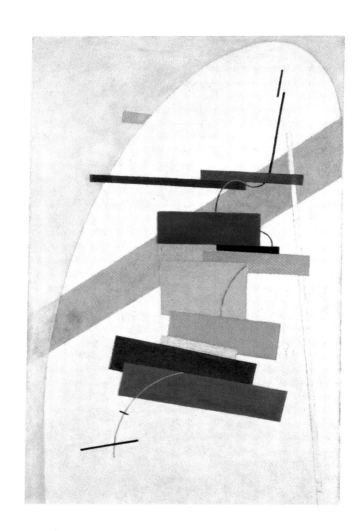

29

ANTOINE PEVSNER

Anchored Cross (La Croix ancrée), 1933

Marble, brass painted black, and crystal, 84.6 cm long (diagonally)
76.2553 PG 60

In 1920 Antoine Pevsner signed the *Realistic Manifesto* drafted by his brother Naum Gabo, proclaiming the intention of Constructivism as they conceived it. They sought to translate their apprehension of an absolute and essential reality as "the realization of our perceptions of the world in the forms of space and time."[1] They believed that space was given form through implications of depth rather than volume and they rejected mass as the basic sculptural element. Line, rendered dynamic through directionality, established kinetic rhythms. The Constructivists advocated the use of contemporary industrial materials; they did not carve or model these materials according to sculptural conventions, but constructed them according to principles of modern technology. In their words, "The plumb-line in our hand, eyes as precise as a ruler, in a spirit as taut as a compass . . . we construct our work as the universe constructs its own, as the engineer constructs his bridges, as the mathematician his formula of the orbits."[2]

In this work Pevsner complicates the delineation of space by using a transparent substance in conjunction with opaque materials. The glass panes echo both the rounded excised outlines of the construction and its angular metal surfaces. The metal ribs anchor the panes of glass and hinge all planes, real and imagined, resulting in a complex structuring of space. Furthermore, they function visually as an Orthodox cross. The icons of Pevsner's native Russia, which had played a crucial role in the development of his notions of perspective, may have suggested the form. (L. F.)

1. *Russian Art of the Avant-Garde: Theory and Criticism, 1902–1934*, The Documents of Twentieth-Century Art, ed. J. E. Bowlt, New York, 1976, p. 213. The entire manifesto, translated by Gabo, appears in this volume.

2. Ibid.

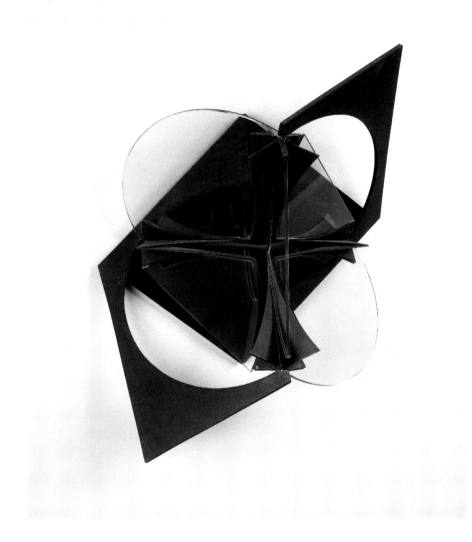

30

PIET MONDRIAN

The Sea, 1914

Charcoal and gouache on paper, mounted on panel; paper 87.6 x 120.3 cm; panel 90.2 x 123 x 1.3 cm
76.2553 PG 38

Piet Mondrian first treated the theme of the sea in naturalistic works of 1909–11, during lengthy sojourns in the village of Domburg on the coast of Dutch Zeeland. He assimilated and adapted the Cubism of Pablo Picasso and Georges Braque in Paris soon after his arrival there in the winter of 1911–12. He returned to the Netherlands in the summer of 1914 and probably in the following war years worked on the studies of the sea that culminated in the *Pier and Ocean* paintings of 1917.[1]

The oval format and grid structure used in these works are devices derived from Cubism. They serve respectively to resolve the problem of the compositional interference of the corners and to organize and unify the picture's elements. For Mondrian the horizontal-vertical arrangement did not have an exclusively pictorial function, as it did for the Cubists, but carried mystical implications. He viewed the horizontal and vertical as basic oppositional principles that could interact to produce a union symbolizing a state of universal harmony.

Although Mondrian's source exists in the natural world, in the motion of waves and their contact with breakwaters, the signs for this source have been reduced to their most essential pictorial form. The strokes are determined by their structural function rather than their descriptive potential, and there is no sense of perspectival recession despite the atmospheric texture of the gouache highlighting. This highlighting evokes the reflection of light on water and also defines planar surfaces. As Mondrian developed the theories of Neo-Plasticism, these suggestions of natural phenomena disappeared. (L. F.)

1. For a discussion of the chronology, see Rudenstine, pp. 555–57.

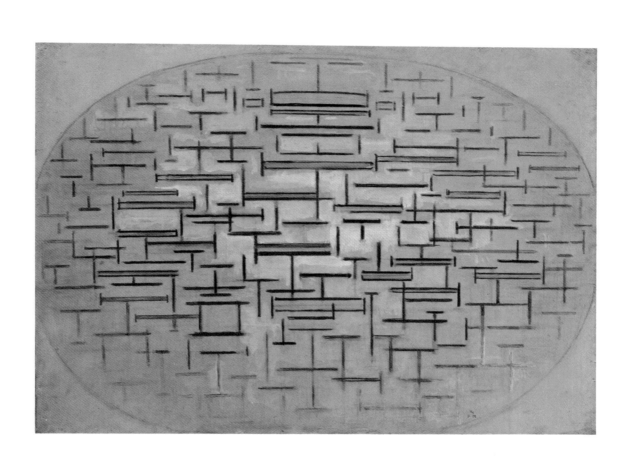

31

PIET MONDRIAN

Composition, 1938–39

Oil on canvas, mounted on wood support; canvas 105.2 x 102.3 cm; wood support 109.1 x 106 x 2.5 cm
76.2553 PG 39

From 1938 to 1940 Piet Mondrian, who had fled wartime Paris, was established in London near his friends Naum Gabo, Barbara Hepworth, and Ben Nicholson. During this period he continued working in the highly reductivist Neo-Plastic mode he had developed in France, in which horizontal and vertical black lines intersect on the canvas in asymmetrically balanced relationships to yield flat white or colored quadrilaterals. The palette is generally restricted to black, white, and primary colors. The present work is among the more coloristically austere examples.

By divorcing form completely from its referential meaning, Mondrian hoped to provide a visual equivalent for the truths that inhabit nature but are concealed in its random, flawed manifestations. He felt that if he could communicate these truths by means of a system of resolved oppositions, a "real equation of the universal and the individual,"[1] the spiritual effect on the viewer would be one of total repose and animistic harmony. In order to effect this transmission the artist must sublimate his personality so that it does not interfere with the viewer's perception of the rhythmic equilibrium of line, dimension, and color. These elements, however, are organized not according to the impersonal dictates of mathematics but rather to the intuition of the artist. Likewise, although the artist's gesture is minimized and the reference to personal experience erased, his presence can be detected in the stroke of the paintbrush and the unevenness of the edge of the transcendent line. The individual consciousness exists in a dialectical relationship with "the absolute," which is realized pictorially through, in Mondrian's words, the "mutual interaction of constructive elements and their inherent relations."[2] Just as the forms and space of the canvas are abstracted from life, so the spiritual plane is removed from, though related to, the work of art. Mondrian sought to unite art, matter, and spirit to discover in all aspects of experience the universal harmony posited in Neo-Plasticism. (L. F.)

1. Quoted in *Theories of Modern Art*, ed. H. B. Chipp, Berkeley and Los Angeles, 1968, p. 350.

2. Ibid., p. 351.

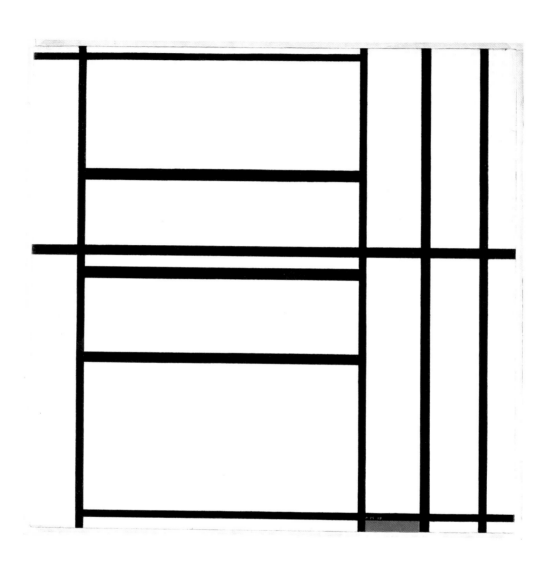

32

THEO VAN DOESBURG

Counter-Composition XIII (Contra-Compositie XIII), 1925–26

Oil on canvas, 49.9 x 50 cm
76.2553 PG 41

About 1924 Theo van Doesburg rebelled against Piet Mondrian's programmatic insistence on the restriction of line to vertical and horizontal orientations, and produced his first *Counter-Composition*. The direction consequently taken by Neo-Plasticism was designated "Elementarism" by van Doesburg, who described its method of construction as "based on the neutralization of positive and negative directions by the diagonal and, as far as color is concerned, by the dissonant. Equilibrated relations are not an ultimate result."[1] Mondrian considered this redefinition of Neo-Plasticism heretical; he was soon to resign from the De Stijl group.

This canvas upholds the Neo-Plastic dictum of "peripheric" composition. The focus is decentralized and there are no empty, inactive areas. The geometric planes are emphasized equally, related by contrasts of color, scale, and direction. One's eyes follow the trajectories of isosceles triangles and stray beyond the canvas to complete mentally the larger triangles sliced off by its edges. The placement of the vertical axis to the left of center and the barely off-square proportions of the support create a sense of shifting balance. (L. F.)

1. Quoted in H. L. C. Jaffé, *De Stijl, 1917–1931: The Dutch Contribution to Modern Art*, Amsterdam, 1956, p. 26.

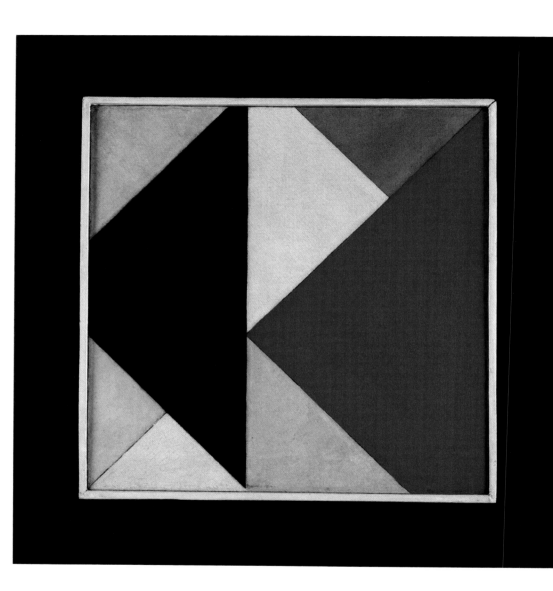

33

GEORGES VANTONGERLOO

Construction of Volumetric Interrelationships Derived from the Inscribed Square and the Square Circumscribed by a Circle (Construction des rapports des volumes émanante du carré inscrit et le carré circonscrit d'un cercle), 1924

Cast cement with paint, 30 cm high, 25.5 cm at widest point
76.2553 PG 59

Georges Vantongerloo, who accepted the De Stijl restriction of line to horizontal and vertical in 1919, based his sculpture on the volumetric translation of this principle. The variation of volume and proportion in his work was determined geometrically, often according to mathematical formulae. Mathematics was for Vantongerloo a convention that established order in the world, a rationalization of nature that could be combined successfully with an aesthetic intention to result in the production of a work of art. In this approach he felt closest to the medieval artist who composed within the constraints of geometric convention, and to the ancient Egyptians, whose solution to the "problem" of the pyramid of Cheops consisted in "the inscribed and circumscribed squares of a circle."[1]

In one of his books Vantongerloo juxtaposed a diagram for the present work with an analytic sketch of the rose window at the cathedral of Amiens.[2] The asymmetry of the De Stijl image distinguishes it from the medieval subject. As the diagram shows and the title indicates, the extensions of the sculpture are determined by the lines of the inscribed and circumscribed squares of a circle. The relationships of its volumes result as much from the creative selectivity of the artist as from mathematical regulation. The effects of changing light produce subtle coloristic modulation and a relationship with the environment approaching that of architecture. (L. F.)

1. G. Vantongerloo, *Paintings, Sculptures, Reflections*, New York, 1948, p. 22.

2. Ibid., p. 23.

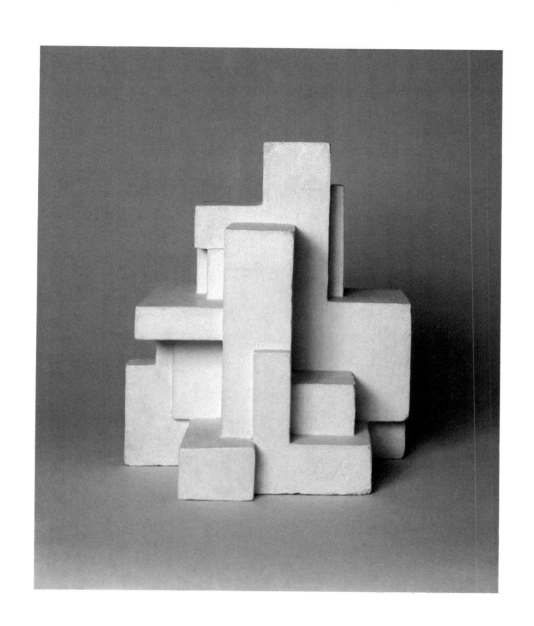

34

AMÉDÉE OZENFANT

Guitar and Bottles (Guitare et bouteilles), 1920

Oil on canvas, 80.5 x 99.8 cm
76.2553 PG 24

Two other versions of this work exist. One of these, *Still Life*, is in the collection of the Solomon R. Guggenheim Museum, New York; the whereabouts of the other is presently unknown. The composition is informed by the Purist aesthetic as developed by Amédée Ozenfant and Le Corbusier in 1918. Drawing on pre-1914 Cubism, particularly the coolly rational interpretation of Juan Gris, they dismissed its subsequent evolution as too decorative and unordered. They felt that the chaos of the natural world should be dispelled by the organizing mechanisms of the human mind. This conviction became a moral imperative that Ozenfant and Le Corbusier attempted to uphold in their work.

Ozenfant used the following metaphor to describe the function of rational thought: "A lens concentrates the diffuse rays of the sun and creates fire by converging those rays. To converge is to refine something in nature, so as to render it more concentrated, compact, penetrative, intense: it helps to facilitate the manifestations of that phenomenon and to render it effective and useful for humanity."[1] Ozenfant's application of this principle to paintings such as *Guitar and Bottles* resulted in compositions that are lucid and geometric but somewhat dry. (L. F.)

1. A. Ozenfant, *Foundations of Modern Art*, trans. J. Rodker, New York, 1952, p. 191.

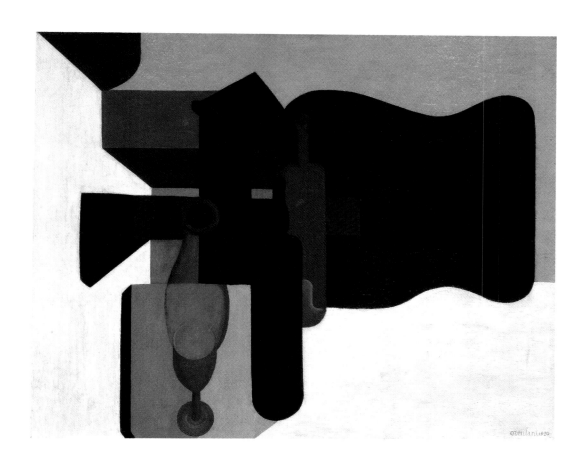

35

JEAN HÉLION

Equilibrium (Equilibre), 1933–34

Oil on canvas, 97.4 x 131.2 cm
76.2553 PG 44

Between 1932 and 1935 Jean Hélion created a series of paintings exploring states of visual equilibrium. Among the earliest of these is *Equilibrium* (Collection Mr. and Mrs. Roy Friedman, Chicago), a simple composition of 1932 in which two curved rectangular shapes are held in balance by two slightly curved lines. In his working journal Hélion recorded the following observations about this work: "In searching for the effect of space and movement on the elements, that is to say in constructing a work in movement, rather in creating equilibrium out of movement, my images have become more pliant. . . . To establish relations between surfaces as complex as those which are defined by curves, it is necessary to arrange nuances." (Quoted in Rudenstine, p. 404, author's translation.)

Following this initial experimentation, Hélion composed several variations on the theme of equilibrium. Generally he worked with drawings and oil studies before reaching the formal solutions of his large canvases. His concern in the present work is to establish a balance between the blocky, simple, essentially rectangular mass on the right with the more complex, more colorful, and varied forms on the left. The construction on the left, which is composed of overlapping and interpenetrating curves, bars, and lines, is not continuous. Careful inspection reveals that the unit of four elements in the upper left corner (the red, gray, and black bars and the green shape) does not touch the forms immediately below it. A similarly strategic use of discontinuous forms occurs in other works in the *Equilibrium* series. In the present painting the subtly disconnected arrangement contributes to the sense of movement and dispersion of the left side of the composition. The multiple hues used at the left also generate visual complexity. The horizontal curves on the left all point to the central white void which is embraced by the more rigidly horizontal dark blue and light green arms of the stable construction on the right. Vibrant red and orange bars unite the edges of the composition with central forms and bind together right and left halves. A state of visual balance is thus achieved without resorting to the purely rectilinear, often programmatic formulations of the De Stijl artists who had influenced Hélion. The *Equilibrium* series, embodying ideas of suspension and tension of two-dimensional forms, inspired Alexander Calder, who was contemporaneously developing his wind-driven mobiles (see cat. no. 68).[1] (E. C. C.)

1. M. Schipper, "Jean Hélion," in *Abstract Painting and Sculpture in America 1927–1944*, exh. cat., Pittsburgh, 1983, p. 168.

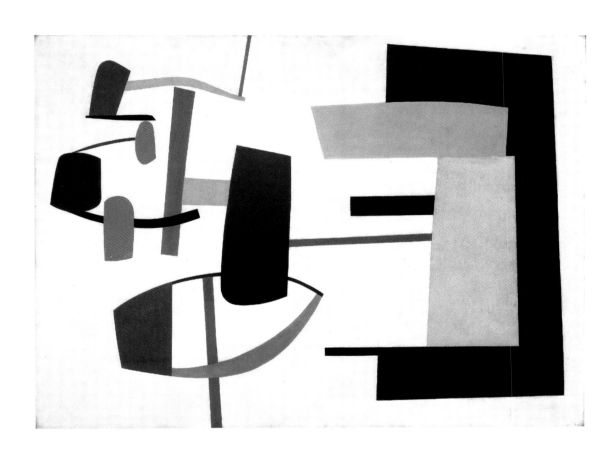

36

GIORGIO DE CHIRICO

The Red Tower (La Tour rouge), 1913

Oil on canvas, 73.5 x 100.5 cm
76.2553 PG 64

Giorgio de Chirico's enigmatic works of 1911 to 1917 provided a crucial inspiration for the Surrealist painters. The dreamlike atmosphere of his compositions results from irrational perspective, the lack of a unified light source, the elongation of shadows, and a hallucinatory focus on objects. Italian piazzas bounded by arcades or classical façades are transformed into ominously silent and vacant settings for invisible dramas. The absence of event provokes a nostalgic or melancholy mood if one senses the wake of a momentous incident; if one feels the imminence of an act, a feeling of anxiety ensues.

De Chirico remarked that "every object has two appearances: one, the current one, which we nearly always see and which is seen by people in general; the other, a spectral or metaphysical appearance beheld only by some individuals in moments of clairvoyance and metaphysical abstraction, as in the case of certain bodies concealed by substances impenetrable by sunlight yet discernible, for instance, by x-ray or other powerful artificial means."[1] Traces of concealed human presences appear in the fraught expanse of this work. One is the partly concealed equestrian monument often identified as Carlo Marochetti's 1861 statue of King Carlo Alberto in Turin,[2] which also appears in the background of de Chirico's *The Departure of the Poet* of 1914 (Private Collection). In addition, in the left foreground, overpainting barely conceals two figures (or statues), one of which resembles a shrouded mythological hero by the nineteenth-century Swiss painter Arnold Böcklin. The true protagonist, however, is the crenellated tower; in its imposing centrality and rotundity it conveys a virile energy that fills the pictorial space. (L. F.)

1. Quoted in W. Rubin, "De Chirico and Modernism," in *De Chirico*, exh. cat., New York, 1982, p. 57.

2. J. T. Soby, *De Chirico*, exh. cat., New York, 1955, pp. 49–50.

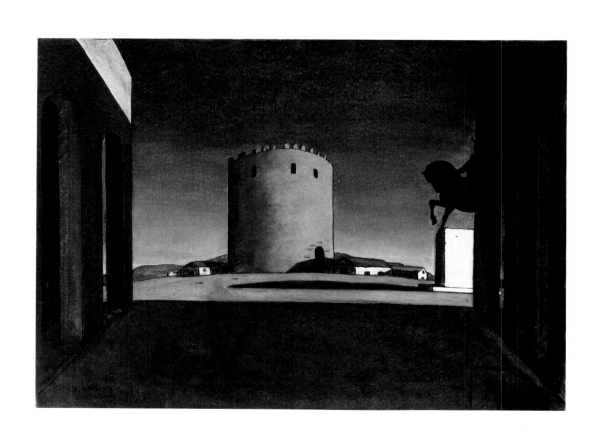

37

GIORGIO DE CHIRICO

The Nostalgia of the Poet (La Nostalgie du poète), 1914

Oil and charcoal on canvas, 89.7 x 40.7 cm
76.2553 PG 65

This work belongs to a series of paintings of 1914 on the subject of the poet, the best known of which is the *Portrait of Guillaume Apollinaire* (Collection Musée National d'Art Moderne, Centre Georges Pompidou, Paris; repr. Rudenstine, p. 162). Recurrent motifs in the sequence are the plaster bust with dark glasses, the mannequin, and the fish mold on an obelisk. These objects, bearing no evident relationships to one another, are compressed here into a narrow vertical format that creates a claustrophobic and enigmatic space.

As in *The Red Tower* (cat. no. 36), the use of inanimate forms imitating or alluding to human beings has complex ramifications. The sculpture at the lower left is a painted representation of a plaster cast from a stone, marble, or metal bust by an imaginary, or at present unidentified, sculptor. The character portrayed could be mythological, historical, symbolical, or fictional. The fish is a charcoal drawing of a metal mold that could produce a baked "cast" of a fish made with an actual fish. The fish has additional connotations as a religious symbol, and the hooklike graphic sign toward which its gaping mouth is directed has its own cryptic allusiveness. The mannequin is a simplified cloth cast of a human figure—a mold on which clothing is shaped to conform to the contours of a person. Each object, though treated as solid and static, dissolves in multiple significations and paradoxes. Such amalgams of elusive meaning in Giorgio de Chirico's strangely intense objects compelled the attention of the Surrealists. (L. F.)

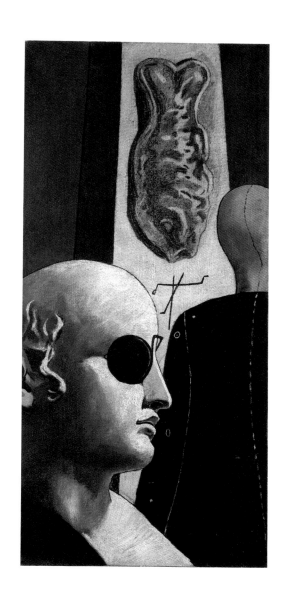

38

MARC CHAGALL

Rain (La Pluie), 1911

Oil (and charcoal?) on canvas, 86.7 x 108 cm
76.2553 PG 63

Marc Chagall's early work is characterized by a neo-primitive style derived primarily from Russian icons and folk art. When he moved from Russia to Paris in the summer of 1910, the artist took with him several of these paintings depicting the life and customs of his native Vitebsk. During the next year he reworked them and also painted new compositions with similar motifs, infused with nostalgia for his homeland, but now adapted according to techniques and concepts he acquired from exposure to current French art.

Nondescriptive, saturated color is used in *Rain* in combination with assertive areas of white and black to produce a highly ornamental and vivid surface. Chagall's use of color was influenced by that of Henri Matisse and Robert Delaunay, whose work he saw almost immediately upon his arrival in Paris. The breaking up of some areas of the composition into shaded planes, for example the roof of the house and the left foreground, has its source in Cubism, though this device is handled somewhat randomly. (L. F.)

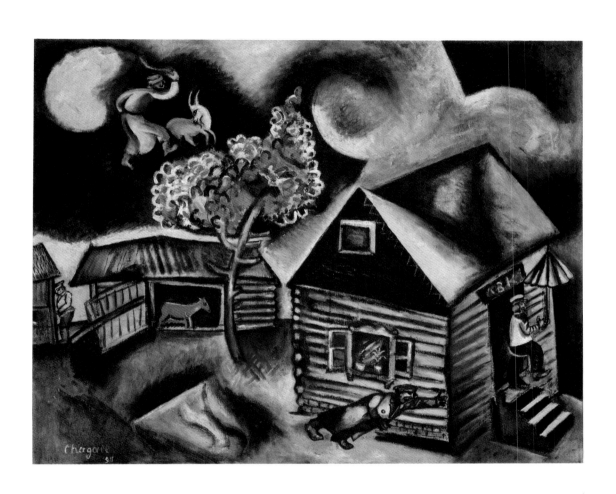

39

PAUL KLEE

Portrait of Mrs. P. in the South (Bildnis der Frau P. im Süden), 1924

Watercolor and oil transfer drawing on paper, mounted on gouache-painted board, 42.5 x 31 cm, including mount
76.2553 PG 89

Paul Klee's vacation in Sicily during the summer of 1924 provided him with the subjects for several watercolors that capture the color, light, and mood of a specific geographical location and cast of characters. This portrait and that of *Frau R. on a Journey to the South*, also of 1924 (present whereabouts unknown), are good-natured caricatures of what might be two prim northern ladies whose absurd hats insufficiently shield them from the intensity of the Mediterranean sun.

The registers that break Frau R. into horizontal sections do not so rigidly stratify Frau P.; her hat dips at a jaunty angle. The vivid, warm color that thickens and thins atmospherically over the surface of the page is incised with simplified graphic contours. The black smudges on the surface result from the use of a transfer technique often employed by Klee in this period. In this technique, one side of a sheet of paper was coated with black oil and laid against a blank support. Then a drawing was placed on top of these two layers and its lines traced with a stylus, transferring the outline to the lower sheet.[1] Finally, watercolor was added.

The heart shape on Frau P.'s chest appears frequently in Klee's work, sometimes as a mouth, nose, or torso. The motif bridged the organic and inorganic worlds for the artist by symbolizing life forces while serving as a "mediating form between circle and rectangle."[2] (L. F.)

1. See J. Glaesmer, *Paul Klee Handzeichnungen I*, Bern, 1973, pp. 258–60.

2. P. Klee, *Notebooks: Volume 2: The Nature of Nature*, ed. J. Spiller, trans. H. Norden, New York, 1973, p. 106.

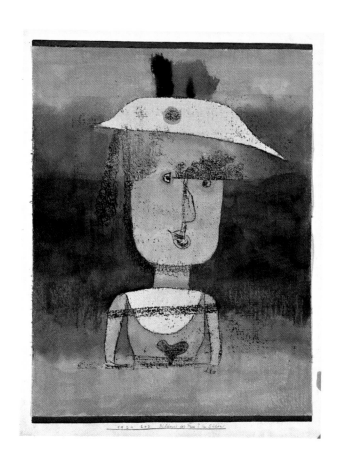

40

PAUL KLEE

Magic Garden (*Zaubergarten*), March 1926

Oil on plaster-filled wire mesh, 52.9 x 44.9 cm, including artist's frame
76.2553 PG 90

Magic Garden was executed in 1926, the year Paul Klee resumed teaching at the Bauhaus at its new location in Dessau. During his Bauhaus period he articulated and taught a complex theoretical program that was supported and clarified by his painting and drawing. Theory, in turn, served to elucidate his art. Based on probing investigation and carefully recorded observation, his work in both areas reveals analogies among the properties of natural, of man-made, and of geometric forms.

Studies of plants illustrating growth processes appear often in Klee's notebooks as well as in his paintings and drawings. He was also interested in architecture and combined images of buildings with vegetal forms in *Magic Garden* and several other works of 1926. Pictorial motifs often arise from geometric exercises: the goblet shape that dominates the lower center of this composition appeared also in a nonrepresentational drawing exploring the development from point to line to surface to volume.

The surface Klee creates with the medium of *Magic Garden* resembles that of a primordial substance worn and textured by its own history. A cosmic eruption seems to have spewed forth forms that are morphologically related but differentiated into various genera. Although excused from the laws of gravity, each of these forms occupies a designated place in a new universe, simultaneously as fixed and mobile as the orbits of planets or the nuclei of organic cells. Klee's cosmic statements are gleefully irreverent; he writes of his work: "Ethical gravity rules, along with hobgoblin laughter at the learned ones."[1] (L. F.)

1. Quoted in W. Grohmann, *Paul Klee*, New York, 1954, p. 191.

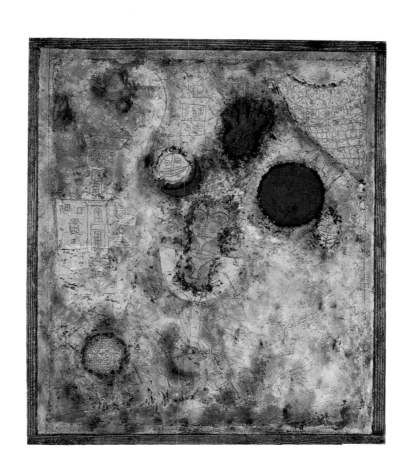

41

FRANCIS PICABIA

Very Rare Picture upon the Earth (Très rare tableau sur la terre), 1915

Oil and metallic paint on board, and silver and gold leaf on wood, 125.7 x 97.8 cm, including artist's painted frame
76.2553 PG 67

In 1915 Francis Picabia abandoned his exploration of abstract form and color to adopt a new machinist idiom that he used until about 1923. Unlike Robert Delaunay or Fernand Léger, who saw the machine as an emblem of a new age, he was attracted to machine shapes for their intrinsic visual and functional qualities. He often used mecanomorphic images humorously as substitutes for human beings; for example, in *Here, This is Stieglitz*, 1915 (Collection The Metropolitan Museum of Art, New York), the photographer Alfred Stieglitz is portrayed as a camera. In *Very Rare Picture on the Earth* a self-generating, almost symmetrical machine is presented frontally, clearly silhouetted against a flat, impassive background. Like Picabia's own *Amorous Parade* of 1917 (Collection Mr. and Mrs. Morton G. Neumann, Chicago) or Marcel Duchamp's *The Bride Stripped Bare by Her Bachelors, Even* of 1915–23 (Collection Philadelphia Museum of Art), the present work might be read as the evocation of a sexual event in mechanical terms. This dispassionate view of sex is consonant with the antisentimental attitudes that were to characterize Dada. The work has also been interpreted as representing an alchemical processor, in part because of the coating of the two upper cylinders with gold and silver leaf respectively.[1]

Not only is *Very Rare Picture on the Earth* one of Picabia's earliest mecanomorphic works, but it has been identified as his first collage.[2] Its mounted wooden forms and integral frame draw attention to the work as object—the picture is not really a picture, making it "very rare" indeed. Thus, an ironic note is added to the humorous pomposity of the inscription at upper left. (L. F.)

1. U. Linde, *Francis Picabia*, exh. cat., Paris, 1976, p. 24.

2. W. A. Camfield, *Francis Picabia: His Art, Life and Times*, Princeton, N. J., 1979, p. 88.

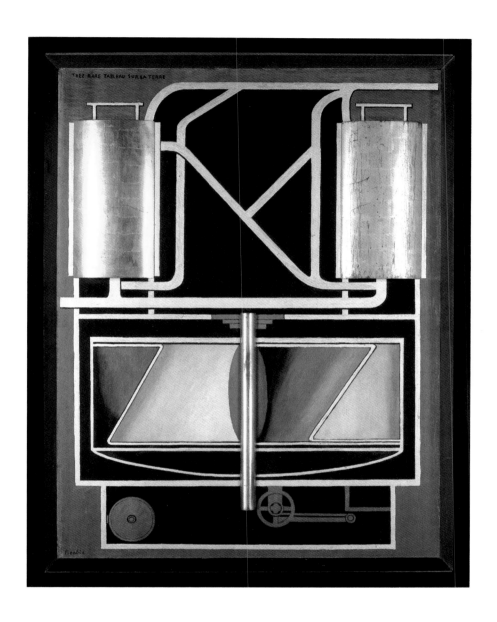

42

MAN RAY

Silhouette, 1916

India ink and charcoal (and gouache?) on board, 51.6 x 64.1 cm
76.2553 PG 68

In 1915 Man Ray abandoned what he called his "Romantic-Expressionist-Cubist" style and adopted a mechanistic, graphic, flattened idiom like that developed by Francis Picabia and Marcel Duchamp during the same period. This drawing is preparatory to his most successful painting in this style, *The Rope Dancer Accompanies Herself with Her Shadows* of 1916 (Collection The Museum of Modern Art, New York; repr. Rudenstine, p. 483), the subject of which was inspired by a vaudeville dancer whose movement he wished to suggest in a series of varying poses.[1] Man Ray's interest in frozen sequential movement may derive from the experiments in photography he initiated about this time.

The particularized features of the figures in this drawing are eliminated to produce two-dimensional patterned forms that are silhouetted against black oval shadows. The dancer is accompanied not only by her shadow but also by music, concisely indicated by the voluted head of an instrument at the lower right of the support, the strings across the bottom, and the music stand at left. The position of her feet on the strings, which may double as a stave, may be meant to convey a specific sequence of notes, as if the dancer were indeed accompanying herself musically. It seems likely that this drawing represents the first stage in the conception of the painting. In the canvas the three positions of the dancer are superimposed and appear at the top of the composition, with the greater part of the field occupied by her distorted, enlarged, and vividly colored cutout shadows. (L. F.)

1. Man Ray discusses the genesis of this work in his autobiography, *Self-Portrait*, Boston and Toronto,1963, pp. 66–67, 71.

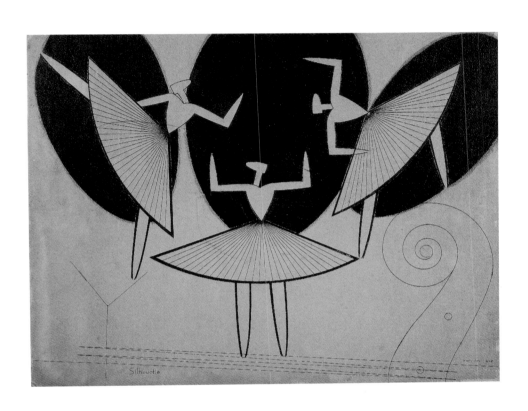

Silhouette

43

MAX ERNST

Little Machine Constructed by Minimax Dadamax in Person (Von minimax dadamax selbst konstruiertes maschinchen), 1919–20

Hand printing (?), pencil and ink frottage, watercolor, and gouache on paper, 49.4 x 31.5 cm
76.2553 PG 70

Little Machine . . . was executed in Cologne the year Dada was established there. It belongs to a series of about fifty works dating from 1919–20, based on diagrams of scientific instruments, in which Max Ernst used printer's plates to reproduce preexisting images. The impressions, once altered by traditional coloristic and modeling effects, occupy a position between found object and artistic product, like his collages.

In both subject and style the series can be compared with Francis Picabia's mecanomorphic drawings and paintings. Ernst shared with Picabia an interest in typography, printed images, and language; many of the forms in the present work can be read as letters. They function as well to describe a mechanical structure that can be seen as a symbol of sexual activity, like Picabia's *Very Rare Picture on the Earth* (cat. no. 41) and his *The Child Carburetor*, 1919 (Collection Solomon R. Guggenheim Museum, New York), or Marcel Duchamp's *The Bride Stripped Bare by Her Bachelors, Even*, 1915–23 (Collection Philadelphia Museum of Art). Ernst's machine is a fantasized solution to the psychological pressures of sexual performance, as announced in the humorously heroic inscription at the bottom of the sheet: *Little machine constructed by minimax dadamax in person for fearless pollination of female suckers at the beginning of the change of life and for other such fearless functions*. The right side of the machine seems to comprise a miniature laboratory for the production of semen, which is indicated as a red drop that courses through passageways to the left side of the apparatus. The drop finally issues from the yellow faucet, accompanied by a whimsically self-assured and cheerful *"Bonjour."* Alternatively, the machine can be seen as a combination of male and female halves. The female (at the right) is dowdy and angular; the more brilliantly colored male (at the left) "fearlessly" points away from her. (L. F.)

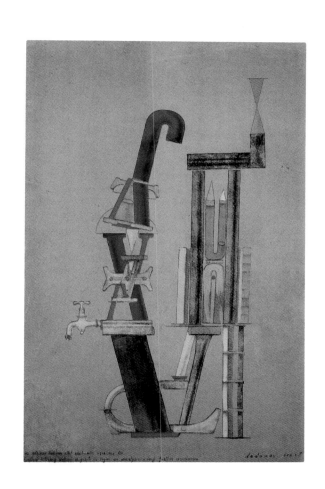

44

MAX ERNST

The Kiss (Le Baiser), 1927
Oil on canvas, 129 x 161.2 cm
76.2553 PG 71

From humorously clinical depictions of erotic events in the Dada period, such as *Little Machine Constructed by Minimax Dadamax in Person* (cat. no. 43), Max Ernst moved on to celebrations of uninhibited sexuality in his Surrealist works. His liaison and marriage with the young Marie-Berthe Aurenche in 1927 may have inspired the erotic subject matter of this painting and others of this year. The major compositional lines of this work may have been determined by the configurations of string that Ernst dropped on a preparatory surface, a procedure according with Surrealist notions of the importance of chance effects. However, Ernst used a coordinate grid system to transfer his string configurations to canvas, thus subjecting these chance effects to conscious manipulation. Visually, the technique produces undulating calligraphic rhythms, like those traced here against the glowing earth and sky colors.

The centralized, pyramidal grouping and the embracing gesture of the upper figure in *The Kiss* have lent themselves to comparison with Renaissance compositions, specifically the *Madonna and Saint Anne* by Leonardo da Vinci (Collection Musée National du Louvre, Paris).[1] The Leonardo work was the subject of a psychosexual interpretation by Sigmund Freud, whose writings were important to Ernst and other Surrealists. The adaptation of a religious subject would add an edge of blasphemy to the exuberant lasciviousness of Ernst's picture. (L. F.)

1. See the interpretation of this work by N. and E. Calas in *The Peggy Guggenheim Collection of Modern Art*, New York, 1966, pp. 112–13.

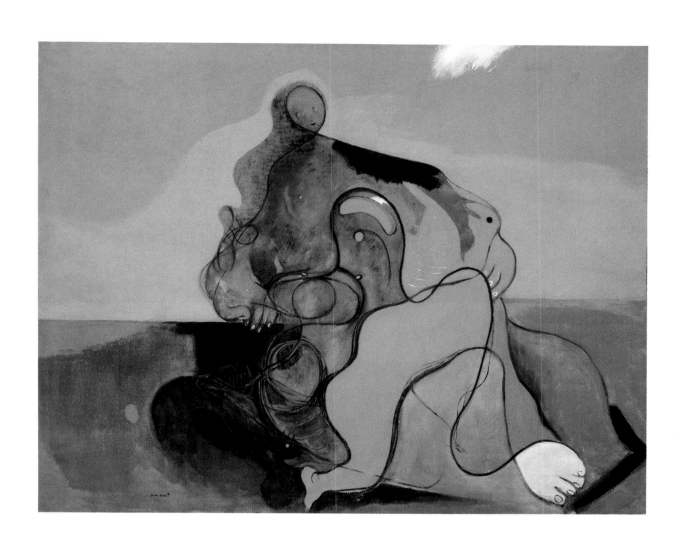

45

MAX ERNST

The Forest (La Forêt), 1927–28

Oil on canvas, 96.3 x 129.5 cm
76.2553 PG 72

André Breton's *Surrealist Manifesto* of 1924 proclaimed "pure psychic automatism" as an artistic ideal, emphasizing inspiration derived from the chance juxtaposition of forms and the haphazard use of materials. Max Ernst came under the influence of Breton's ideas in 1924, and soon thereafter developed his frottage or rubbing technique.[1] In making his first frottages, he dropped pieces of paper at random on floor boards and rubbed them with pencil or chalk, thus transferring the design of the wood grain to the paper. He next adapted this technique to oil painting, scraping paint from prepared canvases laid over materials such as wire mesh, chair caning, leaves, buttons, or twine (see cat. no. 46). His repertory of objects closely parallels that used by Man Ray in his experiments with Rayograms during the same period. Using his grattage (scraping) technique, Ernst covered his canvases completely with pattern and then interpreted the images that emerged, thus allowing texture to suggest composition in a spontaneous fashion. In *The Forest* the artist probably placed the canvas over a rough surface (perhaps wood), scraped oil paint over the canvas, and then rubbed, scraped, and overpainted the area of the trees (Rudenstine, pp. 287–89).

The subject of a dense forest appears often in Ernst's work of the late twenties and early thirties. These canvases, of which *The Quiet Forest*, 1927 (Collection Kunstmuseum Basel), is another example, generally contain a wall of trees, a solar disk, and an apparition of a bird hovering amid the foliage. Ernst's attitude toward the forest as the sublime embodiment of both enchantment and terror can be traced to his experiences in the German forest as a child.[2] His essay "Les Mystères de la forêt," published in *Minotaure* in 1934, vividly conveys his fascination with the various kinds of forests. The Peggy Guggenheim canvas resonates with those qualities he identified with the forests of Oceania: "They are, it seems, savage and impenetrable, black and russet, extravagant, secular, swarming, diametrical, negligent, ferocious, fervent, and likeable, without yesterday or tomorrow. . . . Naked, they dress only in their majesty and their mystery." (Author's translation.) (E. C. C.)

1. For Ernst's own account of frottage see M. Ernst, "Favorite Poets and Painters of the Past," in *Beyond Painting*, New York, 1948, p. 7.

2. M. Ernst, "Some Data on the Youth of M. E. as told by himself," in *Beyond Painting*, New York, 1948, p. 27.

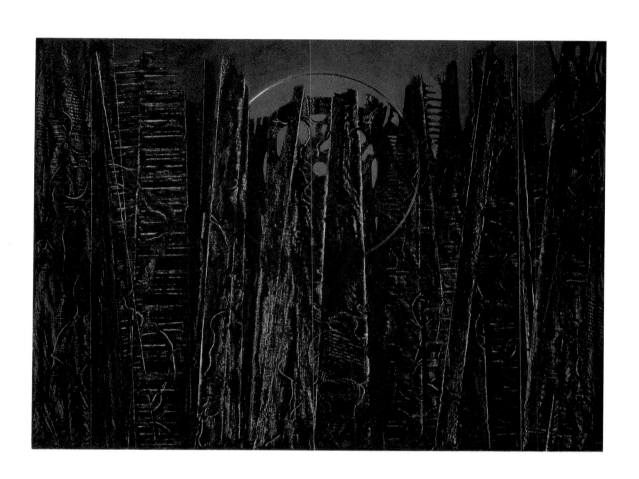

46

MAX ERNST

Zoomorphic Couple (Couple zoomorphe), 1933

Oil on canvas, 91.9 x 73.3 cm
76.2553 PG 75

By 1925 Max Ernst had developed his frottage (rubbing) technique, which he associated with a childhood memory of accidental forms materializing within the grooves of wooden floorboards. He also acknowledged the influence of his later discovery of Leonardo da Vinci's *Treatise on Painting*, in which artists are advised to gaze at the stains on walls until figures and scenes emerge. In the *Hordes* series of 1926–32 Ernst placed twine beneath his canvases and then rubbed pigment over their surfaces. The meanderings of the twine were thus revealed; these chance configurations were then manipulated to elicit imagery. In *Zoomorphic Couple*, the appearance of light, sinuous channels through dark painted areas produces a relieflike effect suggestive of frottage. However, the artist created the effect here by putting paint-laden string or rope on top of the canvas and spraying over it (Rudenstine, p. 299). The image of the bird, which recurs frequently in Ernst's work from 1925, had become an almost obsessive preoccupation by 1930. In the present painting one can discern a vaguely birdlike form and a caressing humanoid arising from the primordial material that gives them their substance. It has been suggested that the atavistic imagery in Ernst's work of this period alludes to the failure of European civilization in the face of the rising National Socialist threat in Germany.[1] (Ernst was blacklisted by the party in 1933 when Hitler became Chancellor of the Third Reich.) Though a sensitivity to the current political climate may be inferred, it is not confirmed by anecdotal detail. The forms have the effect of dream or poetic apparition.

The sense of genesis and evolutionary stirrings in *Zoomorphic Couple* is complemented by the creative inventiveness of the artist, who combines layers of pastel color under spattered, blown, and dripped paint. (L. F.)

1. U. M. Schneede, *Max Ernst*, New York and London, 1972, p. 134.

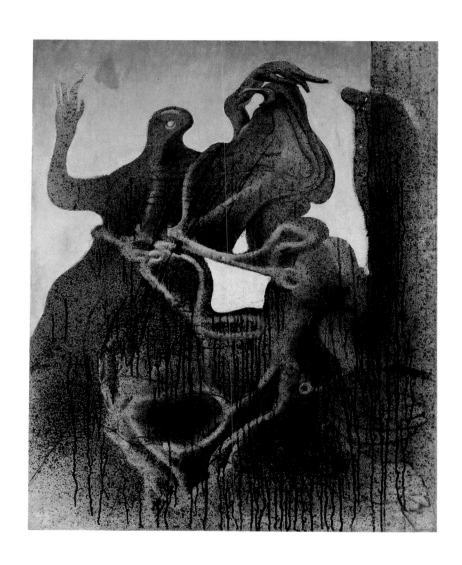

47

MAX ERNST

Attirement of the Bride (La Toilette de la mariée), 1940

Oil on canvas, 129.6 x 96.3 cm
76.2553 PG 78

Attirement of the Bride is an example of Max Ernst's veristic or illusionistic Surrealism, in which a traditional technique is applied to an incongruous or unsettling subject. The theatrical, evocative scene has roots in late nineteenth-century Symbolist painting, especially that of Gustave Moreau. It also echoes the settings and motifs of sixteenth-century German art. The willowy, swollen-bellied figure types recall those of Lucas Cranach the Elder in particular. The architectural backdrop with its strong contrast of light and shadow and its inconsistent perspective shows the additional influence of Giorgio de Chirico, whose work had overwhelmed Ernst when he first saw it in 1919.

The pageantry and elegance of the image are contrasted with its primitivizing aspects—the garish colors, the animal and monster forms—and the blunt phallic symbolism of the poised spearhead. The central scene is contrasted as well with its counterpart in the picture-within-a-picture at the upper left. In this detail the bride appears in the same pose, striding through a landscape of overgrown classical ruins. Here Ernst has used the technique of decalcomania invented in 1935 by Oscar Domínguez, in which diluted paint is pressed onto a surface with an object that distributes it unevenly, such as a pane of glass. A suggestive textured pattern results.

The title of this work had occurred to Ernst at least as early as 1936, when he italicized it in a text in his book *Beyond Painting*. Ernst had long identified himself with the bird, and had invented an alter ego, Loplop, Superior of the Birds, in 1929. Thus one may perhaps interpret the bird-man at the left as a depiction of the artist; the bride may in some sense represent the young English Surrealist artist Leonora Carrington. (L. F.)

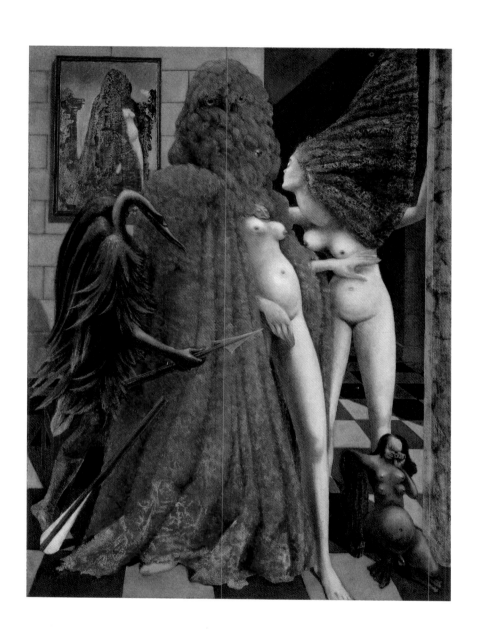

48

MAX ERNST

The Antipope, December 1941–March 1942

Oil on canvas, 160.8 x 127.1 cm
76.2553 PG 80

Max Ernst settled in New York in 1941 after escaping from Europe with the help of Peggy Guggenheim. The same year he executed a small oil on cardboard (now in the Peggy Guggenheim Collection) that became the basis for the large-scale *The Antipope*. When Guggenheim saw the small version, she interpreted a dainty horse-human figure on the right as Ernst, who was being fondled by a woman she identified as herself. She wrote that Ernst conceded that a third figure, depicted in a three-quarter rear view, was her daughter Pegeen; she did not attempt to identify another horse-headed female to the left.[1] When Ernst undertook the large version from December to March he changed the body of the "Peggy" figure into a greenish column and transferred her amorous gesture to a new character, who wears a pink tunic and is depicted in a relatively naturalistic way. The "Pegeen" figure in the center appears to have two faces, one of a flayed horse that looks at the horse-woman at the left. The other, with only its cheek and jaw visible, gazes in the opposite direction, out over the grim lagoon, like a pensive subject conceived by Caspar David Friedrich.

The great upheavals in Ernst's personal life during this period encourage such a biographical interpretation. Despite his marriage to Guggenheim, he was deeply involved with Leonora Carrington at this time, and spent hours riding horses with her. As birds were an obsession for Ernst, so horses were for Carrington. Her identification with them is suggested throughout her collection of stories *La Dame ovale*, published in 1939 with seven illustrations by Ernst, two of which include metamorphosed horse creatures. It seems plausible that the alienated horse-woman of *The Antipope*, who twists furtively to watch the other horse-figure, represents a vision of Guggenheim (Rudenstine, pp. 315–17). Like the triumphal bride in *Attirement of the Bride* (cat. no. 47), she wears an owl headgear. Her irreconcilable separation from her companion is expressed graphically by the device of the diagonally positioned spear that bisects the canvas. The features of the green totemic figure resemble those of Carrington, whose relationship with Ernst was to end soon after the painting was completed, when she moved to Mexico with her husband. (L. F.)

1. See P. Guggenheim, *Out of This Century: Confessions of an Art Addict*, New York, 1979, pp. 261–62.

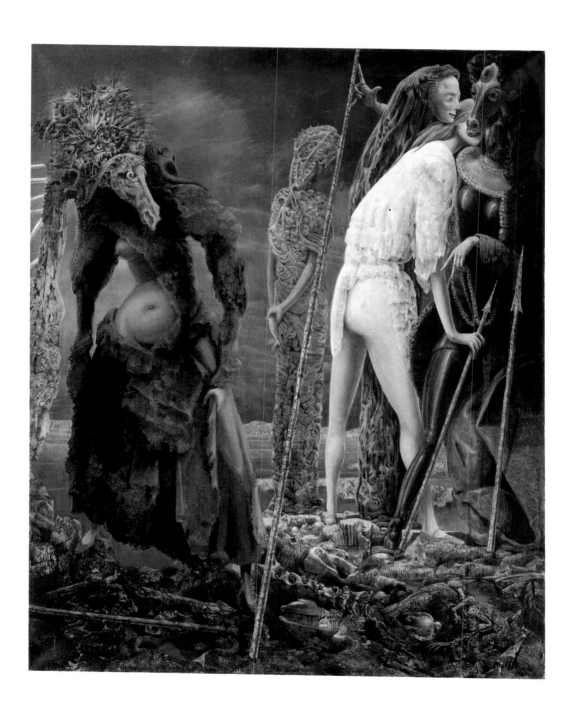

49

JEAN ARP

Large Collage (*Grand collage*), 1955 reconstruction of original of ca. 1918

Paper collage, watercolor, and metallic and oil paint on Masonite, 97.6 x 77.8 cm
76.2553 PG 52

In 1915, shortly before he joined the Zurich Dada group, Jean Arp produced what he described as his "first 'essential' picture," the simplified geometric elements of which he associated with children's building blocks organized in a spirit of play. By 1918 the artist, influenced by the rectilinear strictness of Sophie Taeuber's work, eliminated curves and diagonals from his collages (Rudenstine, pp. 62–64). As the upheaval and anxiety associated with World War I subsided, he concentrated on distilling a world of calm, simplicity, and order in his work. His collages literally emphasized the constructive activity of the artist in opposition to or in disregard of the explicitly destructive, iconoclastic attitudes promulgated by the Dadaists.

Arp based the composition of the present collage on modular rectangles of two sizes distributed along a grid. The proportional ratio of each module is one to one and one-quarter. The only vertically aligned rectangle, at upper center, is inconsistently small and superimposed on another rectangle. The cream-colored areas serve as a ground in which either vertical or horizontal rectangles can be visualized, thereby introducing an element of uncertainty into a composition that at first appears clear and declarative. The way in which collaged elements are integrated with the support results in an ambiguous relationship between figure and ground.

This work, damaged beyond repair, was reconstructed by the artist in 1955 (Rudenstine, p. 60). (L. F.)

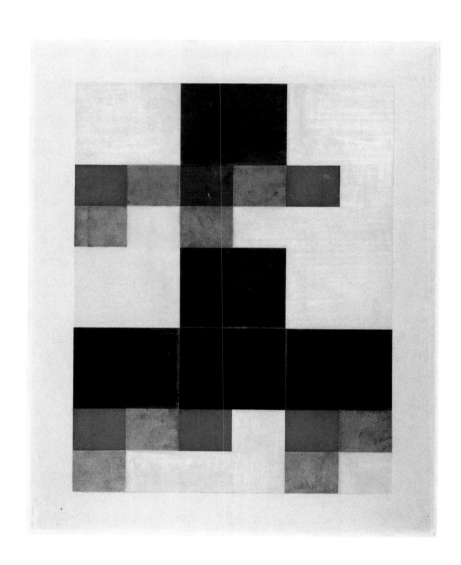

50

JEAN ARP

Overturned Blue Shoe with Two Heels Under a Black Vault (Soulier bleu renversé à deux talons, sous une voûte noire), ca. 1925

Painted wood, 79.3 x 104.6 x 5 cm
76.2553 PG 53

Jean Arp participated in Dada activities in Zurich in the teens; during the mid-twenties he allied himself to a certain extent with Surrealism, which had assimilated many of the tendencies of Dada. Although Arp resisted the program of the Surrealists, he shared their faith in unfettered creativity, their celebration of spontaneity, and their antirational stance.

He executed his first monochrome wood reliefs in 1914, adding the element of color two years later. Comprised of discrete wood forms mounted individually on wood supports, these reliefs are assembled like collages rather than carved. Arp continued to make reliefs throughout his life. By combining aspects of painting, collage, and sculpture, the reliefs of the teens and twenties served in some sense as a bridge to his sculpture in the round. Arp regarded his simplified forms as emblems of natural growth processes. As he wrote: "I looked for new constellations of form such as nature never stops producing. I tried to make forms grow. I put my trust in the example of seeds, stars, clouds, plants, animals, men, and finally in my innermost being."[1] According to Arp, his works carried their own momentum and arrived at organic solutions subject as much to the laws of chance as to his conscious manipulations. He commented on the "ridiculous" analogies of forms that resulted from this process; his descriptive titles, such as that of the present work or *Shirt Front and Fork or Dress with Eye and Navel*, were often correspondingly whimsical. (L. F.)

1. J. Arp, "Looking," in *Arp*, exh. cat., New York, 1958, p. 12.

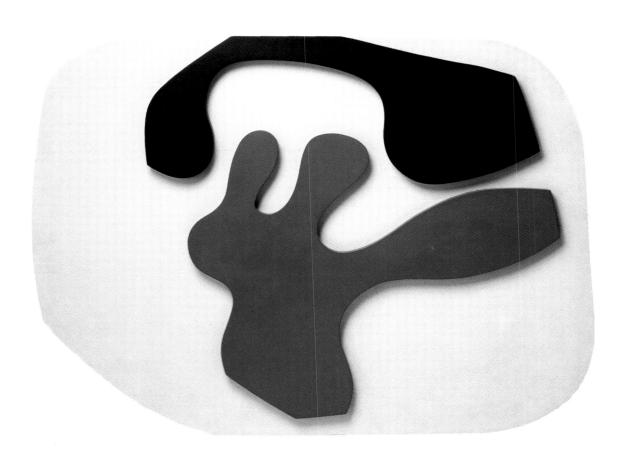

51

KURT SCHWITTERS

Merz Drawing 75 (Merzzeichnung 75), 1920

Collage, gouache, ink, and graphite on papers and fabric, 14.6 x 10 cm, including artist's mat
76.2553 PG 85

Kurt Schwitters, though closely identified with the iconoclastic Dada movement, was also committed to Modernist ideals of pure and self-sufficient art. With a connoisseur's discernment he redeemed objects from the detritus of daily life and incorporated them into his *Merz* works. Even the most raw or worn surfaces are endowed with a poetic grace. The designation *Merz* is derived from the truncation of the *Kommerz*, which appears in an early collage (present whereabouts unknown). Glued or nailed ticket stubs, cigarette wrappings, bits of fabric, wood, tin, and pottery interact in his *Merz* collages to produce compositions of compelling structural authority. These objects lose their conventional associations because of the change of context and the formal manipulations to which they are subjected.

Visually these works are related in some respects to the collages of Pablo Picasso and Georges Braque, the paintings of Robert Delaunay, and the mixed-media sculptures of Umberto Boccioni. Like the Cubists, Schwitters often included printed words or letters, which appealed to him for their intrinsic formal qualities. Here he probably intended a wry comment on his work in the clearly legible words on the cigarette package at the lower right: *made of . . . best old*. Below, he added the inscription: *Mz 75/K. Sch. 20/Zeichnung blass*. Mz stands for *Merzzeichnung* or *Merz Drawing*; *Zeichnung blass* means "pale drawing." Like his other humorously self-deprecating titles (*Nothing At All* or *It's So Lovely*) "pale drawing" seems to be conceived by Schwitters in an irreverent Dada mood. (L. F.)

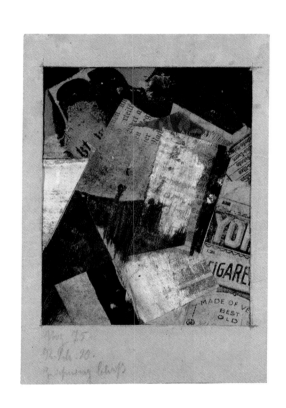

52

KURT SCHWITTERS

Maraak, Variation I (Merzbild), 1930
Oil and assemblage of objects on board, 46 x 37 cm
76.2553 PG 87

Kurt Schwitters abandoned his *Merz* pictures to a large extent during the mid- to late 1920s to concentrate on paintings, constructions, and reliefs in which the influence of Russian Constructivism and the work of his friend Theo van Doesburg is discernable. He eliminated found materials from these compositions and thereby reduced the Dada element of chance they contributed in order to achieve a less idiosyncratic and hence more universal form of expression. This development accorded with his belief in the ascendancy of formal values, which he felt should not be jeopardized by references to anything outside the work of art.

When Schwitters returned to the *Merz* idiom in 1930, he placed more emphasis on the act of painting than he had in his early collages. Though the planes are shaped with the impersonality of geometric contour, they are animated by the variation of rhythmic brushstrokes and the addition of collaged forms. In the tradition of his *Merz* works of the classic period of 1919 to the mid-1920s, the objects he adopted were disposable articles—the top of a corroded tin can and a metal butterfly; the picture once included a broken piece of china to the right of the tin circle and two wooden balls below the butterfly. While the objects function as abstract elements within the flat confines of the support, their projection contradicts the two-dimensionality of the picture plane and implies an extension of the work of art into the observer's world. (L. F.)

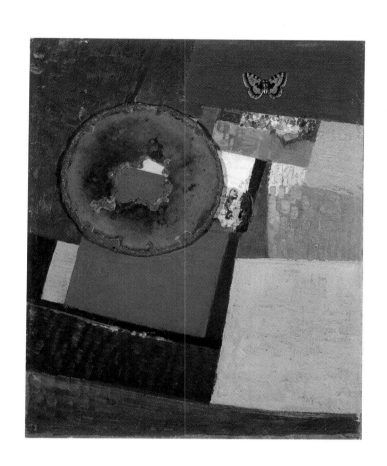

53

JOAN MIRÓ

Painting (Peinture), 1925

Oil on canvas, 114.5 x 145.7 cm
76.2553 PG 91

During the mid- to late 1920s Joan Miró developed a private system of imagery in which the motifs have symbolic meanings that vary according to their context. By studying the constellations of these motifs, one is encouraged to infer meanings appropriate to a particular painting.

In *Painting* two "personages" (the designation Miró used for his abstract figures) and a flame have been identified. The personage on the right can perhaps be read as a female because of the curvaceous nature of the eight-shape, and by analogy with forms in other paintings that are specifically identified by the artist as women. The black dot with radiating lines can be interpreted as the figure's eye receiving rays of light, or as a bodily or verbal emission. The same motif appears in *Personage*, also of 1925, in the collection of the Solomon R. Guggenheim Museum, New York. Moons, stars, suns, or planets float at the upper left of several canvases of the mid-1920s. In the present work the semicircular orange-red image not only carries a cosmic implication, but also possibly doubles as the head of the second personage, probably a male. This head is presented in a combined full-face and profile view, in the manner of Pablo Picasso's Cubist portraits.

The flame, used repeatedly by Miró in this period, may signify sexual excitation in this context. The erotic content that prevails in much of his work in 1925 is particularly explicit in the *Lovers* series, in which two figures approach each other or are united in sexual embrace. The two figures in *Painting* are less clearly conjoined. The submersion of legible subject matter and the ambiguity of the painting's meaning transfer the emphasis to the purely abstract qualities of the work. Line and color articulate a language as complex and poetic as the hieroglyphic signs that constitute the imagery. The generalized ground, rich in texture from the uneven thinning of paint and the use of shadowy black, provides a warm and earthy support for the expressive black lines, the areas of red and yellow, and the staccato rhythm of dots. (L. F.)

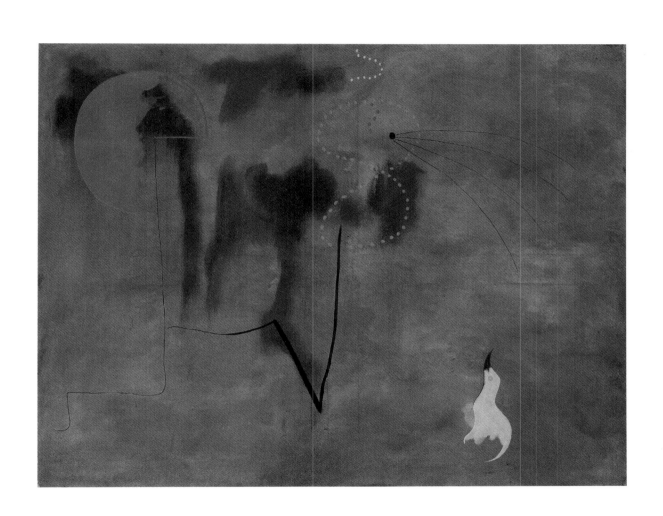

54

JOAN MIRÓ

Dutch Interior II (Intérieur hollandais), summer 1928

Oil on canvas, 92 x 73 cm
76.2553 PG 92

In 1928 Joan Miró returned to Paris from a trip to the Netherlands with several postcard reproductions of works by seventeenth-century Dutch artists. At least two of these have been identified as sources for the *Dutch Interior* paintings in the Museum of Modern Art, New York (repr. Rudenstine, p. 544, fig. h) and the Peggy Guggenheim Collection.[1] The Guggenheim work is a transformation of Jan Steen's *The Dancing Lesson* (Collection Rijksmuseum, Amsterdam; repr. Rudenstine, p. 542, fig. a) and conveys the synthesis of carefully observed, precisely executed detail and imaginative generalization of form that proceeded from Miró's encounter with the Dutch Baroque. In this combination of objective minutiae and abstract vision, *Dutch Interior II* reverts conceptually to works of the early 1920s, such as *The Tilled Field*, 1923–24 (Collection Solomon R. Guggenheim Museum, New York).

The gradual translation of veristic detail into eccentric, evocative form can be followed through preliminary sketches of specific motifs to a meticulously complete preparatory drawing. A conspicuous modification of the Dutch original is Miró's enlargement of and focus on human and animal figures and his concomitant suppression or deemphasis of inanimate objects. Thus a window at the upper center of the Steen has been greatly reduced in size, as though it had been sent hurtling through a vast space. The real subject of the Steen is not the cat, but the sound, movement, and hilarity the dancing lesson provokes. Miró seizes on this anomaly in his version: although the cat serves as the hub of his centrifugal composition, he emphasizes the cacophony and animation of the lesson through the swirling motion of myriad details and the dancing rhythm of points and counterpoints. (L. F.)

1. See W. Erben, *Joan Miró*, New York, 1957, pp. 125–27.

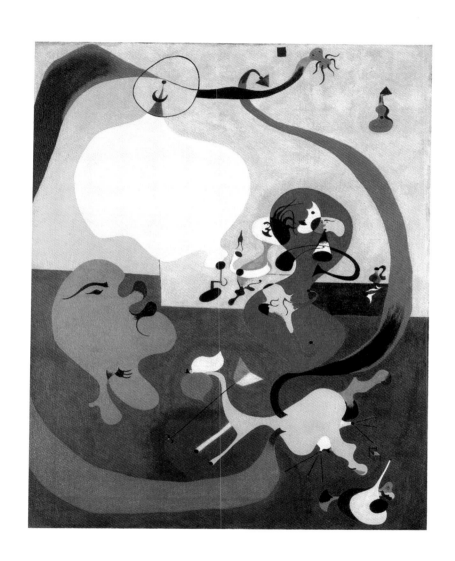

55

JOAN MIRÓ

Seated Woman II (Femme assise II), February 27, 1939

Oil on canvas, 162 x 130 cm
76.2553 PG 93

The expressionistic *Seated Woman II* can be seen as a final manifestation of Joan Miró's *peintures sauvages*, works characterized by violence of execution and imagery. It was painted at a time when Miró, like Pablo Picasso and Julio González (see cat. no. 56), was responding acutely to the events of the Spanish Civil War.

The human figure has been transmogrified here into a grotesque and bestial creature. However, the aggressiveness of imagery and formal elements coexists with fanciful details and cosmic implications. Though the open, saw-toothed mouth imparts a sense of the woman's voraciousness or anguish, her bottle-breast implies her generative force. Her expansive torso constitutes an impenetrable ground, its horizon line described by her squared shoulders, out of which grow the vegetative stems of arms and neck. The bird and fish forms floating through the atmosphere become insignias for air and water, while the moon, star, and planet emblems on the woman's collar broaden the associations to encompass the astral plane. The remaining abstract shapes seem to course slowly in mysterious orbits, passing through and beyond one another, changing color where they intersect. A cohesive universe is created despite the dichotomies of light and dark, nurture and destruction, life and nonexistence. Integration is provided by the repetition of shapes, such as the leaf and oval, which suggests analogies: the woman's pendant becomes a moon or vagina, her hair resembles lines of sight, like those of the fish, or rays of light, and her teeth are equated with the decorative motifs or mountains in the miniature landscape of her collar.

This work postdates by about two months the more generalized *Seated Woman I* (Collection The Museum of Modern Art, New York; repr. Rudenstine, p. 546, fig. a). (L. F.)

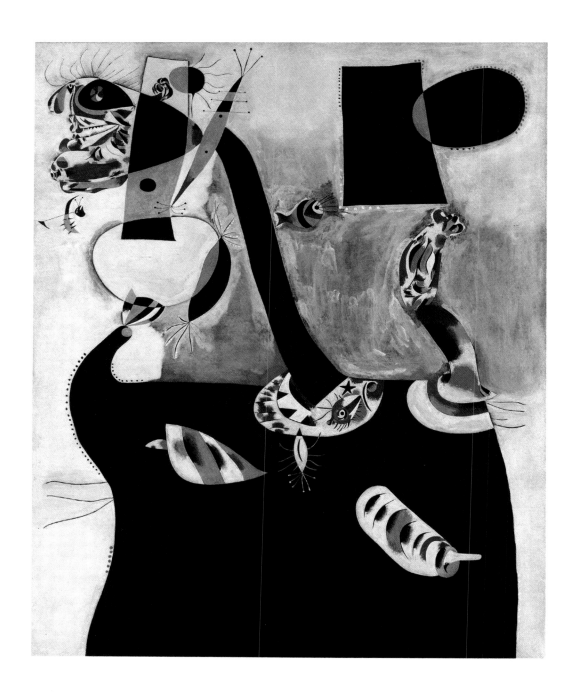

56

JULIO GONZÁLEZ

"Monsieur" Cactus (Cactus Man I), 1939 (cast 1953–54)

Bronze, 64.3 x 25 x 17 cm
76.2553 PG 136

During the late 1930s Julio González worked simultaneously in naturalistic and abstract idioms. His abstract mode constituted an important contribution to the development of avant-garde sculpture in both Europe and the United States. This mode is exemplified by *"Monsieur" Cactus* of 1939, in which he returns to the metamorphic theme of several earlier sculptures. As in works by other Spanish artists living abroad during the Civil War, the figure is anguished—see, for example, Joan Miró's *Seated Woman II* (cat. no. 55) or Pablo Picasso's *Guernica* of 1937 (Collection Museo Nacional del Prado, Madrid). Indeed, several of the more literal preparatory drawings for the sculpture, dating from December of 1938, suggest that the figure is shrieking; the prickly nails intensify the aggressive effect of the work, recalling Picasso's use of nails in his *Guitar* of 1926 (Collection Musée Picasso, Paris). Though the distortion and dislocation of anatomical features make positive identification difficult, with the aid of the drawings one can read a raised arm joined to the hip, its five fingers spread like a cluster of cylindrical cactus stems. The analogous five-fingered block to the left of the torso seems to be lowered to a position just above an angular phallus.

The companion to this sculpture, known as *Cactus Man II* or *"Madame" Cactus*, has been interpreted as the image of the Spanish peasant's defiance of Franco's fascist threat.[1] While the synthesis of human being and cactus may reflect the identification of the Spanish peasant with the land, the metamorphic figure may more generally personify the republican cause. At the end of 1938 Franco launched a major offensive against Catalonia, González's native province, and was to take its capital, Barcelona, in January of 1939, signaling the end of republican hopes. By the time the drawings for the second cactus sculpture appeared in the summer of 1939, Madrid had fallen and Franco's Falange was in full power. (L. F.)

1. E. A. Carmean, "Cactus Man Number Two," *The Museum of Fine Arts, Houston: Bulletin*, fall 1973, p. 41. For a discussion of the titles and the meanings of the two works, see M. Rowell, *Julio González: A Retrospective*, exh. cat., New York, 1983, pp. 188, 195, and Rudenstine, p. 364.

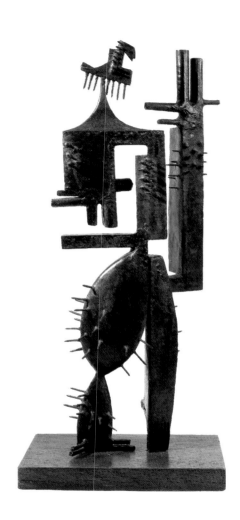

57

ALBERTO GIACOMETTI

Woman with Her Throat Cut (Femme égorgée), 1932 (cast 1940)

Bronze, 23.2 x 89 cm
76.2553 PG 131

In a group of works made between 1930 and 1933, Alberto Giacometti used the Surrealist techniques of shocking juxtaposition and the distortion and displacement of anatomical parts to express the fears and urges of the subconscious. The aggressiveness with which the human figure is treated in these fantasies of brutal erotic assault graphically conveys their content. The female, seen in horror and longing as both victim and victimizer of male sexuality, is often a crustacean or insectlike form. *Woman with Her Throat Cut* is a particularly vicious image: the body is splayed open, disemboweled, arched in a paroxysm of sex and death. Eros and Thanatos, seen here as a single theme, are distinguished and treated separately in two preparatory sketches (Collection Musée National d'Art Moderne, Centre Georges Pompidou, Paris; repr. Rudenstine, p. 344, fig. b).

Body parts are translated into schematic abstract forms like those in *Cage* of 1930–31 (Collection Moderna Museet, Stockholm), which includes the spoon shape of the female torso, the rib and back-bone motif, and the pod shape of the phallus. Here a vegetal form resembling the pelvic bone terminates one arm, and a phalluslike spindle, the only movable part, gruesomely anchors the other; the woman's backbone pins one leg by fusing with it; her slit carotid immobilizes her head. The memory of violence is frozen in the rigidity of rigor mortis. The psychological torment and the sadistic misogyny projected by this sculpture are in startling contrast to the serenity of other contemporaneous pieces by Giacometti, such as *Woman Walking* (cat. no. 58). (L. F.)

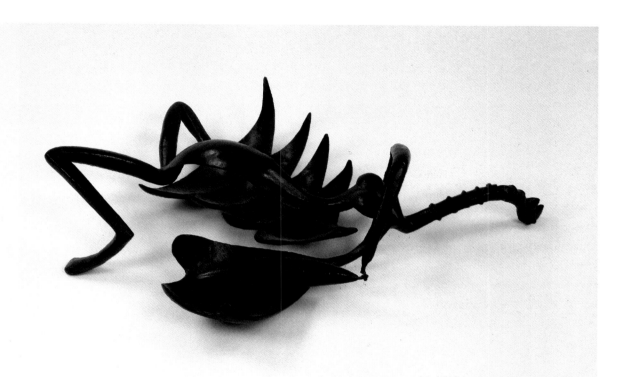

58

ALBERTO GIACOMETTI

Woman Walking (Femme qui marche), 1932

Plaster, 150 x 27.2 cm, including base
76.2553 PG 132

This sculpture is conceived in the rational and formally serene mode Alberto Giacometti pursued concurrently with his dark Surrealist explorations of the subconscious. *Woman Walking* has none of the ferocity of *Woman with Her Throat Cut* (cat. no. 57), though both works were executed during the same period. The graceful, calm plaster seems to have its source in the frontal figures of ancient Egypt, posed with left feet slightly ahead of right in fearless confrontation of death. Despite the pose, *Woman Walking*, like its Egyptian ancestors, conveys no sense of movement. The plane of the body is only slightly inflected by the projections of breasts, belly, and thighs. The long, thin legs are smooth, solid, and columnar. In its flatness, the work evokes the traditions of the highly simplified Cycladic figure and the geometric kouros of archaic Greece. Giacometti is known to have copied works of art at the Louvre, during his travels, and even from reproductions, showing a preference for models characterized by a high degree of stylization. *Woman Walking* also reflects Giacometti's awareness of twentieth-century sculptors, particularly Constantin Brancusi and Alexander Archipenko.

Another plaster version of the sculpture, also probably dating from 1932 (formerly Collection Erica Brausen, London), is distinguished by a triangular cavity in the upper abdomen.[1] The generalization and distortion of form in these works forecast Giacometti's development of the elongated style for which he is best known (see cat. no. 59). (L. F.)

1. For a discussion of the relationship between the two versions, see Rudenstine, pp. 336–40.

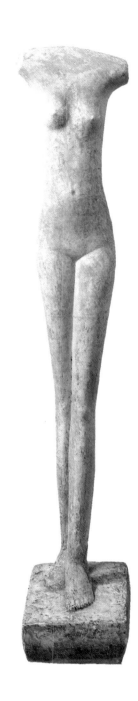

59

ALBERTO GIACOMETTI

Standing Woman ("Leoni") (*Femme debout {"Leoni"}*), 1947 (cast November 1957)

Bronze, 153 cm high, including base
76.2553 PG 134

An early example of the mature style with which Giacometti is usually identified, this figure is more elongated and dematerialized than *Woman Walking* (cat. no. 58), although it retains that sculpture's frontality and immobility. A sense of ghostly fragility detaches the figure from the world around it, despite the crusty materiality of the surfaces, as animated and responsive to light as those of Rodin.

Giacometti exploited the contradictions of perception in the haunting, incorporeal sculptures of this period. His matchstick-sized figures of 1942–46 demonstrate the effect of distance on size and comment on the notion that the essence of an individual persists even as the body appears to vanish, that is, to become nonexistent. Even his large-scale standing women and striding men seem miniaturized and insubstantial. In 1947 the sculptor commented that "lifesize figures irritate me, after all, because a person passing by on the street has no weight; in any case he's much lighter than the same person when he's dead or has fainted. He keeps his balance with his legs. You don't feel your weight. I wanted—without having thought about it—to reproduce this lightness, and that by making the body so thin."[1] Giacometti sought to convey several notions simultaneously in his attenuated plastic forms: one's consciousness of the nonmaterial presence of another person, the insubstantiality of the physical body housing that presence, and the paradoxical nature of perception. The base from which the woman appears to grow like a tree is tilted, emphasizing the verticality of the figure as well as reiterating the contours of the merged feet.

Giacometti had the present cast made expressly for Peggy Guggenheim. (L. F.)

1. Quoted in R. Hohl, *Alberto Giacometti*, New York, 1971, p. 278.

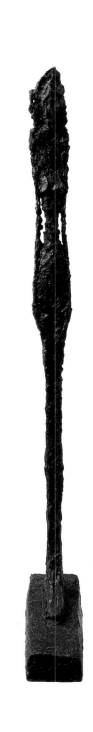

60

ALBERTO GIACOMETTI

Piazza, 1947–48 (cast 1948–49)

Bronze, 21 x 62.5 x 42.8 cm
76.2553 PG 135

In the late 1940s Alberto Giacometti produced attenuated thin figures not only of the life-size height of *Standing Woman* (cat. no. 59), but also on the miniature scale of the figures who inhabit his *Piazza* of 1947–48. Four men stride across a wide plaza, each moving toward the center, yet none apparently directed toward an encounter with another. A single woman, whose stiff posture recalls *Standing Woman*, stands isolated and motionless near the center. The featureless figures exist independently within their haphazardly grouped unity, their multiple, nonconverging paths suggesting individual ambitions and absorptions.

The flat bronze slab on which the figures stand serves both as base and as the plaza setting. Such a tabular format first appears in *The Palace at 4 a.m.*, 1932–33 (Collection The Museum of Modern Art, New York), a highly theatrical work of Giacometti's Surrealist period. Giacometti began placing individual figures on large bases as early as 1942, but only in 1948, in *Three Men Walking*, did a group of attenuated figures appear on a thin square bronze base that also suggests a city square.

Giacometti's scene derives from modern urban experience. He states: "In the street people astound and interest me more than any sculpture or painting. Every second the people stream together and go apart, then they approach each other to get closer to one another. They unceasingly form and re-form living compositions in unbelievable complexity. . . . It's the totality of this life that I want to reproduce in everything I do. . . ."[1]

There are five different casts of this work, and a somewhat larger version with the figures placed in slightly different positions exists in five casts as well (Rudenstine, p. 354). In all of these sculptures, an eye-level examination of the work alters the scale of miniaturization first perceived by the viewer. The vastness of the empty piazza and the anonymity of the figures are revealed by such closeup scrutiny. (E. C. C.)

1. Quoted in *Alberto Giacometti: A Retrospective Exhibition*, exh. cat., New York, 1974, p. 31.

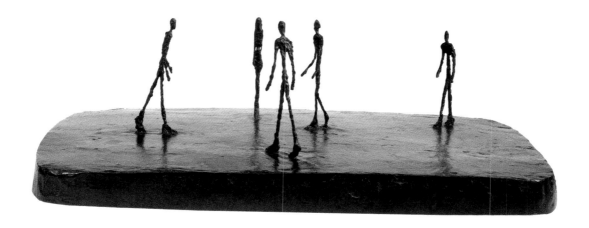

61

YVES TANGUY

Promontory Palace (Palais promontoire), 1931

Oil on canvas, 73 x 60 cm
76.2553 PG 94

Following his trip to Africa in 1930, Yves Tanguy produced a group of landscapes that have been termed *les coulées* (or flowing forms) for their molten character. Other paintings in this sequence include *Neither Legends nor Figures*, ca. 1930 (Private Collection, United States), and *The Armoire of Proteus*, 1931 (Private Collection, Paris).[1] Perhaps the most striking of the series is *Promontory Palace*, in which a rigid multitiered mass dominates a broad, flat plain. This corrugated mesa and other buttes in the center foreground stand firm as the surrounding viscous landscape succumbs to some persistent melting force. The small abstract shapes that inhabit the scene are in various stages of metamorphosis: some appear to melt or ooze, others seem to collapse or deflate, and still others secrete or sputter white liquids or gases. Some of these shapes are disturbingly anthropomorphic. A line of globular forms marches down the incline of the promontory to the edge of a cliff, where two forms have already surrendered and begun to melt over the precipice to join the sea of flowing matter below. A five-fingered, bulbous white mass glides over the ground as if on water. Elsewhere steam emerges, both from the pipe-shaped form at the base of the promontory and from the distant horizon. On the highest peak, or the palace, mysterious sparks emanate from a thornlike tower. To the right a hairlike apparition disappears into the thin atmosphere of an empty sky.

In the natural world such geologic metamorphosis would require intense heat and volcanic activity. Yet Tanguy's restrained grays and muted pinks, accented with cool blue and pale green and yellow, deny the presence of fire and earth. Instead, Tanguy creates a Surrealist terrain where molten and frozen, figurative and abstract, literal and suggestive elements exist in perfect harmony. Tanguy's use of a specific horizon line, his naturalistic modeling of forms, and his depiction of landscape evocative of an actual coastline, permit us a conceptual foothold in known experience. Yet our foothold gives way as Tanguy's abstract shapes transform known experience into a familiar but irrational fantasy. The power of Tanguy's imagery derives from the delicate tension he creates between the logic of sensation and the freedom of imagination. (E. C. C.)

1. For further discussion of this sequence, see *Yves Tanguy: Retrospective (1925–1955)*, exh. cat., Paris, 1982, pp. 50–52, 103–05.

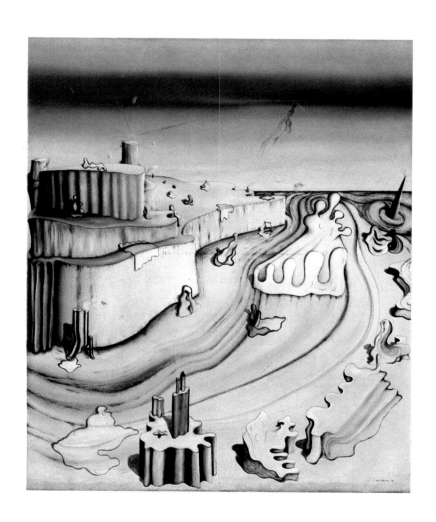

62

YVES TANGUY

The Sun in Its Jewel Case (*Le Soleil dans son écrin*), 1937

Oil on canvas, 115.4 x 88.1 cm
76.2553 PG 95

Yves Tanguy arrived at his lunar or submarine morphology in about 1927, and spent the rest of his artistic career exploring and elaborating it without changing its essential character. His compositions, arrived at in an unpremeditated manner directly on the canvas, recall the landscape of Locronan, in the French province of Brittany, where he spent childhood summers at a house owned by his parents. The repertory of memory was augmented by his experience of Africa during a trip of the early 1930s. After this the light in his paintings became clear and strong and the color schemes more complex. Vegetal forms were replaced by mineral formations. Dolmens and menhirs, stone remnants of prehistoric ages, and fossilized bones were smoothed and tinted in the dream spaces of his canvases. The assertive shadows cast in these landscapes recall those of Giorgio de Chirico, whose example had inspired Tanguy to take up painting in 1923.

The spatial paradox of *The Sun in Its Jewel Case* depends on the merging of sky and earth, achieved through the continuous gradation of color over the surface—there is no horizon line—and the device of a diagonal line of forms shown receding in perspective from lower right to upper left. Acute angles are suggested throughout, by the placement of objects, by the relationship of shadows to objects, or by the things themselves. Geometric precision and a minutely detailed academic technique, in which careful modeling lends plastic solidity to form, heighten the poetic strangeness of Tanguy's world. (L. F.)

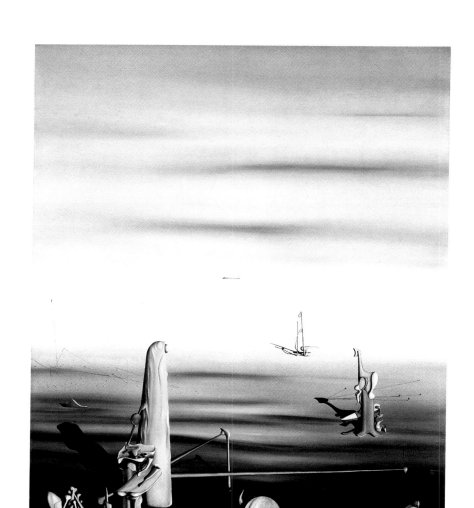

63

RENÉ MAGRITTE

Voice of Space (*La Voix des airs*), 1931

Oil on canvas, 72.7 x 54.2 cm
76.2553 PG 101

Influenced by Giorgio de Chirico, René Magritte sought to strip objects of their usual functions and meanings in order to convey an irrationally compelling image. In *Voice of Space* (of which three other oil versions exist), the bells float in the air; elsewhere they occupy human bodies or replace blossoms on bushes. By distorting the scale, weight, and use of an ordinary object and inserting it into a variety of unaccustomed contexts, Magritte confers on that object a fetishistic intensity. He has written of the jingle bell, a motif that recurs often in his work: "I caused the iron bells hanging from the necks of our admirable horses to sprout like dangerous plants at the edge of an abyss."[1]

The disturbing impact of the bells presented in an unfamiliar setting is intensified by the cool academic precision with which they and their environment are painted. The dainty slice of landscape could be the backdrop of an early Renaissance painting, while the bells themselves, in their rotund and glowing monumentality, impart a mysterious resonance. (L. F.)

1. Quoted in S. Gablik, *Magritte*, Greenwich, Connecticut, 1970, p. 183.

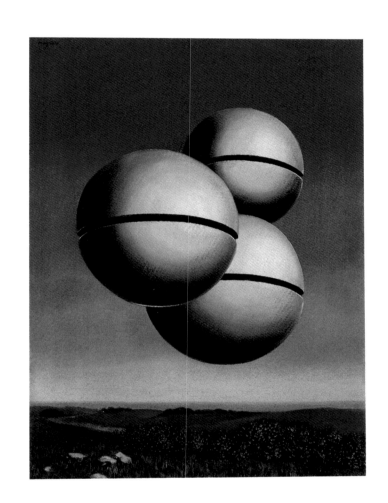

64

RENÉ MAGRITTE

Empire of Light (L'Empire des lumières), 1953–54

Oil on canvas, 195.4 x 131.2 cm
76.2553 PG 102

In *Empire of Light*, numerous versions of which exist (see, for example, those at the Museum of Modern Art, New York, and the Musées Royaux des Beaux-Arts de Belgique, Brussels), a dark, nocturnal street scene is set against a pastel-blue, light-drenched sky spotted with fluffy cumulus clouds. With no fantastic element other than the single paradoxical combination of day and night, René Magritte upsets a fundamental organizing premise of life. Sunlight, ordinarily the source of clarity, here causes the confusion and unease traditionally associated with darkness. The luminosity of the sky becomes unsettling, making the empty darkness below even more impenetrable than it would seem in a normal context. The bizarre subject is treated in an impersonal, precise style, typical of veristic Surrealist painting and preferred by Magritte since the mid-1920s. (L. F.)

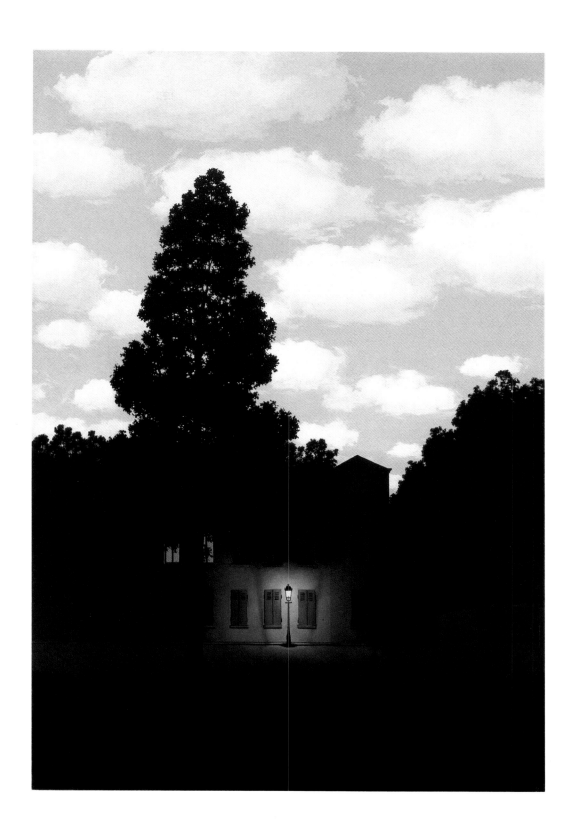

65

SALVADOR DALÍ

Birth of Liquid Desires (*La Naissance des désirs liquides*), 1931–32

Oil and collage on canvas, 96.1 x 112.3 cm
76.2553 PG 100

By the time Salvador Dalí joined the Surrealist group in 1929, he had formulated his "paranoid-critical" approach to art, which consisted in conveying his deepest psychological conflicts to the viewer in the hopes of eliciting an empathetic response. He embodied this theoretical approach in a fastidiously detailed painting style. One of his hallucinatory obsessions was the legend of William Tell, which represented for him the archetypal theme of paternal assault.[1] The subject occurs frequently in his paintings from 1929, when he entered into a liaison with Gala Eluard, his future wife, against his father's wishes. Dalí felt an acute sense of rejection during the early 1930s because of his father's attitude toward him.

Here father, son, and perhaps mother seem to be fused in the grotesque dream-image of the hermaphroditic creature at center. William Tell's apple is replaced by a loaf of bread, with attendant castration symbolism. (Elsewhere Dalí uses a lamb chop to suggest his father's cannibalistic impulses.) Out of the bread arises a lugubrious cloud vision inspired by the imagery of Arnold Böcklin. In one of the recesses of this cloud is an enigmatic inscription in French: "Consigne: gâcher l'ardoise totale?"

Reference to the remote past seems to be made in the two forlorn figures shown in the distant left background, which may convey Dalí's memory of the fond communion of father and child. The infinite expanse of landscape recalls Yves Tanguy's work of the 1920s. The biomorphic structure dominating the composition suggests at once a violin, the weathered rock formations of Port Lligat on the eastern coast of Spain, the architecture of the Catalan visionary Antoni Gaudí, the sculpture of Jean Arp, a prehistoric monster, and an artist's palette. The form has an antecedent in Dalí's own work in the gigantic vision of his mother in *The Enigma of Desire* of 1929 (Collection Staatsgalerie Moderner Kunst, Munich). The repressed, guilty desire of the central figure is indicated by its attitude of both protestation and arousal toward the forbidden flower-headed woman (presumably Gala). The shadow darkening the scene is cast by an object outside the picture and may represent the father's threatening presence, or a more general prescience of doom, the advance of age, or the extinction of life. (L. F.)

1. S. Dalí interviewed by P. Hultén, "L'Enigme de Salvador Dali," *XXe Siècle*, no. 74 (Dec. 1974), p. 92.

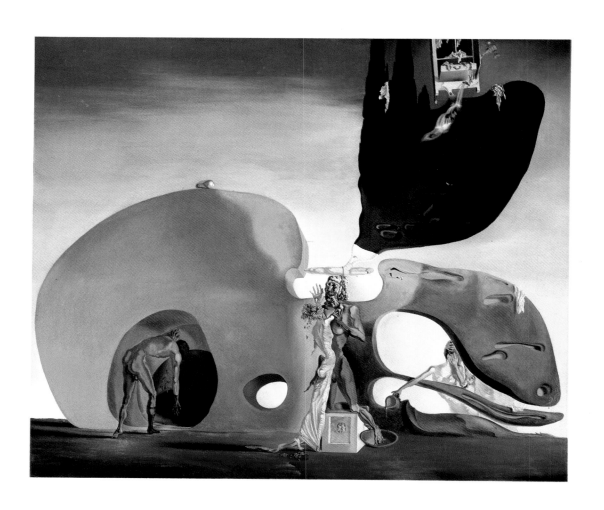

66

PAUL DELVAUX

The Break of Day (*L'Aurore*), July 1937

Oil on canvas, 120 x 150.5 cm
76.2553 PG 103

Like his compatriot René Magritte, Paul Delvaux applied a fastidious, detailed technique to scenes deriving their impact from unsettling incongruities of subject. Influenced by Giorgio de Chirico, he frequently included classicizing details and used perspectival distortion to create rapid, plunging movement from foreground to deep background. Unique to Delvaux is the silent, introspective cast of figures he developed during the mid-1930s. His formidable, buxom nude or seminude women pose immobile with unfocused gazes, their arms frozen in rhetorical gestures, dominating a world through which men, preoccupied and timid, unobtrusively make their way.

Although the fusion of woman and tree in the present picture invites comparison with Greek mythological subjects, the artist has insisted that no such references were intended (Rudenstine, p. 216). The motif of the mirror appears in 1936 in works such as *Woman in a Grotto* (Collection Thyssen-Bornemisza, Lugano) and *The Mirror* (formerly Collection Roland Penrose, London; destroyed during World War II). In *The Break of Day* a new element is introduced; the reflected figure is not present within the scene, but exists outside the canvas field. She is, therefore, in some sense, the viewer, even if that viewer should happen to be male. The irony of the circumstance in which a clothed male viewer could see himself reflected as a nude female torso would have particularly appeared to Marcel Duchamp, who appropriated the detail of the mirror in his collage of 1942 *In the Manner of Delvaux* (Collection Vera and Arturo Schwarz, Milan; repr. Rudenstine, p. 217). (L. F.)

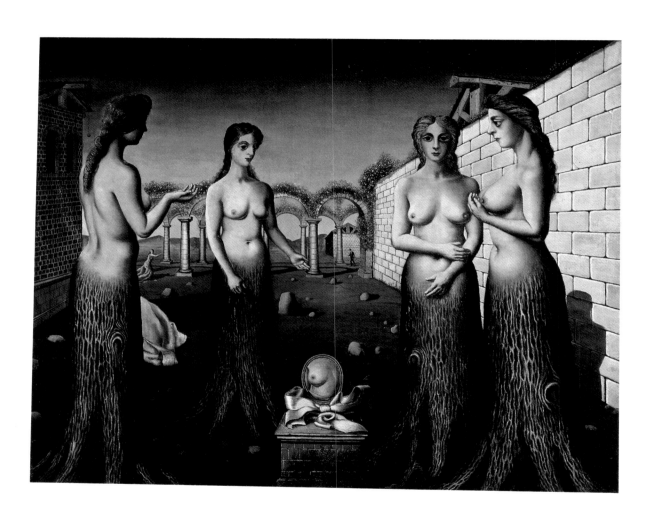

67

VICTOR BRAUNER

The Surrealist (*Le Surréaliste*), January 1947

Oil on canvas, 60 x 45 cm
76.2553 PG III

In *The Surrealist* Victor Brauner borrows motifs from the tarot to create a portrait of himself as a young man. The tarot, a set of seventy-eight illustrated cards used in fortune telling, was a subject of widespread interest to Brauner and other Surrealists. Four of these cards, for example, appeared on André Derain's cover for the December 1933 issue of *Minotaure*. A group including Brauner even produced a deck of cards in 1940–41 that was probably a tarot. One tarot card, the Juggler (the first card in the Marseille tarot deck; repr. Rudenstine, p. 135), provided Brauner with a key prototype for his self-portrait: the Surrealist's large hat, medieval costume, and the position of his arms all derive from this figure who, like Brauner's subject, stands behind a table displaying a knife, a goblet, and coins.[1] The tarot Juggler appropriately symbolizes the creativity of the Surrealist poet, for it refers to the capacity of each individual to create his own personality through intelligence, wit, and initiative, and thus to play with his own future, as the juggler manipulates his baton.

In another tarot deck known as the Waite tarot, the first card of the Major Arcana is the Magician rather than the Juggler, although both share many attributes. A sign of infinity, ∞ (the symbol of life), that appears above the Magician's head is also depicted on the hat of Brauner's Surrealist. Drawing on the Juggler-Magician prototype, Brauner illustrates the traditional signs of the four suits in the tarot deck: wands, cups, swords, and coins (symbols of the elements of natural life—fire, water, air, and earth, respectively). These objects and all natural life are controlled by the Juggler, just as all creative life is at the disposal of the Surrealist poet, who wields his pen as the Juggler brandishes his wand.

Brauner depicted the Juggler and a Popess (a figure from the Marseille Tarot) in another painting of 1947, *The Lovers* (Private Collection, Paris). The inscriptions at either side of that canvas, *Past—Present—Future* and *Fate/Necessity—Will/Magic—Surreality/Liberty*, are written in Brauner's hand on the back of the Peggy Guggenheim canvas. These inscriptions convey the artist's belief that Surrealism could be a path to artistic freedom. (E. C. C.)

1. See N. and E. Calas, *The Peggy Guggenheim Collection of Modern Art*, New York, 1966, pp. 123–24, and Rudenstine, pp. 135–36. Cynthia Goodman's unpublished notes on *The Surrealist* offer the most complete discussion of this tarot iconography.

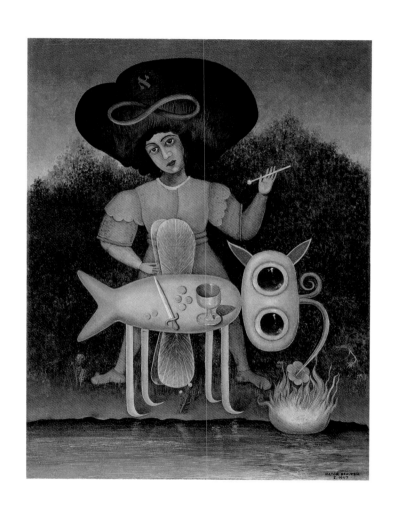

68

ALEXANDER CALDER

Mobile, 1941

Painted aluminum, approximately 214 cm high
76.2553 PG 137

During the early 1930s Alexander Calder, a pioneering figure in the development of kinetic art, created sculptures in which balanced components move, some driven by motor and others impelled by the action of air currents. Marcel Duchamp first applied the descriptive designation "mobiles" to those reliant on air alone. Either suspended or freestanding, these constructions generally consist of flat pieces of painted metal connected by wire veins and stems. Their biomorphic shapes recall the organic motifs of the Surrealist painting and sculpture of his friends Joan Miró and Jean Arp. Calder, a fastidious craftsman, cut, bent, punctured, and twisted his materials entirely by hand, the manual emphasis contributing to the sculptures' evocation of natural form. Shape, size, color, space, and movement combine and recombine in shifting, balanced relationships that provide a visual equivalent to the harmonious but unpredictable activity of nature.

The present mobile is organized as an antigravitational cascade, in which large, heavy, mature shapes sway serenely at the top, while small, undifferentiated, agitated, new growth dips and rocks below. Calder left one leaf unpainted, revealing the aluminum surface and underscoring the sense of variety he considered vital to the success of a work of art. As he wrote: "Disparity in form, color, size, weight, motion, is what makes a composition. . . . It is the apparent accident to regularity which the artist actually controls by which he makes or mars a work."[1] (L. F.)

1. Quoted in J. Lipman, *Calder's Universe,* exh. cat., New York, 1976, p. 33.

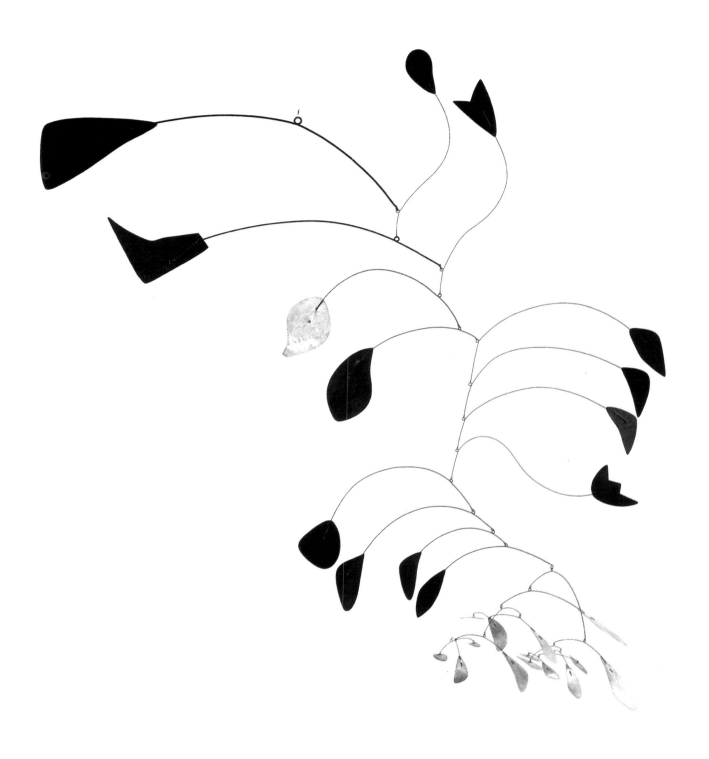

69

ALEXANDER CALDER

Silver Bedhead, winter 1945–46

Silver, 160 x 131 cm
76.2553 PG 138

In New York in the winter of 1945–46, Peggy Guggenheim commissioned Alexander Calder to make a silver bedhead.[1] His design combines fish, insect, and plant motifs in an exuberant conflation of the worlds of sea and garden. The two fish at the lower left are free-hanging elements. Calder also suspended an insect, probably a bee or dragonfly, from a silver link chain that may be dangled from various locations on the sculpture. Since the insect may fly in any of several possible positions, realms of sea and sky are not separated into distinct areas—rather, the bedhead is a whimsical fantasy in which flora and fauna from both regions coexist. The outer curve of a large spiral comprises the basic circular structure of the bedhead, which is elaborated with decorations of hammered and cut silver. Although these botanical forms are fixed permanently in position, their curving, twisting contours nonetheless convey a sense of perpetual natural motion.

Calder first twisted wire into three-dimensional forms in his wire sculptures of the mid-1920s. Subsequently, he twisted, cut, and hammered wire and gold, silver and brass into jewelry for his friends and patrons. It has been suggested that the delicate and slender forms of some of Calder's metal constructions of the early 1940s are indebted to his jewelry of the 1930s, which included both simple animal motifs and curvilinear or spiraling abstract forms.[2] Calder's book illustrations also contributed to the development of a graphic lyricism in his sculpture. Many of the vegetal forms in the bedhead share the spontaneity and inventiveness of Calder's line-etching illustrations. In particular, the soaring zigzag fern motif on the left and the numerous spiral-shaped blossoms anticipate the illustrations executed in 1946 for Eunice Clark's *Fables of La Fontaine* (for example, the "Stag and the Vine").

The compressed, shallow relief of this piece answers neatly the practical demands of Guggenheim's commission for a bedhead. This project allowed Calder to exercise his calligraphic skills not only in the more conventional realm of book illustration but also in drawing on a blank wall with a line of silver metal. The worked surface of the hammered silver, which reflects light in countless directions, adds variety and a three-dimensional presence to each of Calder's lines. (E. C. C.)

1. P. Guggenheim, *Out of This Century: Confessions of an Art Addict*, New York, 1979, p. 318.

2. J. Lipman, *Calder's Universe*, New York, 1976, p. 209.

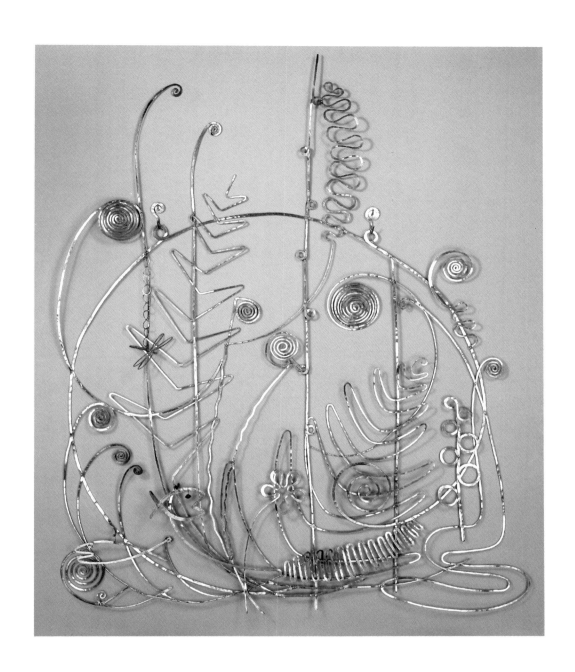

70

JOSEPH CORNELL

Fortune Telling Parrot (Parrot Music Box), ca. 1937–38

Box construction, 40.8 x 22.2 x 17 cm
76.2553 PG 126

Joseph Cornell lived an isolated life with his mother at their home in Flushing, New York, from which he made frequent excursions into Manhattan to gather objects for his constructions. His diaries record his alternating feelings of being trapped at home, and then of release when he escaped to Manhattan. Working on his boxes at home in his cellar became a substitute for traveling, the arrangement of imaginary souvenirs inducing the excitement of voyages.

Fortune Telling Parrot offers many associations with exotic travels. First, the box construction itself resembles the apparatus of a hurdy-gurdy, invoking the bohemian world of the traveling gypsy musician. The crank on the right exterior of the construction turns a broken music box, hidden in the lower-right corner of the sculpture. The music box in turn is attached by a thin rod to the cylinder above it, which is intended to revolve while music plays.

The cylinder is covered with decorations, some of which suggest the paraphernalia and practices of the fortune-teller: playing cards such as the King of Hearts and the Jack of Clubs; the numbers one through nine; a picture of two hands playing cat's cradle, recalling the entertainments of the gypsy; and the picture of a gypsy woman in elaborate costume. Small stars on the cylinder and a map of the constellation of Ursa Minor, "Little Bear," in the lower-left corner of the box, also allude to astrology and divination. The parrot itself is a common attribute of the itinerant fortune-teller. Facing the revolving canister, this bird assumes the role of a soothsayer's assistant. Exotic birds, including parrots, parakeets, and cockatoos, appear in some eighteen boxes by Cornell, the present example being the earliest and the others dating from the forties and fifties (Rudenstine, p. 178). In other boxes, birds are caged and chained on their perches, captured as exotic pets. Cornell recalls in his diary some of the experiences that contributed to his obsession with parrots: "magic windows of yesterday . . . pet shop windows splashed with white tropical plumage / the kind of revelation symptomatic of city wanderings in another era. . . . scintillating songs of Rossini and Bellini and the whole golden age of the bel canto . . . indelible childhood memory of an old German woman a neighbor's pet parrot may have added to the obsession of these . . . feathered friends."[1] (E. C. C.)

1. Quoted in D. Ades, "The Transcendental Surrealism of Joseph Cornell," in *Joseph Cornell*, exh. cat., New York, 1980, p. 37.

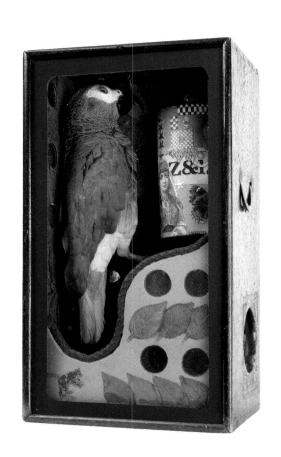

71

JOSEPH CORNELL

Untitled (Pharmacy), ca. 1942

Box construction, 35.5 x 30.6 x 11.1 cm
76.2553 PG 128

Joseph Cornell's obsession with the collection, isolation, combination, and preservation of found objects is revealed in a fastidiously compartmentalized form in the *Pharmacy* boxes of the 1940s and 1950s. Like Marcel Duchamp's *Box in a Valise* of 1941 (an example of which is in the Peggy Guggenheim Collection), this work is a miniature museum dedicated to the protection and presentation of its contents. The care with which the collection has been selected and displayed invests it with a potency the individual objects do not ordinarily convey.[1]

Each apothecary jar presents a diorama of poetically allusive natural or man-made forms. The natural world is present in sand, stones, shells, plant and insect parts, feathers, and wood; the constructed world appears in mechanisms, toys, maps, and prints. The environments invoked range from the seashore, where man's importance is negligible, to the Renaissance palace, one of the most sophisticated expressions of his material and intellectual achievement. Like the alchemist, Cornell transforms ordinary objects into precious things; in one jar he even seems to have fulfilled the ultimate alchemical aspiration of transmuting base metal into gold. By presenting these inviolable jars in a pharmaceutical context, he may also allude to the universal restorative powers that alchemists hoped to discover. The mirroring of the back wall of the box, typical of apothecaries' cabinets, multiplies the contents and reflects the viewer, whom it affords the unexpected opportunity to study the reverse of objects without moving around them. (L. F.)

1. For a discussion of the state of incompletion of this example, see Rudenstine, pp. 187–88.

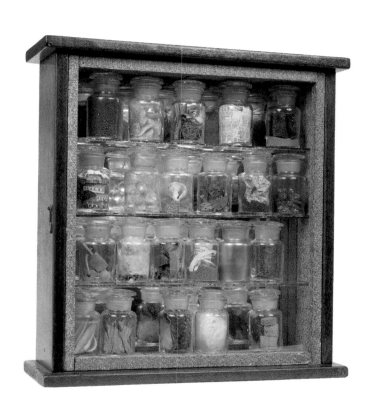

72

ARSHILE GORKY

Untitled, summer 1944

Oil on canvas, 167 x 178.2 cm
76.2553 PG 152

Arshile Gorky spent the greater part of 1944 at Crooked Run Farm in Hamilton, Virginia, where he produced a large number of drawings, many of which were conceived as preliminary studies for paintings. This work is preceded by such a study, a closely related untitled drawing of 1944 (Private Collection; repr. Rudenstine, p. 669, fig. a) that sets out its motifs, their ordering within the composition, and the arrangement of color. Apart from the transformation of an empty contour at the upper center into a solid, anchored black form, only insignificant compositional and coloristic changes appear in the finished painting.

Gorky's enthusiastic response to the natural surroundings of rural Virginia infused his work with expressive freedom. Landscape references appear in *Untitled*; though the white ground is uniform, it is empty at the very top of the canvas, suggesting a slice of sky, while the "earth" below is replete with vegetal shapes and floral colors. A clear gravitational sense is produced by the dripping of paint thinned with turpentine, a technique suggested by Matta. As in *They Will Take My Island* of the same year (Collection Art Gallery of Ontario, Toronto), an aggressive diagonal accent cuts through the upper center of the canvas.

The techniques and content of Surrealism influenced the development of Gorky's language of free, organic, vitally curvilinear forms. Joan Miró's example is particularly evident here, in the disposition of floating abstract units on an indeterminate background, and in details such as flamelike shapes, dotted ovals, and suggestions of genitals. Unlike Miró, however, Gorky enmeshes his forms with one another to create the overall structure. Textured, insubstantial clouds of color occasionally pertain to the graphic form they accompany, but more often are independent elements, as in the work of Vasily Kandinsky. The curves, inflection, and directionality of Gorky's line likewise free it from descriptive function. In his emphasis on the autonomous expressive potential of line, form, and color, Gorky anticipated the concerns of Abstract Expressionism. (L. F.)

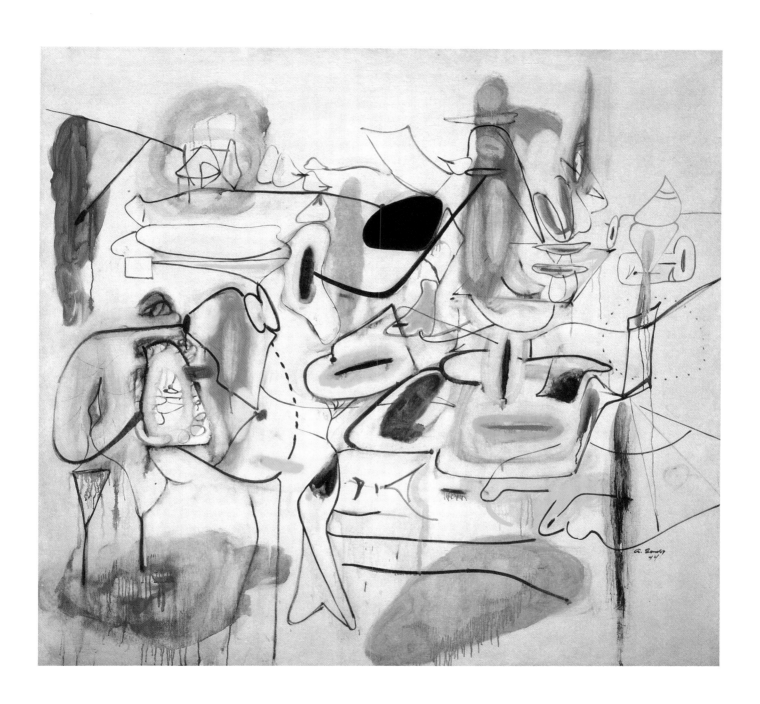

73

JACKSON POLLOCK

The Moon Woman, 1942

Oil on canvas, 175.2 x 109.3 cm
76.2553 PG 141

Like other members of the New York School, Jackson Pollock was influenced in his early work by Joan Miró and Pablo Picasso, and seized on the Surrealists' concept of the unconscious as the source of art. In the late 1930s Pollock introduced imagery based on totemic or mythic figures, ideographic signs, and ritualistic events, which have been interpreted as pertaining to the buried experiences and cultural memories of the psyche.

The Moon Woman suggests the example of Picasso, particularly his *Girl Before a Mirror* of 1932 (Collection The Museum of Modern Art, New York). The palettes are similar, and both artists describe a solitary standing female as if she had been x-rayed, her backbone a broad black line from which her curving contours originate. Frontal and profile views of the face are combined to contrast two aspects of the self, one serene and public, the other dark and interior.

The subject of the moon woman, which Pollock treated in several drawings and paintings of the early 1940s, could have been available to him from various sources. At this time many artists, among them Pollock's friends William Baziotes and Robert Motherwell, were influenced by the fugitive, hallucinatory imagery of Charles Baudelaire and the French Symbolists. In his prose poem "Favors of the Moon" Baudelaire addresses the "image of the fearful goddess, the fateful godmother, the poisonous nurse of all the moonstruck of the world." The poem, which is known to have inspired Baziotes's *Mirror at Midnight*, completed in 1942 (Collection Rudi Blesh, New York), alludes to "ominous flowers that are like the censers of an unknown rite," a phrase uncannily applicable to Pollock's bouquet at the upper right. Although it is possible that Pollock knew the poem, it is likelier that he was affected in a more general way by the interest in Baudelaire and the Symbolists that was pervasive during the period. (L. F.)

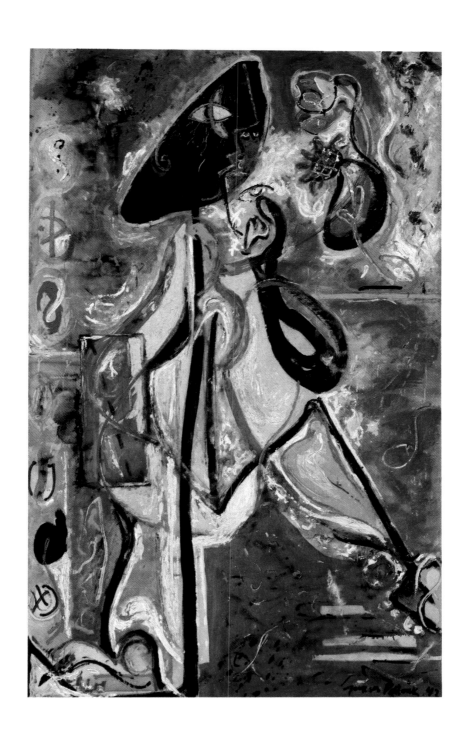

74

JACKSON POLLOCK

Circumcision, January 1946

Oil on canvas, 142.3 x 168 cm
76.2553 PG 145

In this transitional work of 1946 the subtle persistence of the Cubist grid system is felt in the panels that organize the composition and orient major pictorial details in vertical or horizontal positions. However, Jackson Pollock's dependence on Pablo Picasso has virtually dissolved, giving way to a more automatic, fluidly expressive style. Line loses its descriptive function and begins to assume a self-sufficient role, the rhythm, duration, and direction of each brushstroke responding to the artist's instinctual gesture. The compositional focus is multiplied and decentralized and areas of intense activity fill the entire surface. Fragmented figural elements are increasingly integrated into the shallow pictorial space, as background, foreground, and object merge and the texture of the paint gains in importance. By 1945 the vigor and originality of Pollock's work had prompted the critic Clement Greenberg, one of his earliest champions, to write in *The Nation* of April 7: "Jackson Pollock's second one-man show at Art of This Century . . . establishes him, in my opinion, as the strongest painter of his generation and perhaps the greatest one to appear since Miró."

Primitive art forms are alluded to in the crudely drawn arrows, cult and stick figures, and ornamental markings discernable in *Circumcision*. Totemic figures (the rotund being standing at the left and the owl-like creature at upper center) are posed stiffly, observing what seems to be a scene of violence in the center of the canvas. The enactment of a rite of passage is suggested, but the visual evidence does not encourage a specific reading. Pollock's concern with archetypal imagery and pan-cultural rituals and mythologies is evoked with varying degrees of specificity in his work.

Lee Krasner suggested the title to Pollock after the painting was completed (see Rudenstine, pp. 634–35). (L. F.)

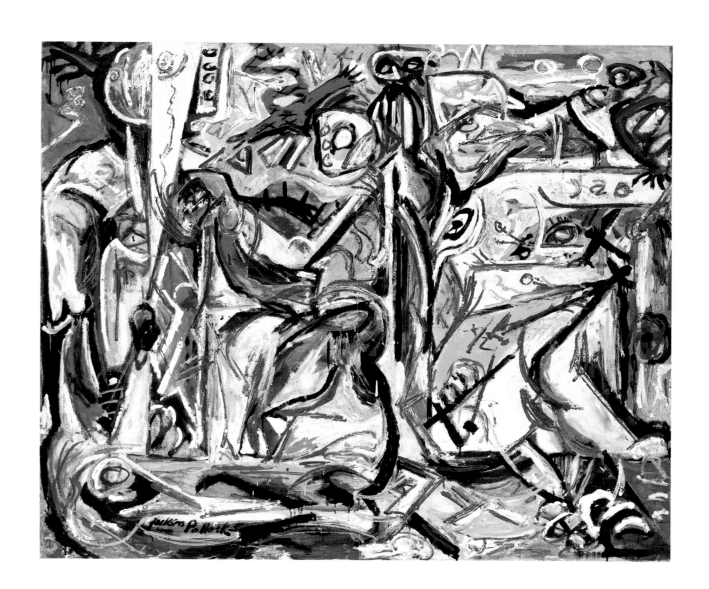

75

JACKSON POLLOCK

Eyes in the Heat, 1946

Oil (and enamel?) on canvas, 137.2 x 109.2 cm
76.2553 PG 149

Eyes in the Heat heralds the poured paintings Jackson Pollock initiated in the winter of 1946–47. It is part of *Sounds in the Grass*, a series of seven canvases that also includes *Croaking Movement* in the Peggy Guggenheim Collection. Pollock had moved to a house on Long Island in 1945, and early the next summer began using one of the bedrooms as a studio. Later in 1946 he arranged with Peggy Guggenheim to have a show at her Art of This Century gallery, to open in January of 1947; in preparation for this exhibition he worked with great intensity on *Sounds in the Grass* and the series *Accabonac Creek*.

Visible effects of the move from New York City to the more rural environment of East Hampton were a lightening of palette and the introduction of themes alluding to nature. Although the light and flora and fauna of Long Island are evoked in a general sense in *Eyes in the Heat*, particularized figurative references are almost entirely submerged in the layers of impasto that build up the surface. Pollock no longer applies paint with a brush, but squeezes pigment onto the canvas directly from the tube, pushing and smearing it with blunt instruments to create a thick, textured crust. One's gaze is carried along broad swaths of color that swoop, careen, double back, rise, and fall rhythmically over the entire canvas. The watchful eyes of creatures concealed in the paint appear here and there, in their proliferation mimicking the restless movement of the viewer's eyes. (L. F.)

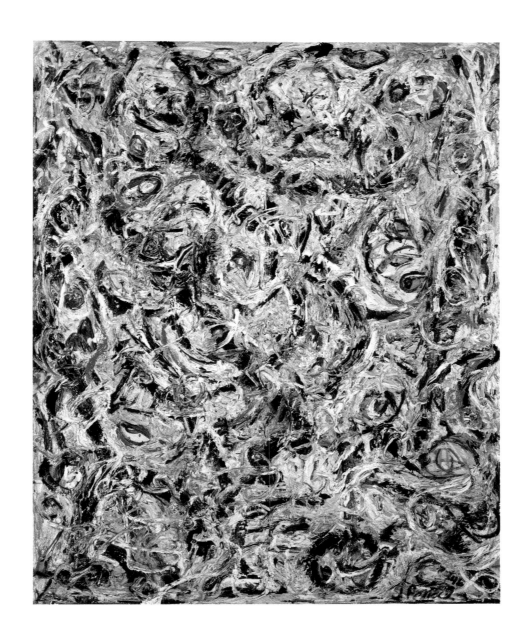

JACKSON POLLOCK

Alchemy, 1947

Oil, aluminum (and enamel?) paint, and string on canvas, 114.6 x 221.3 cm
76.2553 PG 150

Alchemy is one of Jackson Pollock's earliest poured paintings, executed in the revolutionary technique that constituted his most significant contribution to twentieth-century art. After long deliberation before the empty canvas, he used his entire body in a picture-making process that can be described as drawing in paint. By pouring streams of commercial paint onto the canvas from a can with the aid of a stick, Pollock made obsolete the conventions and tools of traditional easel painting. He often tacked the unstretched canvas onto the floor in an approach he likened to that of the Navajo Indian sandpainters, explaining that "on the floor I am more at ease. I feel nearer, more a part of the painting, since this way I can walk around it, work from the four sides and literally be *in* the painting."[1] Surrealist notions of chance and automatism are given full expression in Pollock's classic poured paintings, in which line no longer serves to describe shape or enclose form, but exists as an autonomous event, charting the movements of the artist's body. As the line thins and thickens it speeds and slows, its appearance modified by chance behavior of the medium such as bleeding, pooling, or blistering.

When *Alchemy* is viewed from a distance, its large scale and even emphasis encourage the viewer to experience the painting as an environment. The layering and interpenetration of the labyrinthine skeins give the whole a dense and generalized appearance. The textured surface is like a wall on which primitive signs are inscribed with white pigment squeezed directly from the tube. Interpretations of these markings have frequently relied on the title *Alchemy*; however, this was assigned not by Pollock, but by Ralph Manheim and his wife, neighbors of the Pollocks in East Hampton. (L. F.)

1. J. Pollock, "My Painting," *Possibilities*, no. 1 (winter 1947–48), p. 79.

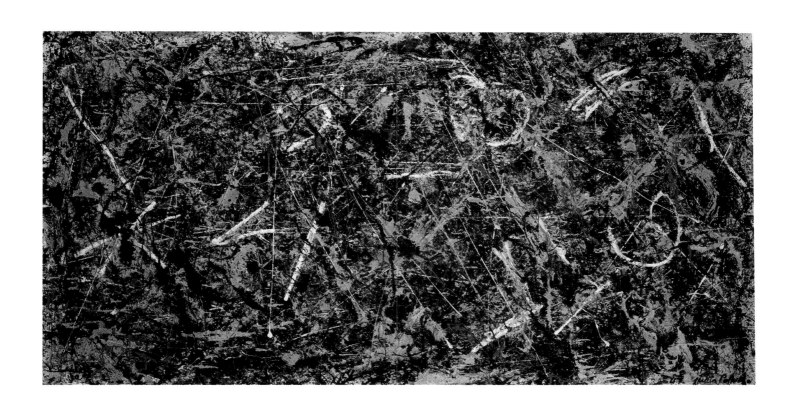

77

JACKSON POLLOCK

Enchanted Forest, 1947
Oil on canvas, 221.3 x 114.6 cm
76.2553 PG 151

Like *Alchemy* (cat. no. 76), *Enchanted Forest* exemplifies Jackson Pollock's mature abstract compositions created by the pouring, dripping, and splattering of paint on large, unstretched canvases. In *Enchanted Forest* Pollock opens up the more dense construction of layered color found in works such as *Alchemy* by allowing large areas of white to breathe amidst the network of moving, expanding line. He also reduces his palette to a restrained selection of gold, black, red, and white. Pollock creates a delicate balance of form and color through orchestrating syncopated rhythms of lines that surge, swell, retreat, and pause only briefly before plunging anew into continuous, lyrical motion. One's eye follows eagerly, pursuing first one dripping rope of color and then another, without being arrested by any dominant focus. Rather than describing a form, Pollock's line thus becomes continuous form itself.

Michael Fried has described Pollock's achievement: "[His] all-over line does not give rise to positive and negative areas. There is no inside or outside to Pollock's line or to the space through which it moves. And that is tantamount to claiming that line, in Pollock's all-over drip paintings of 1947–50, has been freed at last from the job of describing contours and bounding shapes."[1] It is this redefinition of the traditional capacity of the artist's formal means that distinguishes Pollock's art in the history of Modernism. (E. C. C.)

1. M. Fried, *Three American Painters*, exh. cat., Cambridge, Massachusetts, 1965, p. 14.

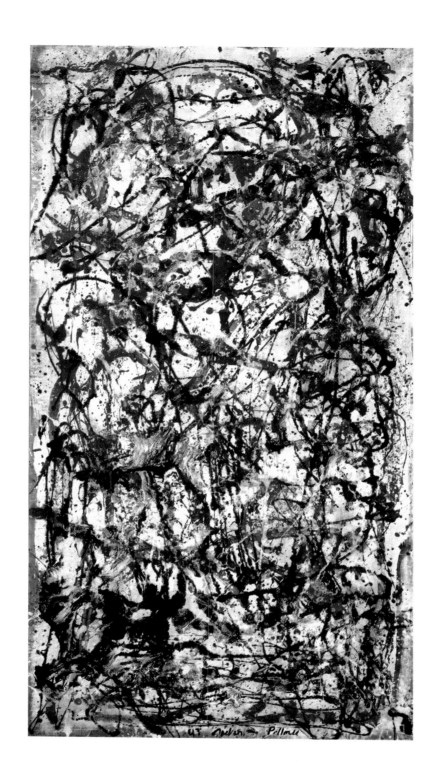

78

WILLIAM BAZIOTES

The Room, 1945
Gouache on board, 45.6 x 61 cm
76.2553 PG 156

William Baziotes and other members of the New York School were influenced by the European Surrealists who had fled'to the United States during World War II. Like the Surrealists, Baziotes used objects in his environment as triggers for the memory of early sensations or as conduits to the unconscious. This procedure produced in him an acutely sensitized state of mind that he attempted to formulate visually in his paintings. Baziotes saw this visual manifestation of states of mind as parallel to the literary achievement of the Symbolist poets and of Marcel Proust, whose work he much admired.

Baziotes makes allusions in his paintings to the external world of objects, but these remain elusive and changeable. He usually added his titles after the compositions had emerged through intuitive decisions. Although the titles do not identify subject matter, they nevertheless guide interpretation. Thus, the title of the present work may encourage one to experience the mood of an interior space illuminated by diffused twilight. An atmosphere of nostalgic reverie is evoked by scumbled, weathered layers of gouache in which pastel colors predominate. Unlike Baziotes's most characteristic works, in which biomorphic shapes float freely on an indefinite background, *The Room* is constructed architectonically. The gridded structure derives from Piet Mondrian and the Cubists, models for Baziotes before his encounter with the Surrealists. (L. F.)

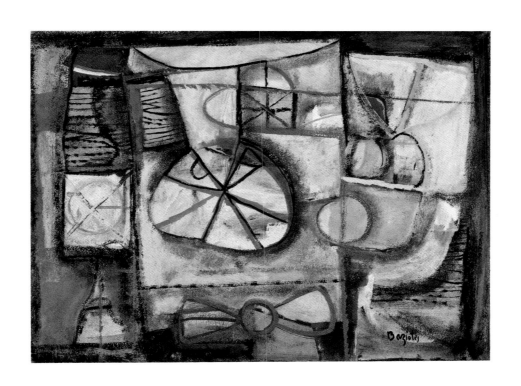

79

ROBERT MOTHERWELL

Personage (Autoportrait), December 9, 1943

Paper collage, gouache, and ink on board, 103.8 x 65.9 cm
76.2553 PG 155

In 1943 Robert Motherwell and Jackson Pollock experimented with collage in response to Peggy Guggenheim's initial preparations for a show of works in the medium at Art of This Century. The exhibition was to include examples by the foremost European practitioners, such as Henri Matisse, Pablo Picasso, and Kurt Schwitters. Though Pollock's interest in the technique soon waned, Motherwell's concern with it endured. *Personage (Autoportrait)* (which has previously been known as *Surprise and Inspiration*, a title assigned by Guggenheim or someone in her circle[1]) was one of several important examples Motherwell produced in 1943–44.

Motherwell acknowledged that the work might, in a sense, evoke an embodiment of self-image (Rudenstine, pp. 585–86). Although a blocky, somewhat mournful figure can be imagined, *Personage (Autoportrait)* is more readily perceived as a nonreferential coloristic and spatial construction. A jagged horizontal-vertical mesh organizes the composition. The alignment of the edges of the cut, torn, and glued paper provides the grid, which has a physical, planar dimension. Not only does the paper structure the work architectonically, but it serves as a support for vigorously applied paint. The energy of handling and the uneven oval shapes separated by a black line in this early collage foreshadow the powerful facture and recurrent motifs of Motherwell's later work. (L. F.)

1. See H. H. Arnason, *Robert Motherwell*, rev. ed., New York, 1982, n. p.

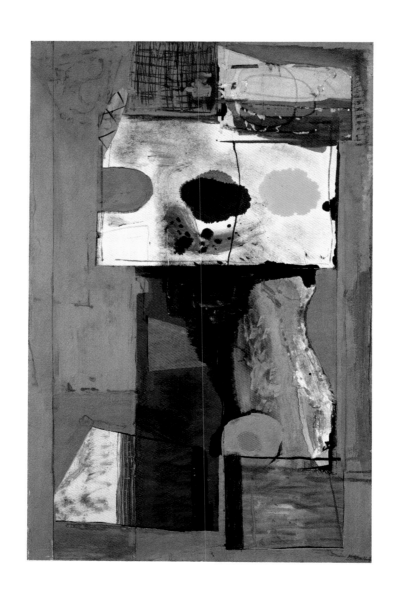

80

MARK ROTHKO

Sacrifice, April 1946

Watercolor, gouache, and india ink on paper, 100.2 x 65.8 cm
76.2553 PG 154

During the late 1930s and early 1940s Mark Rothko, like William Baziotes, Adolph Gottlieb, and Theodoros Stamos, combined mythical themes with primordial imagery in order to express universal experiences. In his work of this period evanescent biomorphic shapes float within an atmospheric haze. Resembling rudimentary life forms or primitive subaquatic plants and creatures, these shapes are intended to provide a visible equivalent of images lodged in the subconscious. Though he drew primarily on his innermost sensations, Rothko also looked toward earlier art. The example of Joan Miró is evoked in *Sacrifice* in the dotted line, the flame, the amorphic personage at the lower left, and in the meandering threadlike tendrils.

Figurative and literary allusions, albeit disguised, persist here. Architectural elements contrast with the aquatic forms and nebulous milieu: the horizontal registers are articulated like moldings, as in an untitled oil painting by Rothko of 1939–40 (Collection Mr. and Mrs. Richard E. Lang, Medina, Washington), in which a frieze of faces appears between an undulating cornice and two ornamental tiers. The title may be inspired by Rothko's interest in Greek tragedy and Friedrich Nietzsche's examination of its origins. Despite the persistence of these references, overtly representational images have disappeared, signaling a move toward the complete abstraction of Rothko's mature style. In its horizontal zoning, cloudlike texture, and blurred contours, *Sacrifice* anticipates his characteristic, fully evolved color-field paintings. (L. F.)

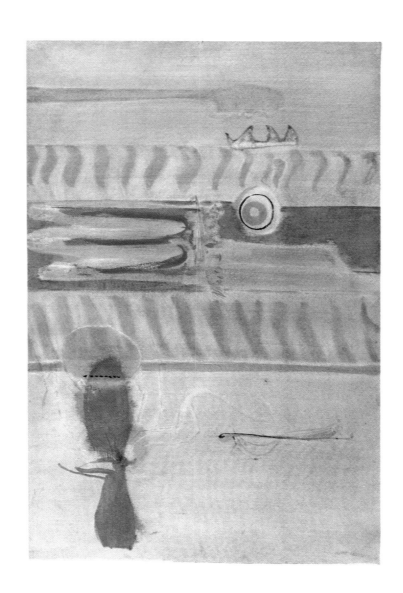

81

CLYFFORD STILL

Jamais, May 1944

Oil on canvas, 165.2 x 82 cm
76.2553 PG 153

Like the examples of William Baziotes, Robert Motherwell, and Mark Rothko in the Peggy Guggenheim Collection (cat. nos. 78–80), *Jamais* dates from the formative, exploratory period of Abstract Expressionism. Although the influence of Surrealism pervaded the work of these artists in the early forties, they were moving toward distinctive independent styles.

Until 1946–47 the single upright figure dominated Clyfford Still's painting. In its elongation and expressionistic distortion, this element is reminiscent of figures painted by Joan Miró and Pablo Picasso in the 1930s. Here the figure is barely particularized, appearing as a black flame or cleft in the blazing environment that surrounds it. Later it was to disappear entirely within the craggy, tenebrous abstractions for which Still is best known. The sphere, which interrupts the thrusting verticality of his tense lines in several of these early works, was also to vanish. Concern with the contrast of light and dark was to become increasingly important and was emphasized by jarring color juxtapositions. The canvas, already large in this example, was to reach monumental proportions and create an impact rivaling that of the viewer's own environment.

The present painting is one of the few by Still bearing its original title. He disdained titles, and discarded those he had given to early works because he considered that they too strongly influenced the observer's experience of the painting. Indeed, *Jamais* (French for "never") lends an air of finality and melancholy to this scene and encourages one to read the figure as howling in protest or despair above a setting sun. (L. F.)

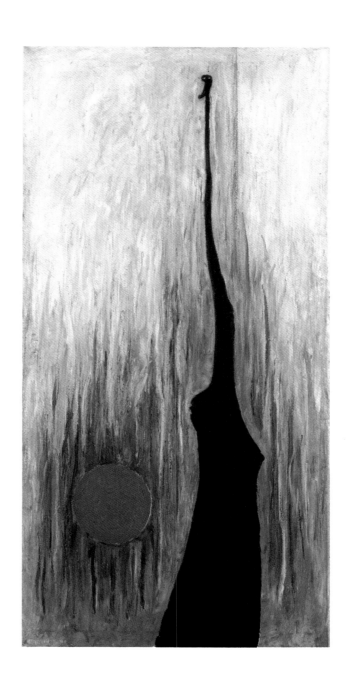

82

WILLEM DE KOONING

Untitled, 1958

Oil on paper, mounted on Masonite, mounted on wood, 58.5 x 74 cm
76.2553 PG 158

Willem de Kooning, like Jackson Pollock and Robert Motherwell, was a leader in the development of Abstract Expressionism, an American movement strongly influenced by European Surrealist notions of automatism and free expression. De Kooning does not use preliminary studies but paints directly on the support, manipulating pigment in vigorous, uninhibited gestures, expressing his subjective apprehensions of the material world in both figurative and abstract compositions. During the late fifties he temporarily abandoned the depiction of the human figure, which had preoccupied him since the beginning of his career, to evoke parkway and urban landscapes in abstract terms. As he wrote: "The pictures done since the *Women*, they're emotions, most of them. Most of them are landscapes and highways and sensations of that, outside the city, or coming from it."[1] The quality of light and the freshness of color in the present painting communicate a sense of landscape. Nevertheless, the subject relates, however indirectly, to the artist's obsession with the image of woman, whose contours he has sublimated in abstract natural forms; it is present here in the flesh tones and the lithe curves playing against an implied grid.

In the late fifties de Kooning reduced the frenzied proliferation of stroke, form, and plane that had characterized his preceding work to effect compositions of relative restraint and clarity. Each area of color, contoured only by the physical edges of the paint, is applied expansively. The broad simplification makes conspicuous the manner of paint application and the resultant textural complexities of the medium. Movement, conflict, and resolution take place on the flat surface of the canvas, while shifting penetrations into an illusory depth are made by color areas that advance and recede according to value, overlap, or shading. (L. F.)

1. Quoted in *Willem de Kooning*, exh. cat., Pittsburgh, 1979, p. 28.

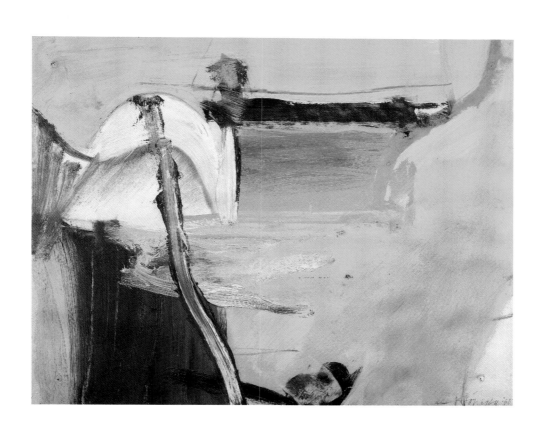

83

RUFINO TAMAYO

Heavenly Bodies, 1946

Oil with sand on canvas, 86.3 x 105 cm
76.2553 PG 119

Rufino Tamayo filtered his pre-Colombian heritage through the pictorial tradition of European Modernism in images of man's confrontation with the forces of nature and the universe. In several paintings of 1946–47 he showed primitive figures gesticulating in terror, awe, or longing at the patterns of astral and planetary orbits.

The lines traversing the sky in *Heavenly Bodies* may represent light emanating from stars or the tails of meteors, and may also indicate the mental constructs that join stars in constellations. These lines dissect the rich blue sky into flat planes and simultaneously provide the illusion of movement through a vast space. The purity of the sky's geometry is contrasted with the unevenly curving contours of the human figure, associated formally with the earth. A setting sun is evoked by the red strip on the hill and is reflected on the man's face. While bearing some relation to Mexican folk art, the treatment of the figure derives more directly from the work of Pablo Picasso. The combination of frontal and profile view, the gaping mouth and conical eye, the shorthand outlining of the face and outstretched childlike hand have analogies in works such as Picasso's *Guernica* of 1937 (Collection Museo Nacional del Prado, Madrid), which Tamayo had occasion to see in New York. (L. F.)

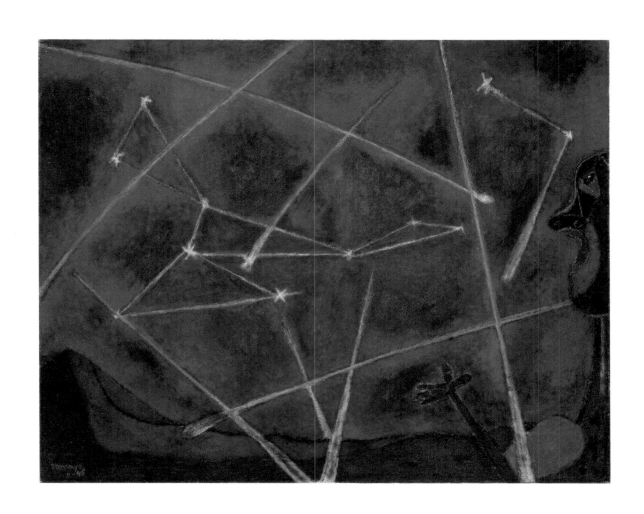

84

HENRY MOORE

Three Standing Figures, 1953

Bronze, 73.2 x 68 x 29 cm, including base
76.2553 PG 194

In its abstraction of the human figure and exaggeration of isolated anatomical features, this work is related to African sculpture and to the Surrealist sculpture of Pablo Picasso and Alberto Giacometti. Within Henry Moore's own body of work, *Three Standing Figures* can be seen in connection with the "shelter" drawings of the early 1940s, in which the artist explored the psychological interaction of groups, and with the monumental *Three Standing Figures* of 1947–49 erected at Battersea Park in London. Classicizing elements of the latter, however remote, endure in the Peggy Guggenheim work. The grouping of three figures, their contrapposto stances, the variety of rhetorical gestures, and the echoes of drapery creases and swags provide visual analogies with ancient sources. Typically, Moore conflates the human figure with the forms of inanimate natural materials such as bone and rock. The perforations through the mass of the sculptured bodies suggest a slow process of erosion by water or wind.

At least three preparatory drawings exist for *Three Standing Figures*, which was cast in bronze from a plaster original in an edition of eight, with one artist's proof (discussed and repr. Rudenstine, p. 580). A ten-inch maquette preceding it in 1952 was also cast in bronze. Neither of the original plasters survives. Moore used bronze increasingly from the late 1940s; he commented on its greater flexibility in comparison with stone, and its relative strength in withstanding the action of the elements. (L. F.)

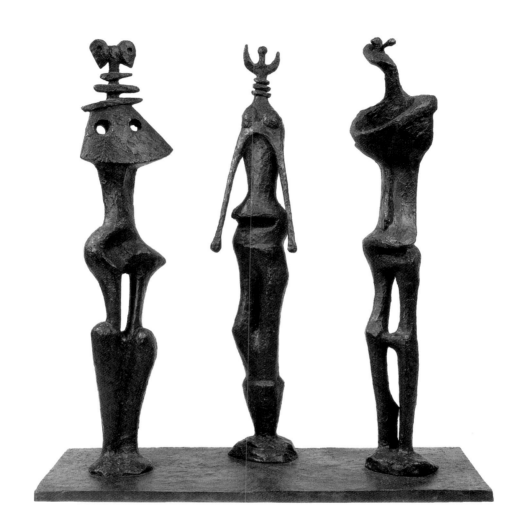

85

BEN NICHOLSON

February 1956 (menhir), 1956

Oil (and ink?) on board, 99.4 x 30 cm
76.2553 PG 46

In the early thirties Ben Nicholson began carving reliefs. By 1934 these were composed of circular and rectilinear elements that he painted white. The first series was completed in 1939. When Nicholson focused again on the form in the mid-1950s, the reliefs became subtly varied in coloration and texture. The present example is particularly severe, the absence of curved or diagonal lines recalling the work of Piet Mondrian, whom Nicholson knew and admired. The muted, chalky color evokes early Italian Renaissance frescoes and shards of classical pottery.

The parenthetical *menhir* (Breton for "long stone") in the title refers to the simple prehistoric stone slabs found throughout western Europe, especially in Brittany. The association is reinforced by the vertical format and the hewn monochromatic surface of the board. The balance of shape, proportion, and placement, apparently so simple, is achieved adroitly. The thickness of the central rectangle decreases gradually from top to bottom, so that the form projects where it meets the upper rectangle, while lying flush above the lower rectangle. This manipulation produces a tapering shadow that softens the strictly perpendicular alignment of the relief to produce a work of austere harmony. (L. F.)

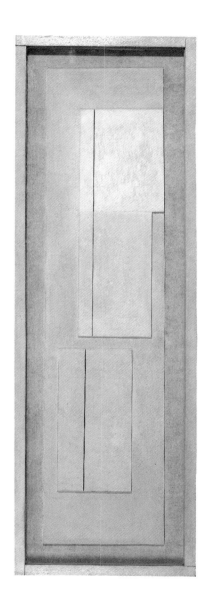

86

GERMAINE RICHIER

Tauromachy (Tauromachie), 1953

Bronze, figure 111.5 cm high; base 95.7 x 52.5 x 3 cm
76.2553 PG 205

Germaine Richier's investigation of the composition and decomposition of organic materials situates her work in the vitalist current of twentieth-century sculpture, which concerns itself with natural processes. In an assault on closed form, she breaks through her heavily worked surfaces to expose the structural armature and hollow spaces within the bodies they describe.

In subject matter and style this sculpture recalls both Pablo Picasso's Surrealist bullfight imagery of the 1930s and his sculptures of the early 1950s. Richier, who was herself familiar with the bullfight, shared with Picasso an interest in its mythic, archaic implications.[1] In addition, the robust three-dimensionality, raw surfaces, and incorporation of found objects in *Tauromachy* may constitute a response to works such as Picasso's *She-Goat* of 1950 and *Goat Skull and Bottle* of 1951–52. Like Henry Moore during the same year (see cat. no. 84), Richier places her forms in situational relationships. As she wrote: "Finally, the sculpture is a *place*, an entity, a synthesis of movements. I don't know if the *Tauromachy* evokes the sand, but no form, it seems to me, can be separated from the universe, the elements. It is therefore something more than an image."[2]

This bronze was produced in an edition of ten. (L. F.)

1. For a discussion of Richier's references to her native Provence, see Rudenstine, pp. 686–87.

2. Quoted in *Art du XXe siècle: Fondation Peggy Guggenheim, Venise*, exh. cat., Paris, 1974, p. 106. Author's translation.

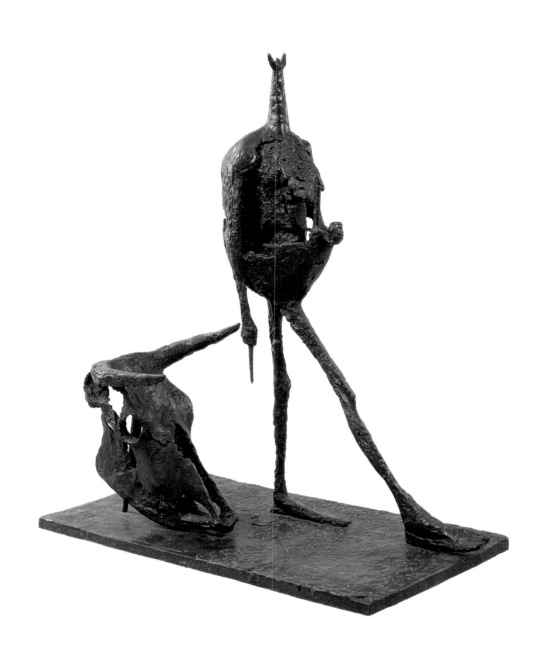

FRANCIS BACON

Study for Chimpanzee, March 1957

Oil and pastel on canvas, 152.4 x 117 cm
76.2553 PG 172

Although Francis Bacon is best known for his alienated and often hideously distorted human figures, animals are the subject of at least a dozen of his canvases. He rarely worked from nature, pre-
ferring photographs, and for images of animals he often consulted Eadweard Muybridge's *Animals
in Motion*, Marius Maxwell's *Stalking Big Game with a Camera in Equatorial Africa*, and pictures from
zoological parks. Intrigued by the disconcerting affinities between simians and human beings, he
first compared them in 1949 in *Head IV (Man with a Monkey)* (formerly Collection Geoffrey Gates,
New York), in which a man's averted face is concealed by that of the monkey he holds.

Like his human subjects, Bacon's animals are shown in formal portraits or candid snapshots in
which they are passive, shrieking, or twisted in physical contortions. The chimpanzee in the Peggy
Guggenheim work is depicted with relative benevolence, though the blurring of the image, reflecting Bacon's interest in frozen motion and the effects of photography and film, makes it difficult to
interpret the pose or expression. In composition and treatment it is close to paintings of simians
executed in the fifties by Graham Sutherland, with whom Bacon became friendly in 1946. The faint,
schematic framing enabled Bacon to "see" the subject better, while the monochrome background
provides a starkly contrasting field that helps to define form. (L. F.)

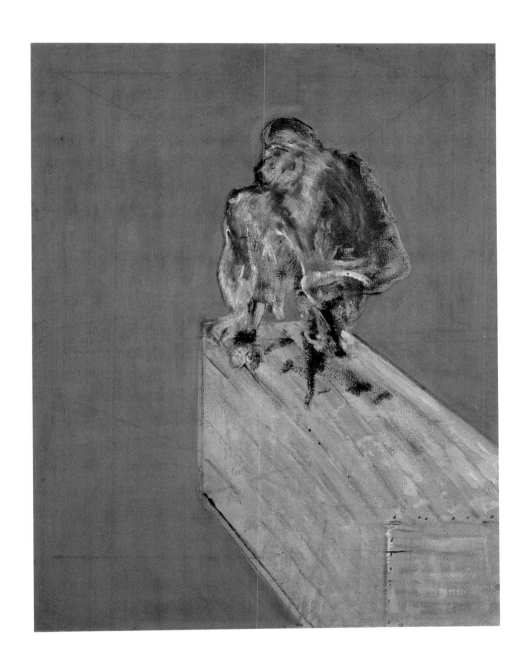

JEAN DUBUFFET

Fleshy Face with Chestnut Hair (*Châtaine aux hautes chairs*), August 1951

Oil-based mixed-media on board, 64.9 x 54 cm
76.2553 PG 121

Jean Dubuffet was attracted to the surfaces of dilapidated walls, pitted roads, and the natural crusts of earth and rock, and during the 1940s and 1950s sought to create an equivalent texture in his art. He experimented with a variety of materials to produce thick, ruggedly tactile surfaces that constitute deliberately awkward, vulgar, and abbreviated imagery, often of grotesque faces or female nudes. Dubuffet made the present work with an oil-based "mortar," applying it with a palette knife, allowing areas to dry partially, then scraping, gouging, raking, slicing, or wiping them before applying more medium. The resulting surface is so thick that incisions providing the contours and delineating features seem to model form in relief. He wrote that this mortar enabled him to "provoke systems of relief in objects where reliefs are least expected, and lent itself, at the same time, to very realistic effects of rugged and stony terrains. I enjoyed the idea that a single medium should have this double (ambiguous) power: to accentuate the actual and familiar character of certain elements (notably in figurations of ground and soils), and yet to precipitate other elements into a world of fantasmagoric irreality."[1]

Dubuffet's aggressively anticultural, antiaesthetic attitude and spontaneity of expression provided an example for members of the COBRA group in Europe, and New York artists such as Claes Oldenburg and Jim Dine. (L. F.)

1. P. Selz and J. Dubuffet, *The Work of Jean Dubuffet*, exh. cat., New York, 1962, p. 66.

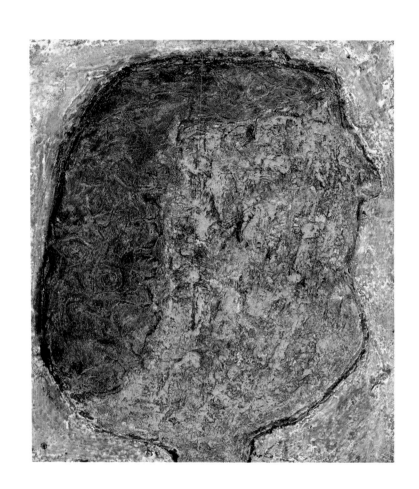

ASGER JORN

Untitled, 1956–57

Oil on canvas, 141 x 110.1 cm
76.2553 PG 175

From about 1948 Asger Jorn filled his canvases with swarming faces and figures, vaporous equivalents of the eccentric visages in crowd scenes by the Belgian artist James Ensor. Their scrawled half-innocent, half-demonic features also have antecedents in the creatures of Jean Dubuffet and Paul Klee. These presences hovering on the surface of the canvas are integrated with their surroundings, scarcely distinguishable as representational forms. In the present canvas blobs of paint and linear contours coalesce into a standing, grinning human figure at the right and a bird in the center; a multitude of faces, less acutely defined, emerge, vanish, and reappear in the seething environment. Wherever two dots can be interpreted as eyes, a face can be imagined.

The sense of fantasy here is complemented by the candied color applied in thicknesses ranging from thin veneer to heavy ridges. Line incises its way through the fluffy space of this layered pigment to determine boundaries and suggest form. The dots of color sprinkled throughout anticipate the pointillism of the artist's *Luxury Paintings* of the early 1960s, in which paint is dripped onto the canvas from a perforated tin can. The accidental revelation of form and the importance of chance in Jorn's work suggest Surrealist concerns. (L. F.)

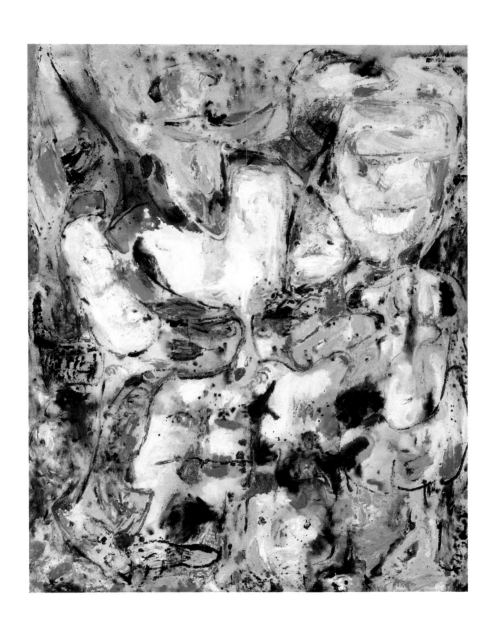

KAREL APPEL

The Crying Crocodile Tries to Catch the Sun, 1956

Oil on canvas, 145.5 x 113.1 cm
76.2553 PG 174

Karel Appel, like Asger Jorn, was a member of the COBRA group, which emphasized material and its spontaneous application. Although the group was short-lived, its concerns have endured in his work. The single standing figures of humans or animals he developed during the 1950s are rendered in a deliberately awkward, naive way, with no attempt at modeling or perspectival illusionism. Thus, the crocodile in this painting is presented as a flat and immobile form, contoured with heavy black lines in the manner of a child's drawing.

Appel's paint handling activates a frenzy of rhythmic movement in *The Crying Crocodile . . .* despite the static monumentality of the subject. Drips and smears are interspersed with veritable stalactites of brilliant, unmodulated color that buckle, ooze, slash, wither, and thread their way over the surface. The physicality of the impasto and its topographic variety allow it to reflect light and cast shadows dramatically, increasing the emotional intensity of violent color contrasts. In 1956 Appel summarized the genesis of his work: "I never try to make a painting; it is a howl, it is naked, it is like a child, it is a caged tiger. . . . My tube is like a rocket writing its own space."[1] (L. F.)

1. Quoted in A. Frankenstein, *Karel Appel*, New York, 1980, p. 52.

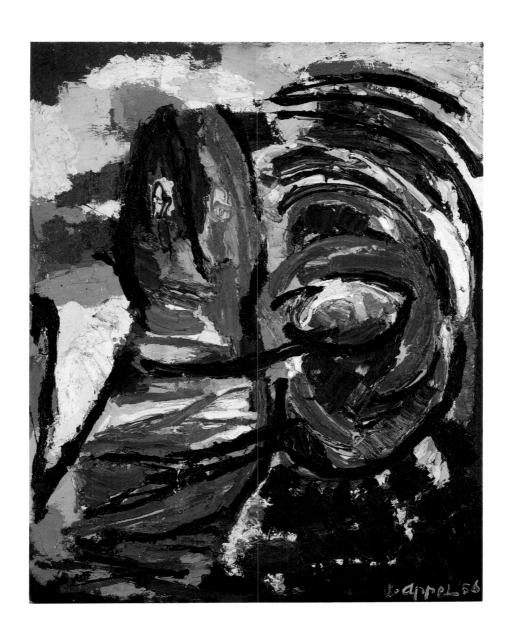

EMILIO VEDOVA

Image of Time (Barrier) (Immagine del tempo {Sbarramento}), 1951

Egg tempera on canvas, 130.5 x 170.4 cm
76.2553 PG 162

Emilio Vedova's work has antecedents in the long tradition of dynamic expression that has existed in Italian art since Tintoretto. Like the Futurists, Vedova sees his work as a response to contemporary social upheavals. Though he shares the emotional pitch of the Futurists, his political position is antithetical to theirs. While they romantically celebrated the aggressive energies of societal conflict, Vedova in his feverish, violent canvases conveys in abstract terms his horror and moral protestation in the face of man's assault on his own kind.

Vedova expressed a political consciousness in his work for the first time during the early 1940s, when his paintings were inspired by the Spanish Civil War. His continuing commitment to social issues gave rise to series such as *Cycle of Protest* and *Image of Time*, initiated during the first years of the 1950s. Although the generating impulse of this turbulent painting is political, its formal preoccupations parallel those of the American Abstract Expressionists Jackson Pollock and, above all, Franz Kline. The drama of the angular, graphic slashes of black on white is heightened with accents of orange-red. Occupying a shallow space, pictorial elements are locked together in formal combat and emotional turmoil. (L. F.)

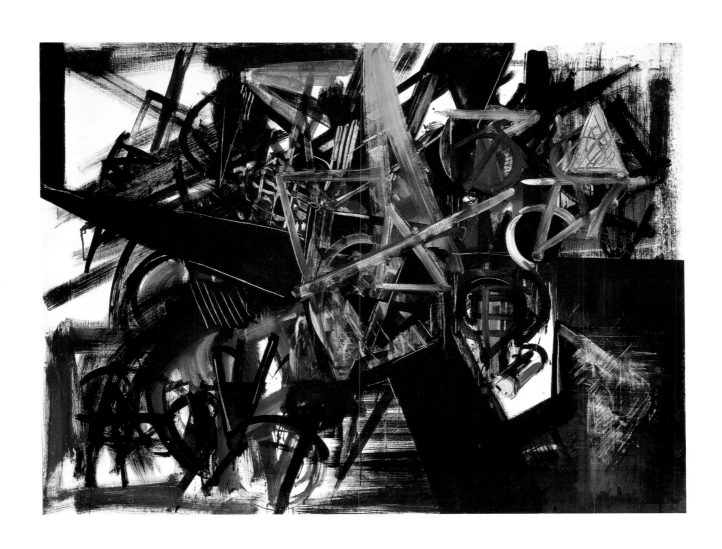

GIUSEPPE SANTOMASO

Secret Life (*Vita segreta*), 1958

Oil on canvas, 73.1 x 49.9 cm
76.2553 PG 161

In resolving the problems of representing color and light, Giuseppe Santomaso relies on the daily experience of his native Venice, fortified by knowledge of classical culture. His development of a non-objective mode of expression for his perceptions of nature was influenced by American abstract art, particularly after his visit in 1957 to New York, where he met Willem de Kooning, Hans Hofmann, Franz Kline, Robert Motherwell, Barnett Newman, and Mark Rothko. Santomaso uses nature as a "visual pretext" (to employ his own term), absorbing it and changing it into pictorial form; the resultant painting derives its impact not from the imitation of nature, but from the tension between art and nature. Life can be imparted to abstract form only through its disposition in an "abstract order." Santomaso refers to the eye's exploratory adventure as it perceives the "secret combination" of things in nature and their "fantastic equivalent" in painting.[1] The title of this work alludes to the encounter of life and art, and draws attention to the hint of a centralized human figure, the structural features of which appear and disappear, easily mistaken for the random patterns seen on a peeling Venetian wall. The romantic colors—rose, gray, smoky blue, warm browns, and ochers—evoke gentle nostalgia. (L. F.)

1. Conversation with the author, June 1981.

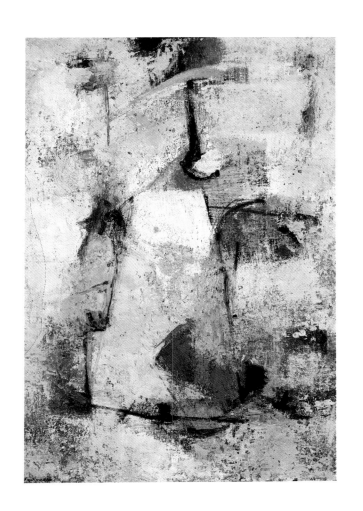

EDMONDO BACCI

Event #247 (Avvenimento #247), 1956

Oil with sand on canvas, 140.2 x 140 cm
76.2553 PG 164

Edmondo Bacci has applied the physicality of action painting to the depiction of the origins of matter in extraterrestrial regions. Like the apocalyptic paintings of the years immediately preceding World War I by artists such as Vasily Kandinsky and Franz Marc, his work comingles themes of cosmic genesis and destruction expressed through swirling atmospheric color. The three primaries, red, blue, and yellow, predominate, defining broad areas against which a wide range of other colors play. The painting is like a scenario in which light is separated from darkness and space from matter. Planetary forms seem to coalesce out of material produced by a cosmic eruption; they prepare to establish their orbits and generate life. The immediacy and drama of the event is conveyed through the tactility of the surface. The paint, mixed with sand, is encrusted on the canvas to form a kind of topographic ground evoking plains, ridges, lakes, and peaks. The activity of the artist in ordering chaos is associated with elemental creational processes within the universe. (L. F.)

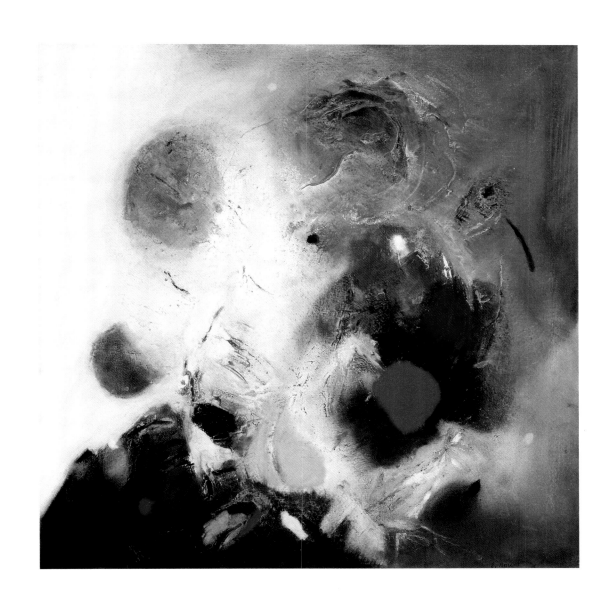

TANCREDI

Composition, 1955

Oil and tempera on canvas, 129.5 x 195 cm
76.2553 PG 166

Where Piet Mondrian used the square as a unit with which to express a notion of space and infinity, Tancredi, who saw his aims as parallel to those of Mondrian, seized on the point as his module. He was intrigued by the point's identity as the determinant sign of location, the smallest indication of presence. Tancredi's ideas about infinite space and the use of the point within it were developed by 1951, when he settled in Venice. This work typifies the crowded, architectonic compositions he painted before his visit to Paris in 1955.

Incomplete circles vibrant with undiluted pigment radiate from pivotal points and swirl throughout the canvas. These appear below, above, and amid rectangular slabs, the whole comprising a multilayered scaffolding of light and color producing the illusion of extensive, textured depth. Density of form and color increases toward the center of the composition, which consequently appears to bulge forward from the corners, illustrating Tancredi's view of space as curved. The vitality of execution and tactile richness reflect the influence of Jackson Pollock. The choppy, animated repetition of color applied with a palette knife resembles that of the French-Canadian painter Jean-Paul Riopelle, with whom Tancredi exhibited in 1954. (L. F.)

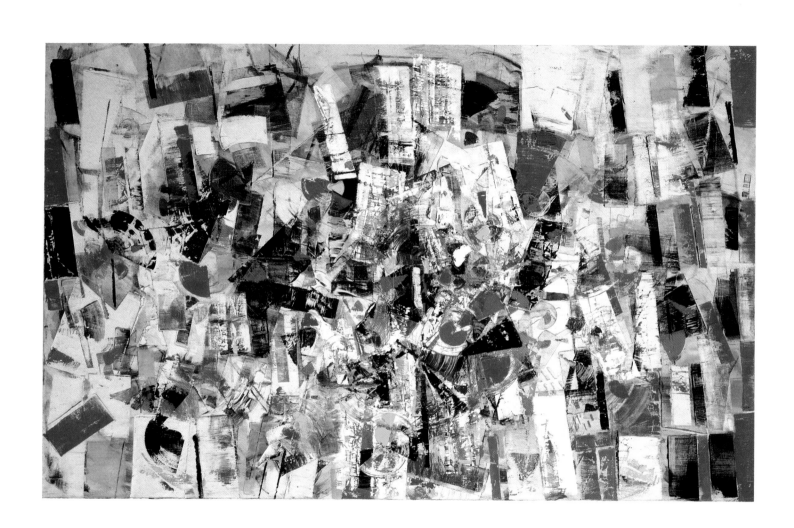

ARNALDO POMODORO

Sphere No. 4 (Sfero No. 4), 1963–64 (cast 1964)

Bronze, 185 cm circumference
76.2553 PG 214

Although the figurative tradition represented by Marino Marini and Giacomo Manzù has flourished in postwar Italian sculpture, an equally energetic commitment to abstraction has been pursued by artists such as Pietro Consagra, Mirko, and the Pomodoro brothers, Giò and Arnaldo. Trained in goldsmithing, Arnaldo Pomodoro combines the meticulous approach and skill of the craftsman with the techniques and aims of the caster of large-scale bronzes. His sculpture, cast from plasters of clay originals, contrasts the intricate detailing of jewelry with geometric breadth and clarity.

Using the basic shapes of cube, cylinder, and sphere, he tears open their pristine, highly polished surfaces to reveal the internal structure of form. Underneath the gleaming skin and solid flesh of the bronze lies a regulating machinery of cogs and gears, which Pomodoro calls "sign systems," akin to the complex interlocking systems of language or of organic bodies. The sphere not only functions as a geometric shape and analogue of a living body or mineral form, but also suggests the globe of the earth. The equatorial rupture produces configurations suggesting land masses, and evokes the earth's core and desiccated ocean beds. By eliminating frontality, Pomodoro invites the viewer to circle the globe, conveying a sense of uninterrupted rotational movement imitating the orbit of planets. (L. F.)

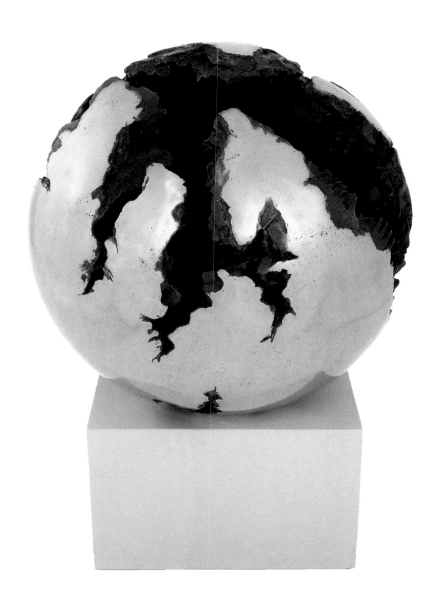

MARINO MARINI

The Angel of the City (L'Angelo della città), 1948 (cast 1950?)

Bronze, 247.9 x 106 cm, including base
76.2553 PG 183

Marino Marini drew on the tradition of Etruscan and Northern European sculpture in developing his themes of the female nude, the portrait bust, and the equestrian figure. By interpreting classical themes in light of modern concerns and with modern techniques, he sought to contribute a mythic image that would be applicable in a contemporary context.

The evolution of the subject of the horse and rider reflects Marini's personal response to that changing context. The theme first appears in his work in 1936, when the proportions of horse and rider are relatively slender and both figures are poised, formal, and calm. By the following year the horse rears and the rider gestures. In 1940 the forms become simplified and more archaic in spirit, and the proportions become squatter. By the late 1940s the horse is planted immobile with its neck extended, strained, ears pinned back, and mouth open, as in the present example, which conveys the qualities characteristic of this period of Marini's work—affirmation and charged strength associated explicitly with sexual potency. Later, the rider becomes increasingly oblivious of his mount, involved in his own visions or anxieties. Eventually he was to topple from the horse as it fell to the ground in an apocalyptic image of lost control, paralleling Marini's feelings of despair and uncertainty about the future of the world. (L. F.)

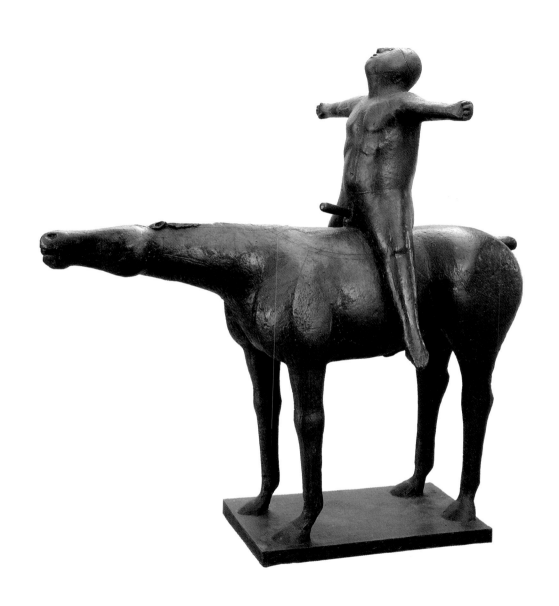

BIOGRAPHIES OF THE ARTISTS

KAREL APPEL
b. 1921

Karel Appel was born on April 25, 1921, in Amsterdam. From 1940 to 1943 he studied at the Rijksakademie van Beeldende Kunsten in Amsterdam. In 1946 his first solo show was held at Het Beerenhuis in Groningen, the Netherlands, and he participated in the *Jonge Schilders* exhibition at the Stedelijk Museum of Amsterdam. About this time Appel was influenced first by Pablo Picasso and Henri Matisse, then by Jean Dubuffet. He was a member of the Nederlandse Experimentele Groep and established the COBRA movement in 1948 with George Constant, Corneille, and others. In 1949 Appel completed a fresco for the cafeteria of the city hall in Amsterdam, which created such controversy that it was covered for ten years.

In 1950 the artist moved to Paris; there the writer Hugo Claus introduced him to Michel Tapié, who organized various exhibitions of his work. Appel was given a solo show at the Palais des Beaux-Arts in Brussels in 1953. He received the UNESCO Prize at the Venice Biennale of 1954, and was commissioned to execute a mural for the restaurant of the Stedelijk Museum in 1956. The following year Appel traveled to Mexico and the United States and won a graphics prize at the Ljubljana Biennial in Yugoslavia. He was awarded an International Prize for Painting at the São Paulo Bienal in 1959. The first major monograph on Appel, written by Claus, was published in 1962. In the late 1960s the artist moved to the Château de Molesmes, near Auxerre, southeast of Paris. Solo exhibitions of his work were held at the Centre National d'Art Contemporain in Paris and the Stedelijk Museum in Amsterdam in 1968, and at the Kunsthalle Basel and the Palais des Beaux-Arts in Brussels in 1969. During the 1950s and 1960s he executed numerous murals for public buildings. A major Appel show opened at the Centraal Museum in Utrecht in 1970, and a retrospective of his work toured Canada and the United States in 1972. Appel lives in Paris and New York.

ALEXANDER ARCHIPENKO
1887–1964

Alexander Archipenko was born on May 30, 1887, in Kiev, Ukraine, Russia. In 1902 he entered the Kiev Art School, where he studied painting and sculpture until 1905. During this time he was impressed by the Byzantine icons, frescoes, and mosaics of Kiev. After a sojourn in Moscow Archipenko moved to Paris in 1908. He attended the Ecole des Beaux-Arts for a brief period and then continued to study independently at the Louvre, where he was drawn to Egyptian, Assyrian, archaic Greek, and early Gothic sculpture. In 1910 he began exhibiting at the Salon des Indépendants, Paris, and the following year showed for the first time at the Salon d'Automne.

In 1912 Archipenko was given his first solo show in Germany at the Folkwang Museum in Hagen. That same year in Paris he opened the first of his many art schools, joined the Section d'Or group, which included Georges Braque, Marcel Duchamp, Fernand Léger, and Pablo Picasso, among others, and produced his first painted reliefs, the *Sculpto-Peintures*. In 1913 Archipenko exhibited at the Armory Show in New York and made his first prints, which were reproduced in the Italian Futurist publication *Lacerba* in 1914. He participated in the Salon des Indépendants in 1914 and the Venice Biennale in 1920. During the war years the artist resided in Cimiez, a suburb of Nice. From 1919 to 1921 he traveled to Geneva, Zurich, Paris, London, Brussels, Athens, and other European cities to exhibit his work. Archipenko's first solo show in the United States was held at the Société Anonyme in New York in 1921.

In 1923 he moved from Berlin to the United States where, over the years, he opened art schools in New York City, Woodstock (New York), Los Angeles, and Chicago. In 1924 Archipenko invented his first kinetic work, *Archipentura*. For the next thirty years he taught throughout the United States at art schools and universities, including the New Bauhaus School of Industrial Arts in Chicago. He became a United States citizen in 1928. Most of Archipenko's work in German museums was confiscated by the Nazis in their purge of "degenerate art." In 1947 he produced the first of his sculptures that are illuminated from within. He accompanied an exhibition of his work throughout Germany in 1955, and at this time began his book *Archipenko: Fifty Creative Years 1908–1958*, published in 1960. Archipenko died on February 25, 1964, in New York.

JEAN ARP

1886–1966

Jean (Hans) Arp was born on September 16, 1886, in Strasbourg, Alsace-Lorraine. In 1904, after leaving the Ecole des Arts et Métiers in Strasbourg, he visited Paris and published his poetry for the first time. From 1905 to 1907 Arp studied at the Kunstschule of Weimar and in 1908 went to Paris, where he attended the Académie Julian. In 1909 he moved to Switzerland and in 1911 was a founder of the Moderner Bund group there. The following year he met Robert and Sonia Delaunay in Paris and Vasily Kandinsky in Munich. Arp participated in the *Erste deutsche Herbstsalon* in 1913 at Der Sturm gallery in Berlin. After returning to Paris in 1914, he became acquainted with Guillaume Apollinaire, Max Jacob, and Pablo Picasso. In 1915 he moved to Zurich, where he executed collages and tapestries, often in collaboration with his future wife, Sophie Taeuber.

In 1916 Hugo Ball opened the Cabaret Voltaire, which was to become the center of Dada activities in Zurich, for a group including Arp, Marcel Janco, Tristan Tzara, and others. Arp continued his involvement with Dada after moving to Cologne in 1919. In 1922 he participated in the *Kongress der Konstruktivisten* in Weimar. Soon thereafter he began contributing to magazines such as *Merz*, *Mécano*, *De Stijl*, and in 1925 *La Révolution surréaliste*. Arp's work appeared in the first exhibition of the Surrealist group at the Galerie Pierre in Paris in 1925. In 1926 he settled in Meudon, France.

In 1931 Arp was associated with the Paris-based group Abstraction-Création and the periodical *Transition*. Throughout the 1930s and until the end of his life he continued to write and publish poetry and essays. In 1942 he fled Meudon for Zurich; he was to make Meudon his primary residence again in 1946. The artist visited New York in 1949 on the occasion of his solo show at Curt Valentin's Buchholz Gallery. In 1950 he was invited to execute a relief for the Harvard Graduate Center in Cambridge, Massachusetts. In 1954 Arp received the International Prize for Sculpture at the Venice Biennale. A large retrospective of his work was held at the Museum of Modern Art in New York in 1958, followed by another at the Musée National d'Art Moderne in Paris in 1962. Arp died on June 7, 1966, in Basel.

EDMONDO BACCI

1913–1978

Edmondo Bacci was born on July 21, 1913, in Venice. He studied with Ettore Tito and Virgilio Guidi at the Accademia di Belle Arti of Venice from 1932 to 1937. His first solo exhibition was held at the Galleria del Cavallino in Venice in 1945. In 1948 he participated in the Venice Biennale for the first of many times. Bacci was included in the first Genoa Biennale in 1951 and in an exhibition of the Movimento Spaziale, the group founded by Lucio Fontana, held in Venice in 1953. He contributed regularly to Spazialismo exhibitions thereafter, among them *Espacialismo* at the Galeria Bonino in Buenos Aires in 1966. From the mid-1950s Bacci received support from Peggy Guggenheim.

An important solo exhibition of Bacci's work took place at the Galleria del Cavallino in 1955. His first solo show in the United States occurred at the Seventy-Five Gallery in New York the following year. Solo exhibitions of his work were held also at the Galleria del Naviglio, Milan, the Galleria d'Arte Selecta, Rome, and the Galleria "La Cittadella" in Ascona, Switzerland, all in 1957. That same year he participated in *Between Space and Earth* at the Marlborough Gallery in London. Bacci was accorded a separate room at the Venice Biennale of 1958, and he received a Prize of the Municipality of Venice at the *Terza biennale dell'incisione italiana contemporanea* in Venice in 1959. He was given shows at the Drian Gallery in London in 1961 and at the Frank Perls Gallery in Beverly Hills the following year. In 1961 he also participated in *Neue italienische Kunst* at Galerie 59 in Aschaffenburg. He executed lithographs to accompany a poem by Guido Ballo, *Il ciè-lo Kàinos*, in 1972. Bacci died on October 16, 1978, in Venice.

FRANCIS BACON

1909–1992

Francis Bacon was born in Dublin on October 28, 1909. At the age of sixteen he moved to London and subsequently lived for about two years in Berlin and Paris. Although Bacon never attended art school he began to draw and work in watercolor about 1926–27. Pablo Picasso's work decisively influenced his painting until the mid-1940s. Upon his return to London in 1929 he established himself as a furniture designer and interior designer. He began to use oils in the fall of that year and exhibited furniture and rugs as well as a few paintings in his studio. His work was included in a group exhibition in London at the Mayor Gallery in 1933. In 1934 the artist organized his own first solo show at Sunderland House, London, which he called Transition Gallery for the occasion. He participated in a group show at Thos. Agnew and Sons in London in 1937.

Bacon painted relatively little after his solo show and in the 1930s and early 1940s destroyed many of his works. He began to paint intensively again in 1944. His first major solo show took place at the Hanover Gallery in London in 1949. From the mid-1940s to the 1950s Bacon's work reflected the influence of Surrealism. In the 1950s Bacon drew on such sources as Velázquez's *Portrait of Pope Innocent X*, Vincent van Gogh's *The Painter on the Road to Tarascon*, and Eadweard Muybridge's photographs. His first solo exhibition outside England was held in 1953 at the Durlacher Brothers, New York. In 1950–51 and 1952 the artist traveled to South Africa. He visited Italy in 1954 when his work was featured in the British Pavilion at the Venice Biennale. His first retrospective was held at the Institute of Contemporary Art, London, in 1955. Bacon was given a solo show at the São Paulo Bienal in 1959. In 1962 the Tate Gallery, London, organized a major Bacon retrospective, a modified version of which traveled to Mannheim, Turin, Zurich, and Amsterdam. Other important exhibitions of his work were held at the Solomon R. Guggenheim Museum, New York, in 1963 and the Grand Palais in Paris in 1971; paintings from 1968 to 1974 were exhibited at the Metropolitan Museum of Art, New York, in 1975. The artist died in Madrid on April 28, 1992.

GIACOMO BALLA

1871–1958

Giacomo Balla was born in Turin on July 18, 1871. In 1891 he studied briefly at the Accademia Albertina di Belle Arti and the Liceo Artistico in Turin and exhibited for the first time under the aegis of the Società Promotrice di Belle Arti in that city. He studied at the University of Turin with Cesare Lombroso about 1892. In 1895 Balla moved to Rome, where he worked for several years as an illustrator, caricaturist, and portrait painter. In 1899 his work was included in the Venice Biennale and in the *Esposizione internazionale di belle arti* at the galleries of the Società degli Amatori e Cultori di Belle Arti in Rome, where he exhibited regularly for the next ten years. In 1900 Balla spent seven months in Paris assisting the illustrator Serafino Macchiati. About 1903 he began to instruct Gino Severini and Umberto Boccioni in divisionist painting techniques. In 1903 his work was exhibited at the *Esposizione internazionale d'arte della città di Venezia* and in 1903 and 1904 at the Glaspalast in Munich. In 1904 Balla was represented in the *Internationale Kunstausstellung* in Düsseldorf, and in 1909 exhibited at the Salon d'Automne in Paris.

Balla signed the second Futurist painting manifesto of 1910 with Boccioni, Carlo Carrà, Luigi Russolo, and Severini, although he did not exhibit with the group until 1913. In 1912 he traveled to London and to Düsseldorf, where he began painting his abstract light studies. In 1913 Balla participated in the *Erste deutsche Herbstsalon* at Der Sturm gallery in Berlin and in an exhibition at the Rotterdamsche Kunstkring in Rotterdam. In 1914 he experimented with sculpture for the first time and showed it in the *Prima esposizione libera futurista* at the Galleria Sprovieri, Rome. He also designed and painted Futurist furniture and designed Futurist "antineutral" clothing. With Fortunato Depero, Balla wrote the manifesto *Ricostruzione futurista dell'universo* in 1915. His first solo exhibitions were held that same year at the Società Italiana Lampade Elettriche "Z" and at the Sala d'Arte A. Angelelli in Rome. His work was also shown in 1915 at the *Panama-Pacific International Exposition* in San Francisco. In 1918 he was given a solo show at the Casa d'Arte Bragaglia in Rome. Balla continued to exhibit in Europe and the United States and in 1935 was made a member of the Accademia di San Luca in Rome. He died on March 1, 1958, in Rome.

WILLIAM BAZIOTES

1912–1963

William Baziotes was born to parents of Greek origin on June 11, 1912, in Pittsburgh. He grew up in Reading, Pennsylvania, where he worked at the Case Glass company from 1931 to 1933, antiquing glass and running errands. At this time he took evening sketch classes and met the poet Byron Vazakas, who became his life-long friend. Vazakas introduced Baziotes to the work of Charles Baudelaire and the Symbolist poets. In 1931 Baziotes saw the Henri Matisse exhibition at the Museum of Modern Art in New York, and in 1933 he moved to that city to study painting. From 1933 to 1936 Baziotes attended the National Academy of Design.

In 1936 he exhibited for the first time in a group show at the Municipal Art Gallery, New York, and was employed by the WPA Federal Art Project as an art teacher at the Queens Museum. Baziotes worked in the easel division of the WPA from 1938 to 1941. He met the Surrealist emigrés in New York in the late thirties and early forties, and by 1940 knew Jimmy Ernst, Matta, and Gordon Onslow-Ford. He began to experiment with Surrealist automatism at this time. In 1941 Matta introduced Baziotes to Robert Motherwell, with whom he formed a close friendship. André Masson invited Baziotes to participate with Motherwell, David Hare, and others in the 1942 exhibition *First Papers of Surrealism* at the Whitelaw Reid Mansion in New York. In 1943 he took part in two group shows at Peggy Guggenheim's Art of This Century, New York, where his first solo exhibition was held the following year. With Hare, Motherwell, and Mark Rothko, Baziotes founded the Subjects of the Artist school in New York in 1948. Over the next decade Baziotes held a number of teaching positions in New York: at the Brooklyn Museum Art School and at New York University from 1949 to 1952; at the People's Art Center, the Museum of Modern Art from 1950 to 1952; and at Hunter College from 1952 to 1962. Baziotes died in New York on June 6, 1963. A memorial exhibition of his work was presented at the Solomon R. Guggenheim Museum, New York, in 1965.

UMBERTO BOCCIONI

1882–1916

Umberto Boccioni was born on October 19, 1882, in Reggio Calabria, Italy. In 1901 he went to Rome, where he studied design with a sign painter and attended the Scuola Libera del Nudo at the Accademia di Belle Arti. In Rome he and Gino Severini learned the techniques of divisionist painting from Giacomo Balla. Boccioni traveled in 1902 to Paris, where he studied Impressionist and Post-Impressionist painting. He participated in the *Mostra dei rifiutati* in 1905 and in the *Esposizione di belle arti* in 1906, both in Rome.

Following a trip to Russia in 1906, Boccioni visited Padua and then moved to Venice, where he spent the winter of 1906–07 taking life-drawing classes at the Accademia di Belle Arti. In 1907 he settled in Milan. In 1909–10 Boccioni began to frequent the Famiglia Artistica, a Milanese artists' society that sponsored annual exhibitions. During this period he associated with Carlo Carrà and Luigi Russolo, and met the poet Filippo Tommaso Marinetti, who had published the first Futurist manifesto in February of 1909. In 1910 Boccioni participated in the formulation of the two Futurist manifestos *Manifesto dei pittori futuristi* and *Manifesto tecnico della pittura futurista*. He, Carrà, Russolo, and Severini signed the first, and were joined by Balla in signing the second. That same year Boccioni's first solo exhibition was held at the Galleria Ca' Pesaro in Venice.

In the fall of 1911 the artist went to Paris, where he met Pablo Picasso and Guillaume Apollinaire through Severini. Boccioni's paintings were shown with those of Carrà, Russolo, and Severini in the first Futurist show in Paris, at the Galerie Bernheim-Jeune in 1912. The exhibition then traveled to London, Berlin, and Brussels. In 1912 Boccioni began concentrating on sculpture, and his *Manifesto tecnico della scultura futurista* was published. From 1912 to 1914 he contributed articles to the Futurist publication *Lacerba*. In 1913 the artist showed sculpture and paintings in a solo show at the Galerie de la Boétie in Paris, and his sculpture was included in the inaugural exhibition of the Galleria Futurista Permanente in Rome. His book *Pittura e scultura futuriste (dinamismo plastico)* appeared in 1914. In July of 1915 Boccioni enlisted in the army with Marinetti, Russolo, and Antonio Sant'Elia. He suffered an accident during cavalry exercises in Sorte near Verona, and died on August 17, 1916.

CONSTANTIN BRANCUSI

1876–1957

Constantin Brancusi was born on February 19, 1876, in the village of Hobitza, Romania. He studied art at the Craiova School of Arts and Crafts from 1894 to 1898 and at the Bucharest School of Fine Arts from 1898 to 1901. Eager to continue his education in Paris, Brancusi arrived there in 1904 and enrolled in the Ecole des Beaux-Arts in 1905. The following year his sculpture was shown at the Salon d'Automne, where he met Auguste Rodin.

Soon after 1907 his mature period began. The sculptor had settled in Paris but throughout these years returned frequently to Bucharest and exhibited there almost every year. In Paris his friends included Marcel Duchamp, Fernand Léger, Henri Matisse, Amedeo Modigliani, and Henri Rousseau. In 1913 five of Brancusi's sculptures were included in the Armory Show in New York. Alfred Stieglitz presented the first solo show of Brancusi's work at his gallery "291" in New York in 1914. Brancusi was never a member of any organized artistic movement, although he associated with Francis Picabia, Tristan Tzara, and many other Dadaists in the early 1920s. In 1921 he was honored with a special issue of *The Little Review*. He traveled to the United States twice in 1926 to attend his solo shows at Wildenstein and at the Brummer Gallery in New York. The following year a major trial was initiated in U.S. Customs Court to determine whether Brancusi's *Bird in Space* was liable for duty as a manufactured object or as a work of art. The court decided in 1928 that the sculpture was a work of art.

Brancusi traveled extensively in the 1930s, visiting India and Egypt as well as European countries. He was commissioned to create a war memorial for a park in Turgu Jiu, Romania, in 1935, and designed a complex that included gates, tables, stools, and an *Endless Column*. In 1937 Brancusi discussed a proposed Temple of Meditation in India with the Maharajah of Indore (who had purchased several of his sculptures), but the project was never realized. After 1939 Brancusi worked alone in Paris. His last sculpture, a plaster *Grand Coq*, was completed in 1949. In 1952 Brancusi became a French citizen. He died in Paris on March 16, 1957.

GEORGES BRAQUE

1882–1963

Georges Braque was born in Argenteuil-sur-Seine on May 13, 1882. He grew up in Le Havre and studied evenings at the Ecole des Beaux-Arts there from about 1897 to 1899. He left for Paris to study under a master-decorator to receive his craftsman certificate in 1901. From 1902 to 1904 he painted at the Académie Humbert in Paris, where he met Marie Laurencin and Francis Picabia. By 1906 Braque's work was no longer Impressionist but Fauve in style; after spending that summer in Antwerp with Othon Friesz, he showed his Fauve work the following year in the Salon des Indépendants in Paris. His first solo show was at D.-H. Kahnweiler's gallery in 1908. From 1909 Pablo Picasso and Braque worked together in developing Cubism; by 1911 their styles were extremely similar. In 1912 they started to incorporate collage elements into their paintings and to experiment with the papier collé (pasted paper) technique. Their artistic collaboration lasted until 1914. Braque was wounded during World War I; upon his recovery in 1917 he began a close friendship with Juan Gris.

After World War I his work became freer and less schematic. His fame grew in 1922 as a result of a major exhibition at the Salon d'Automne in Paris. In the mid-1920s Braque designed the decor for two Sergei Diaghilev ballets. By the end of the decade he had returned to a more realistic interpretation of nature, although certain aspects of Cubism always remained present in his work. In 1931 Braque made his first engraved plasters and began to portray mythological subjects. His first important retrospective took place in 1933 at the Kunsthalle Basel. He won First Prize at the Carnegie International in Pittsburgh in 1937.

During World War II Braque remained in Paris. His paintings at that time, primarily still lifes and interiors, became more somber. In addition to paintings, Braque also made lithographs, engravings, and sculpture. From the late 1940s Braque treated various recurring themes such as birds, ateliers, landscapes, and seascapes. In 1953 he designed stained-glass windows for the church of Varengeville. During the last few years of his life Braque's ill health prevented him from undertaking further large-scale commissions but he continued to paint and make lithographs and jewelry designs. He died in Paris on August 31, 1963.

VICTOR BRAUNER
1903–1966

Victor Brauner was born on June 15, 1903, in Piatra-Neamt, Romania. His father was involved in spiritualism and sent Brauner to evangelical school in Braïla from 1916 to 1918. In 1921 he briefly attended the School of Fine Arts in Bucharest, where he painted Cézannesque landscapes. He exhibited paintings in his subsequent expressionist style at his first solo show at the Galerie Mozart in Bucharest in 1924. Brauner helped found the Dadaist review *75 HP* in Bucharest. He went to Paris in 1925 but returned to Bucharest approximately a year later. In Bucharest in 1929 Brauner was associated with the Dadist and Surrealist review *UNU*.

Brauner settled in Paris in 1930 and became a friend of his compatriot Constantin Brancusi. Then he met Yves Tanguy, who introduced him to the Surrealists by 1933. André Breton wrote an enthusiastic introduction to the catalogue for Brauner's first Parisian solo show at the Galerie Pierre in 1934. The exhibition was not well-received, and in 1935 Brauner returned to Bucharest, where he remained until 1938. That year he moved to Paris, lived briefly with Tanguy, and painted a number of works featuring distorted human figures with mutilated eyes. Some of these paintings, dated as early as 1931, proved gruesomely prophetic when he lost his own eye in a scuffle in 1938. At the outset of World War II Brauner fled to the South of France, where he maintained contact with other Surrealists in Marseille. Later he sought refuge in Switzerland; unable to obtain suitable materials there, he improvised an encaustic from candle wax and developed a graffito technique.

Brauner returned to Paris in 1945. He was included in the *Exposition internationale du surréalisme* at the Galerie Maeght in Paris in 1947. His postwar painting incorporated forms and symbols based on Tarot cards, Egyptian hieroglyphics, and antique Mexican codices. In the fifties Brauner traveled to Normandy and Italy, and his work was shown at the Venice Biennale in 1954 and in 1966. He died in Paris on March 12, 1966.

ALEXANDER CALDER
1898–1976

Alexander Calder was born on July 22, 1898, in Lawnton, Pennsylvania, into a family of artists. In 1919 he received an engineering degree from Stevens Institute of Technology in Hoboken, New Jersey. Calder attended the Art Students League in New York from 1923 to 1926, studying briefly with Thomas Hart Benton and John Sloan, among others. As a freelance artist for the *National Police Gazette* in 1925 he spent two weeks sketching at the circus; his fascination with the subject dates from this time. He also made his first sculpture in 1925; the following year he made several constructions of animals and figures with wire and wood. Calder's first exhibition of paintings took place in 1926 at the Artist's Gallery in New York. Later that year he went to Paris and attended the Académie de la Grande Chaumière. In Paris he met Stanley William Hayter, exhibited at the 1926 Salon des Indépendants and in 1927 began giving performances of his miniature circus. The first show of his wire animals and caricature portraits was held at the Weyhe Gallery, New York, in 1928. That same year he met Joan Miró, who became his lifelong friend. Subsequently Calder divided his time between France and the United States. In 1929 the Galerie Billiet gave him his first solo show in Paris. He met Fernand Léger, Frederick Kiesler, and Theo van Doesburg and visited Mondrian's studio in 1930. Calder began to experiment with abstract sculpture at this time and in 1931 and 1932 introduced moving parts into his work. These moving sculptures were called mobiles; the stationary constructions were to be named *stabiles*. He exhibited with the Abstraction-Création group in Paris in 1933. In 1943 the Museum of Modern Art in New York gave him a major solo exhibition.

During the 1950s Calder traveled widely and executed *Towers* (wall mobiles) and *Gongs* (sound mobiles). He won First Prize for Sculpture at the 1952 Venice Biennale. Late in the decade the artist worked extensively with gouache; from this period he executed numerous major public commissions. In 1964–65 the Solomon R. Guggenheim Museum presented a major Calder retrospective. He began the *Totems* and the *Animobiles*, variations on the standing mobile, in 1966 and 1971, respectively. An important Calder exhibition was held at the Whitney Museum of American Art in New York in 1976. Calder died in New York on November 11, 1976.

MARC CHAGALL

1887–1985

Marc Chagall was born on July 7, 1887, in the Russian town of Vitebsk. From 1906 to 1909 he studied in St. Petersburg at the Imperial School for the Protection of the Arts and with Léon Bakst. In 1910 he moved to Paris, where he associated with Guillaume Apollinaire and Robert Delaunay and encountered Fauvism and Cubism. He participated in the Salon des Indépendants and the Salon d'Automne in 1912. His first solo show was held in 1914 at Der Sturm gallery in Berlin.

Chagall returned to Russia during the war, settling in Vitebsk, where he was appointed Commissar for Art. He founded the Vitebsk Popular Art School and directed it until disagreements with the Suprematists resulted in his resignation in 1920. He moved to Moscow and executed his first stage designs for the State Jewish Chamber Theater there. After a sojourn in Berlin Chagall returned to Paris in 1923 and met Ambroise Vollard. His first retrospective took place in 1924 at the Galerie Barbazanges-Hodebert, Paris. During the 1930s he traveled to Palestine, the Netherlands, Spain, Poland, and Italy. In 1933 the Kunsthalle Basel held a major retrospective of his work.

During World War II Chagall fled to the United States. The Museum of Modern Art, New York, gave him a retrospective in 1946. He settled permanently in France in 1948 and exhibited in Paris, Amsterdam, and London. During 1951 he visited Israel and executed his first sculptures. The following year the artist traveled in Greece and Italy. In 1962 he designed windows for the synagogue of the Hadassah Medical Center near Jerusalem and the cathedral at Metz. He designed a ceiling for the Opéra in Paris in 1964 and murals for the Metropolitan Opera House, New York, in 1965. An exhibition of the artist's work from 1967 to 1977 was held at the Louvre, Paris, in 1977–78. Chagall died in St. Paul de Vence, France, on March 28, 1985.

JOSEPH CORNELL

1903–1972

Joseph Cornell was born on December 24, 1903, in Nyack, New York. From 1917 to 1921 he attended Phillips Academy in Andover, Massachusetts. He was an avid collector of memorabilia and, while working as a woolen-goods salesman in New York for the next ten years, developed his interest in ballet, literature, and opera.

In the early thirties Cornell met Surrealist writers and artists at the Julien Levy Gallery in New York and saw Max Ernst's collage-novel *La Femme 100 têtes*. Cornell's early constructions of found objects were first exhibited in *Surrealism*, presented at the Wadsworth Atheneum in Hartford and subsequently at Julien Levy's gallery in 1932. From 1934 to 1940 Cornell supported himself by working at the Traphagen studio in New York. During these years he became familiar with Marcel Duchamp's readymades and Kurt Schwitters's box constructions. Cornell was included in the 1936 exhibition *Fantastic Art, Dada, Surrealism* at the Museum of Modern Art, New York. Always interested in film and cinematic techniques, he made a number of movies, including *Rose Hobart* of 1931, and wrote two film scenarios. One of these, *Monsieur Phot* of 1933, was published in 1936 in Levy's book *Surrealism*.

Cornell's first solo exhibition took place at the Julien Levy Gallery in 1939 and included an array of objects, a number of them in shadow boxes. During the forties and fifties he made *Medici* boxes, boxes devoted to stage and screen personalities, *Aviary* constructions, *Observatories*, *Night Skies*, *Winter Night Skies*, and *Hotel* boxes. In the early 1960s Cornell stopped making new boxes and began to reconstruct old ones and to work intensively in collage. Major Cornell retrospectives were held in 1967 at the Pasadena Art Museum and the Solomon R. Guggenheim Museum, New York. In 1971 the Metropolitan Museum of Art in New York mounted an exhibition of his collages. Cornell died on December 29, 1972, at his home in Flushing, New York.

SALVADOR DALÍ

1904–1989

Salvador Dalí was born Salvador Felipe Jacinto Dalí y Domenech in the Catalan town of Figueras, Spain, on May 11, 1904. In 1921 he enrolled in the Real Academia de Bellas Artes de San Fernando in Madrid, where he became a friend of Federico García Lorca and Luis Buñuel. His first solo show was held in 1925 at the Galeries Dalmau in Barcelona. In 1926 Dalí was expelled from the Academia and the following year he visited Paris and met Pablo Picasso. He collaborated with Buñuel on the film *Un Chien andalou* in 1928. At the end of the year he returned to Paris and met Tristan Tzara and Paul Eluard. About this time Dalí produced his first Surrealist publications and illustrated the works of Surrealist writers and poets. His first solo show in the United States took place at the Julien Levy Gallery in New York in 1933.

Dalí was censured by the Surrealists in 1934. Toward the end of the decade he made several trips to Italy to study the art of the sixteenth and seventeenth centuries. In 1940 Dalí fled to the United States, where he worked on theatrical productions, wrote, illustrated books, and painted. A major retrospective of his work opened in 1941 at the Museum of Modern Art in New York and traveled throughout the United States. In 1942 Dalí published his autobiography and began exhibiting at M. Knoedler and Co. in New York. He returned to Europe in 1948, settling in Port Lligat, Spain. His first paintings with religious subjects date from 1948–49. In 1954 a Dalí retrospective was held at the Palazzo Pallavicini in Rome and in 1964 an important retrospective of his work was shown in Tokyo, Nagoya, and Kyoto. He continued painting, writing, and illustrating during the 1960s. The Salvador Dalí Museum in Cleveland was inaugurated in 1971, and the Dalinian Holographic Room opened at M. Knoedler and Co., New York, in 1973. In 1980 a major Dalí retrospective was held at the Musée National d'Art Moderne, Centre Georges Pompidou, in Paris, and his work was exhibited at the Tate Gallery, London. The artist died on January 23, 1989, in Figueras.

GIORGIO DE CHIRICO

1888–1978

Giorgio de Chirico was born to Italian parents in Vólos, Greece, on July 10, 1888. In 1900 he began studies at the Athens Polytechnic Institute and attended evening classes in drawing from the nude. About 1906 he moved to Munich, where he attended the Akademie der Bildenden Künste. At this time he became interested in the art of Arnold Böcklin and Max Klinger and the writings of Friedrich Nietzsche and Arthur Schopenhauer. De Chirico moved to Milan in 1909, to Florence in 1910, and to Paris in 1911. In Paris he was included in the Salon d'Automne in 1912 and 1913 and in the Salon des Indépendants in 1913 and 1914. As a frequent visitor to Guillaume Apollinaire's weekly gatherings, he met Constantin Brancusi, André Derain, Max Jacob, and others. Because of the war, in 1915 de Chirico returned to Italy, where he met Filippo de Pisis in 1916 and Carlo Carrà in 1917; they formed the group that was later called the Scuola Metafisica.

The artist moved to Rome in 1918, and was given his first solo exhibition at the Casa d'Arte Bragaglia in that city in the winter of 1918–19. In this period he was one of the leaders of the Gruppo Valori Plastici, with whom he showed at the Nationalgalerie in Berlin. From 1920 to 1924 he divided his time between Rome and Florence. A solo exhibition of de Chirico's work was held at the Galleria Arte in Milan in 1921, and he participated in the Venice Biennale for the first time in 1924. In 1925 the artist returned to Paris, where he exhibited that year at Léonce Rosenberg's Galerie l'Effort Moderne. In Paris his work was shown at the Galerie Paul Guillaume in 1926 and 1927 and at the Galerie Jeanne Bucher in 1927. In 1928 he was given solo shows at the Arthur Tooth Gallery in London and the Valentine Gallery in New York. In 1929 de Chirico designed scenery and costumes for Sergei Diaghilev's production of the ballet *Le Bal*, and his book *Hebdomeros* was published. The artist designed for the ballet and opera in subsequent years, and continued to exhibit in Europe, the United States, Canada, and Japan. In 1945 the first part of his book *Memorie della mia vita* appeared. De Chirico died on November 20, 1978, in Rome, his residence for over thirty years.

WILLEM DE KOONING

b. 1904

Willem de Kooning was born on April 24, 1904, in Rotterdam. From 1916 to 1925 he studied at night at the Academie voor Beeldende Kunsten en Technische Wetenschappen, Rotterdam, while apprenticed to a commercial art and decorating firm and later working for an art director. In 1924 he visited museums in Belgium and studied further in Brussels and Antwerp. De Kooning came to the United States in 1926 and settled briefly in Hoboken, New Jersey. He worked as a house painter before moving to New York in 1927, where he met Stuart Davis, Arshile Gorky, and John Graham. He took various commercial art and odd jobs until 1935–36, when he was employed in the mural and easel divisions of the WPA Federal Art Project. Thereafter he painted full-time. In the late 1930s his abstract as well as figurative work was primarily influenced by the Cubism and Surrealism of Pablo Picasso and also by Gorky, with whom he shared a studio.

In 1938 de Kooning started his first series of *Women*, which would become a major recurrent theme. During the 1940s he participated in group shows with other artists who would form the New York School of Abstract Expressionism. De Kooning's first solo show, which took place at the Egan Gallery in New York in 1948, established his reputation as a major artist; it included a number of the allover black-and-white abstractions he had initiated in 1946. The *Women* of the early 1950s were followed by abstract urban landscapes, *Parkways*, rural landscapes, and, in the 1960s, a new group of *Women*.

In 1968 de Kooning visited the Netherlands for the first time since 1926 for the opening of his major retrospective at the Stedelijk Museum in Amsterdam. In Rome in 1969 he executed his first sculptures—figures modeled in clay and later cast in bronze—and in 1970–71 he began a series of life-size figures. In 1974 the Walker Art Center in Minneapolis organized a show of de Kooning's drawings and sculpture that traveled throughout the United States, and in 1978 the Solomon R. Guggenheim Museum, New York, mounted an important exhibition of his recent work. In 1979 de Kooning and Eduardo Chillida received the Andrew W. Mellon Prize, which was accompanied by an exhibition at the Museum of Art, Carnegie Institute, in Pittsburgh. De Kooning lives in the Springs, East Hampton, Long Island, where he settled in 1963.

ROBERT DELAUNAY

1885–1941

Robert-Victor-Félix Delaunay was born in Paris on April 12, 1885. In 1902, after secondary education, he apprenticed in a studio for theater sets in Belleville. In 1903 he started painting and by 1904 was exhibiting, that year and in 1906 at the Salon d'Automne and from 1904 until World War I at the Salon des Indépendants. Between 1905 and 1907 Delaunay became friendly with Henri Rousseau and Jean Metzinger and studied the color theories of M. E. Chevreul; he was then painting in a Neo-Impressionist manner. Paul Cézanne's work also influenced Delaunay around this time. From 1907–08 he served in the military in Laon and upon returning to Paris he had contact with the Cubists. The period 1909–10 saw the emergence of Delaunay's personal style: he painted his first Eiffel Tower in 1909. In 1910 Delaunay married the painter Sonia Terk, who became his collaborator on many projects.

Delaunay's participation in exhibitions in Germany and association with advanced artists working there began in 1911, the year Vasily Kandinsky invited him to participate in the first Blaue Reiter (Blue Rider) exhibition in Munich. At this time he became friendly with Guillaume Apollinaire, Albert Gleizes, and Henri Le Fauconnier. In 1912 Delaunay's first solo show took place at the Galerie Barbazanges, Paris, and he began his *Windows* pictures. Inspired by the lyricism of color of the *Windows*, Apollinaire invented the term "Orphism" or "Orphic Cubism" to describe Delaunay's work. In 1913 Delaunay painted his *Circular Form* or *Disc* pictures.

From 1914 to 1920 Delaunay lived in Spain and Portugal and became friends with Sergei Diaghilev, Leonide Massine, Diego Rivera, and Igor Stravinsky. He designed the decor for the Ballets Russes in 1918. By 1920 he had returned to Paris, where, in 1922, a major exhibition of his work was held at Galerie Paul Guillaume and he began his second *Eiffel Tower* series. In 1924 he undertook his *Runner* paintings and in 1925 executed frescoes for the Palais de l'Ambassade de France at the *Exposition internationale des arts décoratifs* in Paris. In 1937 he completed murals for the Palais des Chemins de Fer and Palais de l'Air at the Paris World's Fair. His last works were decorations for the sculpture hall of the Salon des Tuileries in 1938. In 1939 he helped organize the exhibition *Réalités nouvelles*. Delaunay died in Montpellier on October 25, 1941.

PAUL DELVAUX

b. 1897

Paul Delvaux was born on September 23, 1897, in Antheit, Belgium. At the Académie Royale des Beaux-Arts in Brussels he studied architecture from 1916 to 1917 and decorative painting from 1918 to 1919. During the early 1920s he was influenced by James Ensor and Gustave De Smet. In 1936 Delvaux shared an exhibition at the Palais des Beaux-Arts in Brussels with René Magritte, a fellow member of the Belgian group Les Compagnons de l'Art.

Delvaux was given solo exhibitions in 1938 at the Palais des Beaux-Arts, Brussels, and the London Gallery, the latter organized by E. L. T. Mesens and Roland Penrose. That same year he participated in the *Exposition internationale du surréalisme* at the Galerie des Beaux-Arts in Paris, organized by André Breton and Paul Eluard, and an exhibition of the same title at the Galerie Robert in Amsterdam. The artist visited Italy in 1938 and 1939. His first retrospective was held at the Palais des Beaux-Arts in Brussels in 1944–45. Delvaux executed stage designs for Jean Genet's *Adame Miroire* in 1947 and collaborated with Eluard on the book *Poèmes, peintures et dessins*, published in Geneva and Paris the next year. After a brief sojourn in France in 1949, the following year he was appointed professor at the Ecole Supérieure d'Art et d'Architecture in Brussels, a position he retained until 1962. From the early 1950s he executed a number of mural commissions in Belgium. About the middle of the decade Delvaux settled in Boitsfort, and in 1956 he traveled to Greece.

From 1965 to 1966 Delvaux served as president and director of the Académie Royale des Beaux-Arts of Belgium, and about this time he produced his first lithographs. Retrospectives of his work were held at the Palais des Beaux-Arts in Lille in 1965, at the Musée des Arts Décoratifs in Paris in 1969, and at the Museum Boymans-van Beuningen in Rotterdam in 1973. Also in 1973 he was awarded the Rembrandt Prize of the Johann Wolfgang Stiftung. A Delvaux retrospective was shown at the National Museum of Modern Art in Tokyo and the National Museum of Modern Art of Kyoto in 1975. In 1977 he became an associate member of the Académie des Beaux-Arts of France. Delvaux lives and works in Brussels.

JEAN DUBUFFET

1901–1985

Jean Dubuffet was born in Le Havre on July 31, 1901. He attended art classes in his youth and in 1918 moved to Paris to study at the Académie Julian, which he left after six months. During this time Dubuffet met Raoul Dufy, Max Jacob, Fernand Léger, and Suzanne Valadon and became fascinated with Hans Prinzhorn's book on psychopathic art. He traveled to Italy in 1923 and South America in 1924. Then Dubuffet gave up painting for about ten years, working as an industrial draftsman and later in the family wine business. He committed himself to becoming an artist in 1942.

Dubuffet's first solo exhibition was held at the Galerie René Drouin in Paris in 1944. During the 1940s the artist associated with André Breton, Georges Limbour, Jean Paulhan, and Charles Ratton. His style and subject matter in this period owed a debt to Paul Klee. From 1945 he collected Art Brut, spontaneous, direct works by untutored individuals, such as mental patients. The Pierre Matisse Gallery gave him his first solo show in New York in 1947.

From 1951 to 1952 Dubuffet lived in New York. He then returned to Paris, where a retrospective of his work took place at the Cercle Volney in 1954. His first museum retrospective occurred in 1957 at the Schloss Morsbroich, Leverkusen, Germany. Major Dubuffet exhibitions have since been held at the Musée des Arts Décoratifs, Paris, the Museum of Modern Art, New York, the Art Institute of Chicago, the Stedelijk Museum, Amsterdam, the Tate Gallery, London, and the Solomon R. Guggenheim Museum. His paintings of L'Hourloupe, a series begun in 1962, were exhibited at the Palazzo Grassi in Venice in 1964. A collection of Dubuffet's writings, *Prospectus et tous écrits suivants*, was published in 1967, the same year he started his architectural structures. Soon thereafter he began numerous commissions for monumental outdoor sculptures. In 1971 he produced his first theater props, the "practicables." A major Dubuffet retrospective was presented at the Akademie der Künste, Berlin, the Museum Moderner Kunst, Vienna, and the Joseph-Haubrichkunsthalle, Cologne, in 1980–81. In 1981 the Solomon R. Guggenheim Museum observed the artist's eightieth birthday with an exhibition. Dubuffet died in Paris on May 12, 1985.

MARCEL DUCHAMP

1887–1968

Henri-Robert-Marcel Duchamp was born on July 28, 1887, near Blainville, France. In 1904 he joined his artist brothers, Jacques Villon and Raymond Duchamp-Villon, in Paris, where he studied painting at the Académie Julian until 1905. Duchamp's early works were Post-Impressionist in style. He exhibited for the first time in 1909 at the Salon des Indépendants and the Salon d'Automne in Paris. His paintings of 1911 were directly related to Cubism but emphasized successive images of a single body in motion. In 1912 he painted the definitive version of *Nude Descending a Staircase*; this was shown at the Salon de la Section d'Or of that same year and subsequently created great controversy at the Armory Show in New York in 1913.

Duchamp's radical and iconoclastic ideas predated the founding of the Dada movement in Zurich in 1916. By 1913 he had abandoned traditional painting and drawing for various experimental forms including mechanical drawings, studies, and notations that would be incorporated in a major work, *The Bride Stripped Bare by Her Bachelors, Even* of 1915–23. In 1914 Duchamp introduced his readymades—common objects, sometimes altered, presented as works of art—which had a revolutionary impact upon many painters and sculptors. In 1915 Duchamp came to New York, where his circle included Katherine Dreier and Man Ray, with whom he founded the Société Anonyme, as well as Louise and Walter Arensberg, Francis Picabia, and other avant-garde figures.

After playing chess avidly for nine months in Buenos Aires, Duchamp returned to France in the summer of 1919 and associated with the Dada group in Paris. In New York in 1920 he made his first motor-driven constructions and invented Rrose Sélavy, his feminine alter ego. Duchamp moved back to Paris in 1923 and seemed to have abandoned art for chess but in fact continued his artistic experiments. From the mid-1930s he collaborated with the Surrealists and participated in their exhibitions. Duchamp settled permanently in New York in 1942 and became a United States citizen in 1955. During the 1940s he associated and exhibited with the Surrealist emigrés in New York, and in 1946 began *Etant donnés*, a major assemblage on which he worked secretly for the next twenty years. He died in the Paris suburb of Neuilly-sur-Seine on October 2, 1968.

RAYMOND DUCHAMP-VILLON

1876–1918

Raymond Duchamp-Villon was born Pierre-Maurice-Raymond Duchamp on November 5, 1876, in Damville, near Rouen. From 1894 to 1898 he studied medicine at the University of Paris. When illness forced him to abandon his studies, he decided to make a career in sculpture, until then an avocation. During the early years of the century he moved to Paris, where he exhibited for the first time at the Salon de la Société Nationale des Beaux-Arts in 1902. His second show was held at the same Salon in 1903, the year he settled in Neuilly-sur-Seine. In 1905 he had his first exhibition at the Salon d'Automne and a show at the Galerie Legrip in Rouen with his brother, the painter Jacques Villon; he moved with him to Puteaux two years later.

His participation in the jury of the sculpture section of the Salon d'Automne began in 1907 and was instrumental in promoting the Cubists in the early 1910s. Around this time he, Villon, and their other brother, Marcel Duchamp, attended weekly meetings of the Puteaux group of artists and critics. In 1911 he exhibited at the Galerie de l'Art Contemporain in Paris; the following year his work was included in a show organized by the Duchamp brothers at the Salon de la Section d'Or at the Galerie de la Boétie. Duchamp-Villon's work was exhibited at the Armory Show in New York in 1913 and the Galerie André Groult in Paris, the Galerie S. V. U. Mánes in Prague, and Der Sturm gallery in Berlin in 1914. During World War I Duchamp-Villon served in the army in a medical capacity, but was able to continue work on his major sculpture *The Horse*. He contracted typhoid fever in late 1916 while stationed at Champagne; the disease ultimately resulted in his death on October 9, 1918, in the military hospital at Cannes.

MAX ERNST

1891–1976

Max Ernst was born on April 2, 1891, in Bruhl, Germany. He enrolled in the University at Bonn in 1909 to study philosophy, but soon abandoned this pursuit to concentrate on art. At this time he was interested in psychology and the art of the mentally ill. In 1911 Ernst became a friend of August Macke and joined the Rheinische Expressionisten group in Bonn. Ernst showed for the first time in 1912 at the Galerie Feldman in Cologne. At the *Sonderbund* exhibition of that year in Cologne he saw the work of Paul Cézanne, Edvard Munch, Pablo Picasso, and Vincent van Gogh. In 1913 he met Guillaume Apollinaire and Robert Delaunay and traveled to Paris. Ernst participated that same year in the *Erste deutsche Herbstsalon*. In 1914 he met Jean Arp, who was to become a lifelong friend.

Despite military service throughout World War I, Ernst was able to continue painting and to exhibit in Berlin at Der Sturm in 1916. He returned to Cologne in 1918. The next year he produced his first collages and founded the short-lived Cologne Dada movement with Johannes Theodor Baargeld; they were joined by Arp and others. In 1921 Ernst exhibited for the first time in Paris, at the Galerie au Sans Pareil. He was involved in Surrealist activities in the early 1920s with Paul Eluard and André Breton. In 1925 Ernst executed his first frottages; a series of frottages was published in his book *Histoire naturelle* in 1926. He collaborated with Joan Miró on designs for Sergei Diaghilev that same year. The first of his collage-novels, *La Femme 100 têtes*, was published in 1929. The following year the artist collaborated with Salvador Dalí and Luis Buñuel on the film *L'Age d'or*.

His first American show was held at the Julien Levy Gallery, New York, in 1932. In 1936 Ernst was represented in *Fantastic Art, Dada, Surrealism* at the Museum of Modern Art in New York. In 1939 he was interned in France as an enemy alien. Two years later Ernst fled to the United States with Peggy Guggenheim, whom he married early in 1942. After their divorce he married Dorothea Tanning and in 1953 resettled in France. Ernst received the Grand Prize for painting at the Venice Biennale in 1954, and in 1975 the Solomon R. Guggenheim Museum gave him a major retrospective, which traveled in modified form to the Musée National d'Art Moderne, Paris, in 1975. He died on April 1, 1976, in Paris.

ALBERTO GIACOMETTI

1901–1966

Alberto Giacometti was born on October 10, 1901, in Borgonovo, Switzerland, and grew up in the nearby town of Stampa. His father Giovanni was a Post-Impressionist painter. From 1919 to 1920 he studied painting at the Ecole des Beaux-Arts and sculpture and drawing at the Ecole des Arts et Métiers in Geneva. In 1920 he traveled to Italy, where he was impressed by the works of Paul Cézanne and Alexander Archipenko at the Venice Biennale. He was also deeply affected by primitive and Egyptian art and by the masterpieces of Giotto and Tintoretto. In 1922 Giacometti settled in Paris, making frequent visits to Stampa. From time to time over the next several years he attended Antoine Bourdelle's sculpture classes at the Académie de la Grande Chaumière.

In 1927 the artist moved into a studio with his brother Diego, his lifelong companion and assistant, and exhibited his sculpture for the first time at the Salon des Tuileries, Paris. His first show in Switzerland, shared with his father, was held at the Galerie Aktuaryus in Zurich in 1927. The following year Giacometti met André Masson, and by 1930 he was a participant in the Surrealist circle. His first solo show took place in 1932 at the Galerie Pierre Colle in Paris. In 1934 his first American solo exhibition opened at the Julien Levy Gallery in New York. During the early 1940s he became friends with Simone de Beauvoir, Pablo Picasso, and Jean-Paul Sartre. From 1942 Giacometti lived in Geneva, where he associated with the publisher Albert Skira.

He returned to Paris in 1946. In 1948 he was given a solo show at the Pierre Matisse Gallery in New York. The artist's friendship with Samuel Beckett began around 1951. In 1955 he was honored with major retrospectives at the Arts Council Gallery in London and the Solomon R. Guggenheim Museum. He received the Sculpture Prize at the Carnegie International in Pittsburgh in 1961 and the First Prize for Sculpture at the Venice Biennale of 1962, where he was given his own exhibition area. In 1965 Giacometti exhibitions were organized by the Tate Gallery in London, the Museum of Modern Art in New York, the Louisiana Museum in Humlebaek, Denmark, and the Stedelijk Museum in Amsterdam. That same year he was awarded the Grand National Prize for Art by the French government. Giacometti died on January 11, 1966, in Chur, Switzerland.

ALBERT GLEIZES

1881–1953

Albert Gleizes was born in Paris on December 8, 1881. He worked in his father's fabric design studio after completing secondary school. While serving in the army from 1901 to 1905, Gleizes began to paint seriously. He exhibited for the first time at the Société Nationale des Beaux-Arts, Paris, in 1902, and participated in the Salon d'Automne in 1903 and 1904.

With several friends, including the writer René Arcos, Gleizes founded the Abbaye de Créteil outside Paris in 1906. This utopian community of artists and writers scorned bourgeois society and sought to create a nonallegorical, epic art based on modern themes. The Abbaye closed in 1908 due to financial difficulties. In 1909 and 1910 Gleizes met Robert Delaunay, Henri Le Fauconnier, Fernand Léger, and Jean Metzinger. In 1910 he exhibited at the Salon des Indépendants, Paris, and the Jack of Diamonds in Moscow. The following year he wrote the first of many articles. In collaboration with Metzinger, Gleizes wrote *Du cubisme*, published in 1912. The same year Gleizes helped found the Section d'Or.

In 1914 Gleizes again saw military service. His paintings had become abstract by 1915. Travels to New York, Barcelona, and Bermuda during the next four years influenced his stylistic evolution. His first solo show was held at the Galeries Dalmau, Barcelona, in 1916. Beginning in 1918 Gleizes became deeply involved in a search for spiritual values, as reflected in his painting and writing. In 1927 he founded Moly-Sabata, another utopian community of artists and craftsmen, in Sablons. His book, *La Forme et l'histoire*, published in 1932, examines Romanesque, Celtic, and Oriental art. In the 1930s Gleizes participated in the Abstraction-Création group. Later in his career Gleizes executed several large commissions, including the murals for the Paris World's Fair of 1937. In 1947 a major Gleizes retrospective took place in Lyons at the Chapelle du Lycée Ampère. From 1949 to 1950 Gleizes worked on illustrations for Pascal's *Pensées*. He executed a fresco, *Eucharist*, for the chapel Les Fontaines at Chantilly in 1952. Gleizes died in Avignon on June 23, 1953.

JULIO GONZÁLEZ

1876–1942

Julio González was born in Barcelona on September 21, 1876. With his older brother Joan he worked in his father's metalsmith shop; during the evenings they took classes at the Escuela de Bellas Artes. González exhibited metalwork at the *Exposición de bellas artes e industrias artísticas* in Barcelona in 1892, 1896, and 1898, and at the *World's Columbian Exposition* in Chicago in 1893. In 1897 he began to frequent Els Quatre Gats, a café in Barcelona, where he met Pablo Picasso.

In 1900 González moved to Paris; there he began to associate with Pablo Gargallo, Juan Gris, Manolo Hugué, Max Jacob, and Jaime Sabartés. His first embossed metalwork was produced in 1900. He exhibited with the Société Nationale des Beaux-Arts in 1903, 1909, and frequently during the early twenties. González participated in the Salon des Indépendants in 1907 and occasionally thereafter. He first exhibited paintings at the Salon d'Automne in 1909, and showed both sculpture and paintings there regularly during the teens and twenties. In 1918 González worked at the Renault factory at Boulogne-Billancourt, where he learned techniques of autogenous welding he used later in iron sculptures. In 1920 he became reacquainted with Picasso.

González's first solo exhibition, which included paintings, sculpture, drawings, jewelry, and objets d'art, was held in 1922 at the Galerie Povolovsky in Paris. The following year he was given a solo show of works in similarly varied media at the Galerie du Caméléon in Paris. In 1923 González participated in the first Salon du Montparnasse, Paris, with Raoul Dufy, Paco Durrio, Friesz, and others. In 1924 he was included in the exhibition *Les Amis du Montparnasse* at the Salon des Tuileries and the Salon d'Automne in Paris. He made his first iron sculptures in 1927. From 1928 to 1931 González provided technical assistance to Picasso in executing sculptures in iron. In 1930 he was given a solo sculpture exhibition at the Galerie de France in Paris, and the following year showed at the Salon des Surindépendants for the first time. In 1937 he contributed to the Spanish Pavilion of the World's Fair in Paris and *Cubism and Abstract Art* at the Museum of Modern Art in New York. That same year he moved to Arcueil, near Paris, where he died on March 27, 1942.

ARSHILE GORKY

1904–1948

Arshile Gorky was born Vosdanik Adoian in the village of Khorkom, province of Van, Armenia, on April 15, 1904. The Adoians became refugees from the Turkish invasion; Gorky himself left Van in 1915 and arrived in the United States about March 1, 1920. He stayed with relatives in Watertown, Massachusetts, and with his father, who had settled in Providence, Rhode Island. By 1922 he lived in Watertown and taught at the New School of Design in Boston. In 1925 he moved to New York and changed his name to Arshile Gorky. He entered the Grand Central School of Art in New York as a student but soon became an instructor of drawing; from 1926 to 1931 he was a member of the faculty. Throughout the 1920s Gorky's painting was influenced by Georges Braque, Paul Cézanne, and, above all, Pablo Picasso.

In 1930 Gorky's work was included in a group show at the Museum of Modern Art in New York. During the thirties he associated closely with Stuart Davis, Willem de Kooning, and John Graham; he shared a studio with de Kooning late in the decade. Gorky's first solo show took place at the Mellon Galleries in Philadelphia in 1931. From 1935 to 1937 he worked under the WPA Federal Art Project on murals for Newark Airport. His involvement with the WPA continued into 1941. Gorky's first solo show in New York was held at the Boyer Galleries in 1938. The San Francisco Museum of Art exhibited his work in 1941.

In the 1940s he was profoundly affected by the work of European Surrealists, particularly Joan Miró, André Masson, and Matta. By 1944 he met André Breton and became a friend of other Surrealist emigrés in this country. Gorky's first exhibition at the Julien Levy Gallery in New York took place in 1945. From 1942 to 1948 he worked for part of each year in the countryside of Connecticut or Virginia. A succession of personal tragedies, including a fire in his studio that destroyed much of his work, a serious operation, and an automobile accident, preceded Gorky's death by suicide on July 21, 1948, in Sherman, Connecticut.

JUAN GRIS

1887–1927

Juan Gris was born José Victoriano Carmelo Carlos González-Pérez in Madrid on March 23, 1887. He studied mechanical drawing at the Escuela de Artes y Manufacturas in Madrid from 1902 to 1904, during which time he contributed drawings to local periodicals. From 1904 to 1905 he studied painting with the academic artist José Maria Carbonero. In 1906 he moved to Paris, where he lived for most of the remainder of his life. His friends in Paris included Georges Braque, Fernand Léger, and Pablo Picasso and the writers Guillaume Apollinaire, Max Jacob, and Maurice Raynal. Although he continued to submit humorous illustrations to journals such as *L'Assiette au beurre*, *Le Charivari*, and *Le Cri de Paris*, Gris began to paint seriously in 1910. By 1912 he had developed a personal Cubist style.

He exhibited for the first time in 1912: at the Salon des Indépendants in Paris, Galeries Dalmau in Barcelona, Der Sturm gallery in Berlin, the Salon de la Société Normande de Peinture Moderne in Rouen, and the Salon de la Section d'Or in Paris. That same year D.-H. Kahnweiler signed Gris to a contract that gave Kahnweiler exclusive rights to the artist's work. Gris became a good friend of Henri Matisse in 1914 and over the next several years formed close relationships with Jacques Lipchitz and Jean Metzinger. After Kahnweiler fled Paris at the outbreak of World War I, Gris signed a contract with Léonce Rosenberg in 1916. His first major solo show was held at Rosenberg's Galerie l'Effort Moderne in Paris in 1919. The following year Kahnweiler returned and once again became Gris's dealer.

In 1922 the painter first designed ballet sets and costumes for Sergei Diaghilev. Gris articulated most of his aesthetic theories during 1924 and 1925. He delivered his definitive lecture, "Des possibilités de la peinture," at the Sorbonne in 1924. Major Gris exhibitions took place at the Galerie Simon in Paris and the Galerie Flechtheim in Berlin in 1923 and at the Galerie Flechtheim in Düsseldorf in 1925. As his health declined, Gris made frequent visits to the south of France. Gris died in Boulogne-sur-Seine on May 11, 1927.

JEAN HÉLION

b. 1904

Jean Hélion was born on April 21, 1904, in Couterne, France. He entered the Institut Industriel du Nord in Lille to study chemistry in 1920 but left the following year to become an architectural apprentice in Paris. He painted while working as an architectural draftsman in the early 1920s. Hélion attracted the attention of the collector Georges Bine in 1925 and was soon able to devote himself entirely to painting. In 1927 he met Joaquín Torres-García, who collaborated on *L'Acte*, a short-lived magazine founded by Hélion and others.

Hélion first exhibited at the Salon des Indépendants in 1928. Shortly thereafter he became acquainted with Jean Arp, Piet Mondrian, and Antoine Pevsner. By 1929 his work was nonfigurative. With Theo van Doesburg and others in 1930 he formed the artists' association Art Concret and the periodical of the same name. This group was succeeded by Abstraction-Création the next year. In 1931, after traveling through Europe and the Soviet Union, Hélion returned to Paris, where he met Marcel Duchamp, Max Ernst, and Tristan Tzara. His first solo show was held at the Galerie Pierre in Paris in 1932. That same year Hélion made his first visit to New York, where he was given a solo exhibition at the John Becker Gallery at the end of 1933. After returning to Europe from a second trip to the United States in 1934, he met Jacques Lipchitz, Joan Miró, and Ben Nicholson. In 1936 he settled in the United States, dividing his time between Virginia and New York. That year solo shows of his work took place at the Galerie Cahiers d'Art in Paris and the Valentine Gallery in New York. The artist traveled to Paris in 1938 on the occasion of his solo exhibition at the Galerie Pierre, and he became a friend of Paul Eluard, Matta, and Yves Tanguy.

Shortly after joining the French army in 1940 he was taken prisoner and sent to a camp in Pomerania and then Stettin. Hélion escaped in 1942 and that same year made his way to France and then the United States. In 1943 he began to paint in a figurative style again. His book *They Shall Not Have Me* was published in 1943, a year in which he was given solo shows at the Arts Club of Chicago and Peggy Guggenheim's Art of This Century, New York. Hélion returned to Paris in 1946. Throughout the 1950s and 1960s his work was shown in Europe and New York. During the 1970s he exhibited primarily in France. Hélion now lives in Paris.

ASGER JORN

1914–1973

Asger Jorn was born Asger Oluf Jørgensen in Vejrum, Jutland, Denmark, on March 3, 1914. He visited Paris in the fall of 1936, where he studied at Fernand Léger's Académie Contemporaine. During the war Jorn remained in Denmark, painting canvases that reflect the influence of James Ensor, Vasily Kandinsky, Paul Klee, and Joan Miró and contributing to the magazine *Helhesten*.

Jorn traveled to Swedish Lapland in the summer of 1946, met George Constant in Paris that fall, and spent six months in Djerba, Tunisia, in 1947–48. His first solo exhibition in Paris took place in 1948 at the Galerie Breteau. At about the same time the COBRA (an acronym for Copenhagen, Brussels, Amsterdam) movement was founded by Karel Appel, Constant, Corneille, Christian Dotremont, Jorn, and Joseph Noiret. The group's unifying doctrine was the complete freedom of expression with an emphasis on color and brushwork. Jorn edited monographs of the Bibliothèque Cobra before disassociating himself from the movement.

In 1951 Jorn returned, poor and ill, to Silkeborg, his hometown in Denmark. He began his intensive work in ceramics in 1953. The following year he settled in Albisola, Italy, and participated in a continuation of COBRA called Mouvement International pour un Bauhaus Imaginiste. Jorn's activities included painting, collage, book illustration, prints, drawings, ceramics, tapestries, commissions for murals, and, in his last years, sculpture. He participated in the Situationist International movement from 1957 to 1961 and worked on a study of early Scandinavian art between 1961 and 1965. After the mid-1950s Jorn divided his time between Paris and Albisola. His first solo show in New York took place in 1962 at the Lefebre Gallery. From 1966 Jorn concentrated on oil painting and traveled frequently, visiting Cuba, England and Scotland, the United States, and the Orient. Jorn died on May 1, 1973, in Aarhus, Denmark.

VASILY KANDINSKY

1866–1944

Vasily Kandinsky was born on December 4, 1866, in Moscow. In 1886–92 he studied law and economics at the University of Moscow, where he lectured after graduation. In 1896 he declined a teaching position in order to study art in Munich with Anton Ažbe from 1897 to 1899 and at the Akademie with Franz von Stuck in 1900. Kandinsky taught in 1901–03 at the art school of the Phalanx, a group he had cofounded in Munich. One of his students, Gabriele Münter, would be his companion until 1914. In 1902 Kandinsky exhibited for the first time with the Berlin Secession and produced his first woodcuts. In 1903 and 1904 he began his travels in Italy, the Netherlands, and North Africa and his visits to Russia. He showed at the Salon d'Automne in Paris from 1904.

In 1909 Kandinsky was elected president of the newly founded Neue Künstlervereinigung München (NKVM). The group's first show took place at the Moderne Galerie Thannhauser in Munich in 1909. In 1911 Kandinsky and Franz Marc began to make plans for the Blaue Reiter (Blue Rider) almanac. Kandinsky's *Über das Geistige in der Kunst* (*On the Spiritual in Art*) was published in December 1911. He and Marc withdrew from the NKVM in that month, and shortly thereafter the Blaue Reiter's first exhibition was held at the Moderne Galerie. In 1912 the second Blaue Reiter show was held at the Galerie Hans Goltz, Munich, and the *Almanach der Blaue Reiter* appeared. Kandinsky's first solo show was held at Der Sturm gallery in Berlin in 1912. In 1913 one of his works was included in the Armory Show in New York and the *Erste deutsche Herbstsalon* in Berlin. Kandinsky lived in Russia from 1914 to 1921, principally in Moscow, where he held a position at the People's Commissariat of Education.

Kandinsky began teaching at the Bauhaus in Weimar in 1922. In 1923 he was given his first solo show in New York by Société Anonyme, of which he became vice-president. Lyonel Feininger, Alexej Jawlensky, Kandinsky, and Paul Klee made up the Blaue Vier (Blue Four) group, formed in 1924. He moved with the Bauhaus to Dessau in 1925 and became a German citizen in 1928. The Nazi government closed the Bauhaus in 1933 and later that year Kandinsky settled in Neuilly-sur-Seine near Paris; he acquired French citizenship in 1939. Fifty-seven of his works were confiscated by the Nazis in the 1937 purge of "degenerate art." Kandinsky died on December 13, 1944, in Neuilly.

PAUL KLEE

1879–1940

Paul Klee was born on December 18, 1879, in Munchenbuchsee, Switzerland, into a family of musicians. His childhood love of music was always to remain profoundly important in his life and work. From 1898 to 1901 Klee studied in Munich, first with Heinrich Knirr, then at the Akademie under Franz von Stuck. Upon completing his schooling, he traveled to Italy: this was the first in a series of trips abroad that nourished his visual sensibilities. He settled in Bern in 1902. A series of his satirical etchings was exhibited at the Munich *Secession* in 1906. That same year Klee married and moved to Munich. Here he gained exposure to Modern art. Klee's work was shown at the Kunstmuseum Bern in 1910 and at Heinrich Thannhauser's Moderne Galerie in Munich in 1911.

Klee met Alexej Jawlensky, Vasily Kandinsky, August Macke, Franz Marc, and other avant-garde figures in 1911; he participated in important shows of advanced art, including the second Blaue Reiter (Blue Rider) exhibition, 1912, and the *Erste deutsche Herbstsalon*, 1913. In 1912 he visited Paris for the second time, where he saw the work of Pablo Picasso and Georges Braque and met Robert Delaunay. Klee helped found the Neue Münchner Secession in 1914. Color became central to his art only after a revelatory trip to North Africa in 1914.

In 1920 a major Klee retrospective was held at the Galerie Hans Goltz, Munich; his *Schöpferische Konfession* (*Creative Credo*) was published; he was also appointed to the faculty of the Bauhaus. Klee taught at the Bauhaus in Weimar from 1921 to 1926 and in Dessau from 1926 to 1931. During his tenure he was in close contact with other Bauhaus masters such as Kandinsky and Lyonel Feininger. In 1924 the Blaue Vier (Blue Four), consisting of Feininger, Jawlensky, Kandinsky, and Klee, was founded. Among his notable exhibitions of this period were his first in the United States at the Société Anonyme, New York, 1924; his first major show in Paris the following year at the Galerie Vavin-Raspail; and an exhibition at the Museum of Modern Art, New York, 1930. Klee went to Düsseldorf to teach at the Akademie in 1931, shortly before the Nazis closed the Bauhaus. Forced by the Nazis to leave his position in Düsseldorf in 1933, Klee settled in Bern. Major Klee exhibitions took place in Bern and Basel in 1935 and in Zurich in 1940. Klee died on June 29, 1940, in Muralto-Locarno, Switzerland.

FRANTIŠEK KUPKA

1871–1957

František Kupka was born on September 22, 1871, in Opocno in eastern Bohemia. From 1889 to 1892 he studied at the Prague Academy. At this time he painted historical and patriotic themes. In 1892 Kupka enrolled at the Akademie der Bildenden Künste in Vienna where he concentrated on symbolic and allegorical subjects. He exhibited at the Kunstverein, Vienna, in 1894. His involvement with theosophy and Eastern philosophy dates from this period. By spring 1896 Kupka had settled in Paris; there he attended the Académie Julian briefly and then studied with J. P. Laurens at the Ecole des Beaux-Arts.

Kupka worked as an illustrator of books and posters and, during his early years in Paris, became known for his satirical drawings for newspapers and magazines. In 1906 he settled in Puteaux, a suburb of Paris, and that same year exhibited for the first time at the Salon d'Automne. Kupka was deeply impressed by the first Futurist Manifesto, published in 1909 in *Le Figaro*. Kupka's work became increasingly abstract around 1910–11, reflecting his theories of motion, color, and the relationship between music and painting. In 1911 he attended meetings of the Puteaux group. In 1912 he exhibited at the Salon des Indépendants in the Cubist room, although he did not wish to be identified with any movement.

La Création dans les arts plastiques (*Creation in the Visual Arts*), a book Kupka completed in 1913, was published in Prague in 1923. In 1921 his first solo show in Paris was held at Galerie Povolozky. In 1931 he was a founding member of Abstraction-Création together with Jean Arp, Albert Gleizes, Jean Hélion, Auguste Herbin, Theo van Doesburg, and Georges Vantongerloo; in 1936 his work was included in the exhibition *Cubism and Abstract Art* at the Museum of Modern Art, New York, and in an important show with Alphonse Mucha at the Jeu de Paume, Paris. A major retrospective of his work took place at the Galerie S. V. U. Mánes in Prague in 1946. The same year Kupka participated in the Salon des Réalités Nouvelles, Paris, where he continued to exhibit regularly until his death. During the early 1950s he gained general recognition and had several solo shows in New York. Kupka died in Puteaux on June 24, 1957. Important Kupka retrospectives were held at the Musée National d'Art Moderne, Paris, in 1958 and the Solomon R. Guggenheim Museum, New York, in 1975.

HENRI LAURENS

1885–1954

Henri Laurens was born on February 18, 1885, in Paris, where he attended drawing classes in 1899. The sculpture he produced during the early years of the twentieth century reflects the influence of Auguste Rodin. In 1911 the sculptor entered into a lifelong friendship with Georges Braque, who introduced him to Cubism. Laurens participated for the first time in the Salon des Indépendants in Paris in 1913, and two years later met Juan Gris, Amedeo Modigliani, and Pablo Picasso. From 1916 Laurens executed Cubist collages and constructions. He became a friend of Pierre Reverdy in 1915 and illustrated the writer's *Poèmes en prose* that same year.

The artist was given a solo show at Léonce Rosenberg's Galerie l'Effort Moderne in Paris in 1917, and signed a contract there the following year. During the 1920s he executed designs for various architectural projects and stage decors. From 1932 to 1933 he divided his time between Paris and nearby Etang-la-Ville, where his neighbors were Aristide Maillol and Ker-Xavier Roussel. Laurens contributed substantially to the World's Fair in Paris in 1937. In 1938 he shared an exhibition with Braque and Picasso that traveled from Oslo to Stockholm and Copenhagen. His work was shown in 1945 at the Galerie Louis Carré in Paris and in 1947 at the Buchholz Gallery in New York. About this time Laurens made prints for book illustrations. He was represented at the Venice Biennale in 1948 and 1950. An important exhibition of his work was organized by the Palais des Beaux-Arts in Brussels in 1949, and a major Laurens retrospective took place at the Musée National d'Art Moderne in Paris in 1951. The following year he received a commission for a monumental sculpture for the University of Caracas. He exhibited extensively in Europe and the United States during the early 1950s, and received the Prize of the IV Centenary of São Paulo at the São Paulo Bienal in 1953. Laurens died in Paris on May 5, 1954.

FERNAND LÉGER

1881–1955

Jules Fernand Henri Léger was born on February 4, 1881, in Argentan, Normandy. After apprenticing with an architect in Caen from 1897 to 1899, Léger settled in Paris in 1900 and supported himself as an architectural draftsman. He was refused entrance to the Ecole des Beaux-Arts, but nevertheless attended classes there; he also studied at the Académie Julian. Léger's earliest known works, which date from 1905, were primarily influenced by Impressionism. The experience of seeing the Paul Cézanne retrospective at the Salon d'Automne in 1907 and his contact with the early Cubism of Pablo Picasso and Georges Braque had an extremely significant impact on the development of his personal style. In 1910 he exhibited with Braque and Picasso at D.-H. Kahnweiler's gallery, where he was given a solo show in 1912. From 1911 to 1914 Léger's work became increasingly abstract, and he started to limit his color to the primaries and black and white.

Léger served in the military from 1914 to 1917. His "mechanical" period, in which figures and objects are characterized by tubular, machine-like forms, began in 1917. During the early 1920s he collaborated with the writer Blaise Cendrars on films and designed sets and costumes for Rolf de Maré's *Ballet suédois*; in 1923–24 he made his first film without a plot, *Ballet mécanique*. Léger opened an atelier with Amédée Ozenfant in 1924 and in 1925 presented his first murals at Le Corbusier's Pavillon de l'Esprit Nouveau at the *Exposition internationale des arts décoratifs*. In 1931 he visited the United States for the first time. In 1935 the Museum of Modern Art, New York, and the Art Institute of Chicago presented exhibitions of his work. Léger lived in the United States from 1940 to 1945 but returned to France after the war. In the decade before his death Léger's wide-ranging projects included book illustrations, monumental figure paintings and murals, stained-glass windows, mosaics, polychrome ceramic sculptures, and set and costume designs. In 1955 he won the Grand Prize at the São Paulo Bienal. Léger died on August 17, 1955, at his home in Gif-sur-Yvette, France. The Musée National Fernand Léger was founded in 1957 in Biot.

JACQUES LIPCHITZ

1891–1973

Chaim Jacob Lipschitz was born on August 22, 1891, in Druskieniki, Lithuania. At age eighteen he moved to Paris, where he attended the Ecole des Beaux-Arts and the Académie Julian and soon met Georges Braque, Juan Gris, and Pablo Picasso. In 1912 he began exhibiting at the Salon National des Beaux-Arts and the Salon d'Automne. Lipchitz's first solo show was held at Léonce Rosenberg's Galerie l'Effort Moderne in Paris in 1920. Two years later he executed five bas-reliefs for the Barnes Foundation in Merion, Pennsylvania. In 1924 the artist became a French citizen and the following year moved to Boulogne-sur-Seine. He received a commission from the Vicomte Charles de Noailles in 1927 for the sculpture *Joy of Life*.

Lipchitz's first important retrospective took place at Jeanne Bucher's Galerie de la Renaissance in Paris in 1930. The Brummer Gallery in New York hosted his first large show in the United States in 1935. In 1941 Lipchitz fled Paris for New York, where he began exhibiting regularly at the Buchholz Gallery (later the Curt Valentin Gallery). He settled in Hastings-on-Hudson, New York, in 1947. In 1954 a Lipchitz retrospective traveled from the Museum of Modern Art in New York to the Walker Art Center in Minneapolis and the Cleveland Museum of Art. In 1958 Lipchitz collaborated with the architect Philip Johnson on the Roofless Church in New Harmony, Indiana. This same year he became a United States citizen. His series of small bronzes *To the Limit of the Possible* was shown at Fine Arts Associates in New York in 1959. He visited Israel for the first time in 1963. From 1964 to 1966 Lipchitz showed annually at the Marlborough-Gerson Gallery in New York. Beginning in 1963 he spent several months of each year casting in Pietrasanta, Italy.

From 1970 until 1973 he worked on large-scale commissions for the Municipal Plaza in Philadelphia, Columbia University in New York, and the Hadassah Medical Center near Jerusalem. These projects were completed by Lipchitz's wife, Yulla, after his death. In 1972 the artist's autobiography was published on the occasion of an exhibition of his sculpture at the Metropolitan Museum of Art in New York. Lipchitz died on May 26, 1973, on Capri, and was buried in Jerusalem.

EL LISSITZKY

1890–1941

El Lissitzky was born Lazar Markovich Lisitskii on November 23, 1890, in Pochinok, in the Russian province of Smolensk, and grew up in Vitebsk. He pursued architectural studies at the Technische Hochschule in Darmstadt from 1909 to 1914, when the outbreak of World War I precipitated his return to Russia. In 1916 he received a diploma in engineering and architecture from the Riga Technological University.

Lissitzky and Kazimir Malevich were invited by Marc Chagall to join the faculty of the Vitebsk Popular Art School in 1919; there Lissitzky taught architecture and graphics. That same year he executed his first Proun (acronym in Russian for "project for the affirmation of the new") and formed part of the Unovis group. In 1920 he became a member of Inkhuk (Institute for Artistic Culture) in Moscow and designed his book *Pro dva kvadrata* (*About Two Squares*). The following year he taught at Vkhutemas (Higher State Art-Technical Studios) with Vladimir Tatlin and joined the Constructivist group. The Constructivists exhibited at the *Erste russische Kunstausstellung* designed by Lissitzky at the Galerie van Diemen in Berlin in 1922. During this period he collaborated with Ilya Ehrenburg on the journal *Veshch/Gegenstand/Objet*.

In 1923 the artist experimented with new typographic design for a book by Vladimir Mayakovski, *Dlya golosa* (*For the Voice*), and visited Hannover where his work was shown under the auspices of the Kestner-Gesellschaft. Also in 1923 Lissitzky created his Proun environment for the *Grosse Berliner Kunstausstellung* and executed his lithographic suites *Proun* and *Victory over the Sun* (illustrating the opera by Alexei Kruchenykh and Mikhail Matiushin), before traveling to Switzerland for medical treatment. In 1924 he worked with Kurt Schwitters on the issue of the periodical *Merz* called "Nasci," and with Arp on the book *Die Kunstismen* (*The Isms of Art*). The next year he returned to Moscow to teach at Vkhutemas-Vkhutein (Higher State Art-Technical Studios-Higher State Art-Technical Institute), which he continued to do until 1930. During the mid-1920s Lissitzky stopped painting in order to concentrate on the design of typography and exhibitions. He created a room for the *Internationale Kunstausstellung* in Dresden in 1926 and another at the Niedersächsisches Landesmuseum in Hannover in 1927. He died on December 30, 1941, in Moscow.

RENÉ MAGRITTE

1898–1967

René François Ghislain Magritte was born on November 21, 1898, in Lessines, Belgium. He studied intermittently between 1916 and 1918 at the Académie Royale des Beaux-Arts in Brussels. Magritte first exhibited at the Centre d'Art in Brussels in 1920. After completing military service in 1921, he worked briefly as a designer in a wallpaper factory. In 1923 he participated with Lyonel Feininger, El Lissitzky, László Moholy-Nagy, and the Belgian Paul Joostens in an exhibition at the Cercle Royal Artistique in Antwerp. In 1924 he collaborated with E. L. T. Mesens on the review *Oesophage*.

In 1927 Magritte was given his first solo exhibition at the Galerie le Centaure in Brussels. Later that year the artist left Brussels to establish himself in Le Perreux-sur-Marne, near Paris, where he frequented the Surrealist circle, which included Jean Arp, André Breton, Salvador Dalí, Paul Eluard, and Joan Miró. In 1928 Magritte took part in the *Exposition surréaliste* at the Galerie Goemans in Paris. He returned to Belgium in 1930, and three years later was given a solo show at the Palais des Beaux-Arts in Brussels. Magritte's first solo exhibition in the United States took place at the Julien Levy Gallery in New York in 1936 and the first in England at the London Gallery in 1938. He was represented as well in the 1936 *Fantastic Art, Dada, Surrealism* exhibition at the Museum of Modern Art in New York.

Throughout the 1940s Magritte showed frequently at the Galerie Dietrich in Brussels. During the following two decades he executed various mural commissions in Belgium. From 1953 he exhibited frequently at the galleries of Alexander Iolas in New York, Paris, and Geneva. Magritte retrospectives were held in 1954 at the Palais des Beaux-Arts in Brussels and in 1960 at the Museum for Contemporary Arts, Dallas, and the Museum of Fine Arts in Houston. On the occasion of his retrospective at the Museum of Modern Art in New York in 1965, Magritte traveled to the United States for the first time, and the following year he visited Israel. Magritte died on August 15, 1967, in Brussels, shortly after the opening of a major exhibition of his work at the Museum Boymans-van Beuningen in Rotterdam.

KAZIMIR MALEVICH

1878–1935

Kazimir Severinovich Malevich was born on February 26, 1878, near Kiev, Russia. He studied at the Moscow Institute of Painting, Sculpture, and Architecture in 1903. During the early years of his career he experimented with various Modernist styles and participated in avant-garde exhibitions, such as those of the Moscow Artists' Association, which included Vasily Kandinsky and Mikhail Larionov, and the *Jack of Diamonds* of 1910 in Moscow. Malevich showed his neo-primitivist paintings of peasants at the exhibition *Donkey's Tail* in 1912. After this exhibition he broke with Larionov's group. In 1913, with composer Mikhail Matiushin and writer Alexei Kruchenykh, Malevich drafted a manifesto for the First Futurist Congress. That same year he designed the sets and costumes for the opera *Victory over the Sun* by Matiushin and Kruchenykh. Malevich showed at the Salon des Indépendants in Paris in 1914.

At the *o.10 Last Futurist Exhibition* in Petrograd in 1915, Malevich introduced his non-objective, geometric Suprematist paintings. In 1919 he began to explore the three-dimensional applications of Suprematism in architectural models. Following the Bolshevik Revolution in 1917, Malevich and other advanced artists were encouraged by the Soviet government and attained prominent administrative and teaching positions. Malevich began teaching at the Vitebsk Popular Art School in 1919; he soon became its director. In 1919–20 he was given a solo show at the *Sixteenth State Exhibition* in Moscow, which focused on Suprematism and other non-objective styles. Malevich and his students at Vitebsk formed the Suprematist group Unovis. From 1922 to 1927 he taught at the Institute of Artistic Culture in Petrograd and between 1924 and 1926 he worked primarily on architectural models with his students.

In 1927 Malevich traveled with an exhibition of his paintings to Warsaw and also went to Berlin, where his work was shown at the *Grosse Berliner Kunstausstellung*. In Germany he met Jean Arp, Naum Gabo, Le Corbusier, and Kurt Schwitters and visited the Bauhaus where he met Walter Gropius. The Tretiakov Gallery in Moscow gave Malevich a solo exhibition in 1929. Because of his connections with German artists he was arrested in 1930, and many of his manuscripts were destroyed. In his final period he painted in a representational style. Malevich died in Leningrad on May 15, 1935.

MAN RAY

1890–1976

Man Ray (a pseudonym adopted by the artist) was born on August 27, 1890, in Philadelphia, and moved to New York with his family seven years later. In New York he frequented Alfred Stieglitz's gallery "291" in 1911 and attended classes at the Ferrer Center in 1912. In 1915 his first solo show was held at the Daniel Gallery, New York. About this time he took up photography, the medium for which he was to become best known. He entered into a lifelong friendship with Marcel Duchamp, with whom he and Walter Arensberg founded the Society of Independent Artists in 1916. With Duchamp, Katherine Dreier, Henry Hudson, and Andrew McLaren, Man Ray established the Société Anonyme, which he named, in 1920. Before the artist moved from New York to Paris in 1921, Man Ray and Duchamp published the single issue of *New York Dada*.

In Paris Man Ray was given a solo exhibition at the Librairie Six in 1921. His first Rayographs (photographic images produced without a camera) were published in *Les Champs délicieux, rayographies* in 1922, the year the artist participated in the *Salon Dada* at the Galerie Montaigne in Paris. With Jean Arp, Giorgio de Chirico, Max Ernst, André Masson, Joan Miró, and Pablo Picasso, he was represented in the first Surrealist exhibition at the Galerie Pierre in Paris in 1925. From 1923 to 1929 he made the films *Le Retour à la raison*, *Emak Bakia*, *L'Etoile de mer*, and *Les Mystères du château de dé*. In 1932 Man Ray's work was included in *Dada, 1916–1932* at the Galerie de l'Institut in Paris and in a Surrealist show at the Julien Levy Gallery in New York. He collaborated with Paul Eluard on the books *Facile* in 1935 and *Les Mains libres* in 1937. In 1936 he went to New York on the occasion of the *Fantastic Art, Dada, Surrealism* exhibition at the Museum of Modern Art, in which his work appeared.

The artist left France in 1940, shortly before the German occupation, making his way to Hollywood and then to New York. In 1951 he returned to Paris, where he was given a solo show at the Galerie Berggruen. In 1959 a solo exhibition of Man Ray's work was held at the Institute of Contemporary Art in London. His autobiography *Self Portrait* was published in 1963. Ten years later the Metropolitan Museum of Art in New York presented 125 of his photographic works. Man Ray died on November 18, 1976, in Paris.

LOUIS MARCOUSSIS
1878–1941

Louis Marcoussis was born Ludwig Casimir Ladislas Markus in Warsaw on November 14, 1878. In 1901 he entered the Academy of Fine Arts of Cracow to study painting with Jan Grzegorz Stanislawski. In 1903 Markus moved to Paris, where he worked briefly under Jules Lefebvre at the Académie Julian and became a friend of Roger de La Fresnaye and Robert Lotiron. He exhibited for the first time at the Salon d'Automne in 1905 and at the Salon des Indépendants in 1906, and was often represented in both salons in subsequent years.

In Paris he made his living by selling caricatures to satirical periodicals, including *La Vie parisienne* and *Le Journal*. He frequented the cafés, such as the Rotonde, Cirque Médrano, and the Ermitage, where he met Edgar Degas about 1906 and Guillaume Apollinaire, Georges Braque, and Pablo Picasso in 1910. In 1907 Markus abandoned painting; when he began to paint again in 1910, he discarded his earlier Impressionist style to adopt the new Cubist idiom. About 1911, at the suggestion of Apollinaire, he began calling himself Marcoussis, the name of a village near Monthéry. In 1912 the artist participated in the Salon de la Section d'Or at the Galerie de la Boétie in Paris. By this time his circle included Juan Gris, Max Jacob, Fernand Léger, Jean Metzinger, and Francis Picabia. He served in the army from 1914 to 1919, returning to Poland for a visit after his demobilization.

Marcoussis exhibited in 1921 at Der Sturm gallery in Berlin with Albert Gleizes, Jacques Villon, and others. He had his first solo show at Galerie Pierre, Paris, in 1925. This was followed by solo exhibitions in 1928 at the Galerie le Centaure in Brussels, a city he visited on that occasion, and at the Galerie Georges Bernheim in Paris in 1929. In 1930 the artist made the first of many trips to England and met Helena Rubinstein, who became his supporter. In 1934–35 he stayed for several months in the United States, where solo shows of his prints opened at the Arts Club of Chicago in 1934 and M. Knoedler and Co. in New York in 1935. Marcoussis worked almost exclusively in graphics from 1930 to 1937; a retrospective of his prints took place at the Palais des Beaux-Arts in Brussels in 1936. The artist traveled to England and Italy in 1938, and during the following year was given a solo exhibition at the London Gallery in London. In 1940, as the German army advanced, Marcoussis left Paris for Cusset, near Vichy, where he died on October 22, 1941.

MARINO MARINI
1901–1980

Marino Marini was born in the Tuscan town of Pistoia on February 27, 1901. He attended the Accademia di Belle Arti in Florence in 1917. Although he never abandoned painting, Marini devoted himself primarily to sculpture from about 1922. From this time his work was influenced by Etruscan art and the sculpture of Arturo Martini. Marini succeeded Martini as professor at the Scuola d'Arte de Villa Reale in Monza, near Milan, in 1929, a position he retained until 1940. During this period Marini traveled frequently to Paris, where he associated with Massimo Campigli, Giorgio de Chirico, Alberto Magnelli, and Filippo Tibertelli de Pisis. In 1936 he moved to Tenero-Locarno, in the Ticino canton, Switzerland; during the following few years the artist often visited Zurich and Basel, where he became a friend of Alberto Giacometti, Germaine Richier, and Fritz Wotruba. In 1936 he received the Prize of the Quadriennale of Rome. He accepted a professorship in sculpture at the Accademia di Belle Arti di Brera, Milan, in 1940.

In 1946 the artist settled permanently in Milan. He participated in *Twentieth-Century Italian Art* at the Museum of Modern Art in New York in 1944. Curt Valentin began exhibiting Marini's work at his Buchholz Gallery in New York in 1950, on which occasion the sculptor visited the city and met Jean Arp, Max Beckmann, Alexander Calder, Lyonel Feininger, and Jacques Lipchitz. On his return to Europe, he stopped in London, where the Hanover Gallery had organized a solo show of his work, and there met Henry Moore. In 1951 a Marini exhibition traveled from the Kestner-Gesellschaft Hannover to the Kunstverein in Hamburg and the Haus der Kunst of Munich. He was awarded the Grand Prize for Sculpture at the Venice Biennale in 1952 and the Feltrinelli Prize at the Accademia dei Lincei in Rome in 1954. One of his monumental sculptures was installed in the Hague in 1959.

Retrospectives of Marini's work took place at the Kunsthaus Zürich in 1962 and at the Palazzo Venezia in Rome in 1966. His paintings were exhibited for the first time at Toninelli Arte Moderna in Milan in 1963–64. In 1973 a permanent installation of his work opened at the Galleria d'Arte Moderna in Milan, and in 1978 a Marini show was presented at the National Museum of Modern Art in Tokyo. Marini died on August 6, 1980, in Viareggio.

JEAN METZINGER

1883–1956

Jean Metzinger was born in Nantes, France, on June 24, 1883. At the age of twenty he moved to Paris to pursue a career as a painter. One of his early friends in Paris was Robert Delaunay. About 1908 he met the writer Max Jacob, who introduced him to Guillaume Apollinaire and his circle, which included Georges Braque and Pablo Picasso. Picasso was to have a significant influence on Metzinger from this time to about 1923. In 1910 Metzinger exhibited for the first time at the Salon des Indépendants. In 1910 and 1911 he published several articles on contemporary painting and afterwards periodically contributed to the literature on Modern art. Metzinger was the first to note in print that Picasso and Braque had dismissed traditional perspective and merged multiple views of an object in a single image; his article on this subject appeared in *Pan* in 1910.

In 1911, with Robert Delaunay, Albert Gleizes, and Fernand Léger, Metzinger participated in the controversial Salle 41 at the Salon des Indépendants, the first formal group exhibition of Cubist painters. His work was represented at the Salon d'Automne in Paris that same year. Metzinger collaborated with Gleizes in 1912 on *Du cubisme*, in which a theoretical foundation for Cubism was proposed. During that year he was a founder of the Section d'Or and exhibited at the Galerie de la Boétie in Paris with other members of the group, including Alexander Archipenko, Roger de La Fresnaye, Gleizes, Juan Gris, Léger, and Louis Marcoussis. In 1913 Metzinger's work was again shown at the Salon d'Automne, and he continued to exhibit in the principal salons of Paris thereafter. This same year he took part in an exhibition at Der Sturm gallery in Berlin and shared a show at the Galerie Berthe Weill in Paris with Gleizes and Léger. In 1916 Metzinger showed with Jean Crotti, Marcel Duchamp, and Gleizes at the Montross Gallery in New York. After army service during World War I Metzinger returned in 1919 to Paris, where he lived for the remainder of his life. Among his solo exhibitions were those at the Leicester Galleries in London in 1930, the Hanover Gallery in London in 1932, and the Arts Club of Chicago in 1953. The artist died in Paris on November 3, 1956.

JOAN MIRÓ

1893–1983

Joan Miró Ferra was born in Barcelona on April 20, 1893. At the age of fourteen he went to business school in Barcelona and also attended La Lonja, the academy of fine arts in the same city. Upon completing three years of art studies he took a position as a clerk. After suffering a nervous breakdown he abandoned business and resumed his art studies, attending Francesc Galí's Escola d'Art in Barcelona from 1912 to 1915. Miró received early encouragement from the dealer José Dalmau, who gave him his first solo show at his gallery in Barcelona in 1918. In 1917 he met Francis Picabia.

In 1919 Miró made his first trip to Paris, where he met Pablo Picasso. From 1920 Miró divided his time between Paris and Montroig. In Paris he associated with the poets Max Jacob, Pierre Reverdy, and Tristan Tzara and participated in Dada activities. Dalmau organized Miró's first solo show in Paris, at the Galerie la Licorne in 1921. His work was included in the Salon d'Automne of 1923. In 1924 Miró joined the Surrealist group. His solo show at the Galerie Pierre in Paris in 1925 was a major Surrealist event; Miró was included in the first Surrealist exhibition at the Galerie Pierre that same year. He visited the Netherlands in 1928 and began a series of paintings inspired by Dutch masters. This year he also executed his first papiers collés and collages. In 1929 he started his experiments in lithography, and his first etchings date from 1933. During the early 1930s he made Surrealist sculpture-objects incorporating painted stones and found objects. In 1936 Miró left Spain because of the Civil War; he returned in 1941.

An important Miró retrospective was held at the Museum of Modern Art in New York in 1941. That year Miró began working in ceramics with Josep Lloréns i Artigas and started to concentrate on prints; from 1954 to 1958 he worked almost exclusively in these two mediums. In 1958 Miró was given a Guggenheim International Award for murals for the UNESCO Building in Paris; the following year he resumed painting, initiating a series of mural-sized canvases. During the 1960s he began to work intensively in sculpture. A major Miró retrospective took place at the Grand Palais in Paris in 1974. In 1978 the Musée National d'Art Moderne, Centre Georges Pompidou, Paris, exhibited over five hundred works in a major retrospective of his drawings. Miró died on December 25, 1983, in Palma de Mallorca, Spain.

PIET MONDRIAN

1872–1944

Piet Mondrian was born Pieter Cornelis Mondriaan, Jr., on March 7, 1872, in Amersfoort, the Netherlands. He studied at the Rijksakademie van Beeldende Kunsten, Amsterdam, from 1892 to 1897. Until 1908, when he began to take annual trips to Domburg in Zeeland, Mondrian's work was naturalistic—incorporating successive influences of academic landscape and still-life painting, Dutch Impressionism, and Symbolism. In 1909 a major exhibition of his work (with that of Jan Sluyters and C. R. H. Spoor) was held at the Stedelijk Museum, Amsterdam, and that same year he joined the Theosophic Society. In 1909 and 1910 he experimented with Pointillism and by 1911 had begun to work in a Cubist mode. After seeing original Cubist works by Georges Braque and Pablo Picasso at the first *Moderne Kunstkring* exhibition in 1911 in Amsterdam, Mondrian decided to move to Paris. In Paris from 1912 to 1914 he began to develop an independent abstract style.

Mondrian was visiting the Netherlands when World War I broke out and prevented his return to Paris. During the war years in Holland he further reduced his colors and geometric shapes and formulated his non-objective Neo-Plastic style. In 1917 Mondrian became one of the founders of De Stijl. This group, which included Theo van Doesburg and Georges Vantongerloo, extended its principles of abstraction and simplification beyond painting and sculpture to architecture and graphic and industrial design. Mondrian's essays on abstract art were published in the periodical *De Stijl*. In July 1919 he returned to Paris; there he exhibited with De Stijl in 1923, but withdrew from the group after van Doesburg reintroduced diagonal elements into his work around 1925. In 1930 Mondrian showed with Cercle et Carré (Circle and Square) and in 1931 joined Abstraction-Création.

World War II forced Mondrian to move to London in 1938 and then to settle in New York in October 1940. In New York he joined American Abstract Artists and continued to publish texts on Neo-Plasticism. His late style evolved significantly in response to the city. In 1942 his first solo show took place at the Valentine Dudensing Gallery, New York. Mondrian died on February 1, 1944, in New York. In 1971 the Solomon R. Guggenheim Museum organized a centennial exhibition of his work.

HENRY MOORE

1898–1987

Henry Spencer Moore was born on July 30, 1898, in Castleford, Yorkshire. Despite an early desire to become a sculptor, Moore began his career as a teacher in Castleford. After military service in World War I he attended Leeds School of Art on an ex-serviceman's grant. In 1921 he won a Royal Exhibition Scholarship to study sculpture at the Royal Academy of Art in London. Moore became interested in the Mexican, Egyptian, and African sculpture he saw at the British Museum. He was appointed Instructor of Sculpture at the Royal Academy in 1924, a post he held for the next seven years. A Royal Academy traveling scholarship allowed Moore to visit Italy in 1925; there he saw the frescoes of Giotto and Masaccio and the late sculpture of Michelangelo. Moore's first solo show of sculpture was held at the Warren Gallery, London, in 1928.

In the 1930s Moore was a member of Unit One, a group of advanced artists organized by Paul Nash, and was a close friend of Barbara Hepworth, Ben Nicholson, and the critic Herbert Read. From 1932 to 1939 he taught at the Chelsea School of Art. He was an important force in the English Surrealist movement, although he was not entirely committed to its doctrines; Moore participated in the *International Surrealist Exhibition* at the New Burlington Galleries, London, in 1936. In 1940 Moore was appointed an official war artist and was commissioned by the War Artists Advisory Committee to execute drawings of life in underground bomb shelters. From 1940 to 1943 the artist concentrated almost entirely on drawing. His first retrospective took place at Temple Newsam, Leeds, in 1941. In 1943 he received a commission from the Church of St. Matthew, Northampton, to carve a Madonna and Child; this sculpture was the first in an important series of family-group sculptures. Moore was given his first major retrospective abroad by the Museum of Modern Art, New York, in 1946. He won the International Prize for Sculpture at the Venice Biennale of 1948.

Moore executed several important public commissions in the 1950s, among them *Reclining Figure*, 1956–58, for the UNESCO Building in Paris. In 1963 the artist was awarded the British Order of Merit. In 1978 an exhibition of his work organized by the Arts Council of Great Britain was held at the Serpentine in London, at which time he gave many of his sculptures to the Tate Gallery, London. Moore died in Much Hadham, Hertfordshire, on August 31, 1986.

ROBERT MOTHERWELL

1915–1991

Robert Motherwell was born on January 4, 1915, in Aberdeen, Washington. He was awarded a fellowship to the Otis Art Institute in Los Angeles at age eleven, and in 1932 studied painting briefly at the California School of Fine Arts in San Francisco. Motherwell received a B.A. from Stanford University in 1937 and enrolled for graduate work later that year in the Department of Philosophy at Harvard University, Cambridge, Massachusetts. He traveled to Europe in 1938 for a year of study abroad. His first solo show was presented at the Raymond Duncan Gallery in Paris in 1939.

In September of 1940 Motherwell settled in New York City, where he entered Columbia University to study art history with Meyer Schapiro, who encouraged him to become a painter. In 1941 Motherwell traveled to Mexico with Matta for six months. After returning to New York, his circle came to include William Baziotes, Willem de Kooning, Hans Hofmann, and Jackson Pollock. In 1942 Motherwell was included in the exhibition *First Papers of Surrealism* at the Whitelaw Reid Mansion, New York. In 1944 Motherwell became editor of the Documents of Modern Art series of books, and he contributed frequently to the literature on Modern art from that time.

A solo exhibition of Motherwell's work was held at Art of This Century in 1944. In 1946 he began to associate with Herbert Ferber, Barnett Newman, and Mark Rothko, and spent his first summer in East Hampton, Long Island. This year Motherwell was given solo exhibitions at the Arts Club of Chicago and the San Francisco Museum of Art, and he participated in *Fourteen Americans* at the Museum of Modern Art in New York. The artist subsequently taught and lectured throughout the United States, and continued to exhibit extensively in the United States and abroad. A Motherwell exhibition took place at the Städtische Kunsthalle, Düsseldorf, the Museum des 20. Jahrhunderts, Vienna, and the Musée d'Art Moderne de la Ville de Paris in 1976–77. He was given important solo exhibitions at the Royal Academy, London, and the National Gallery, Washington, D.C., in 1978. A retrospective of his works organized by the Albright-Knox Art Gallery, Buffalo, traveled in the United States from 1983 to 1985. From 1971 the artist lived and worked in Greenwich, Connecticut. He died on July 16, 1991, in Cape Cod, Massachusetts.

BEN NICHOLSON

1894–1982

Ben Nicholson was born on April 10, 1894, in Denham, Buckinghamshire, England. Both his parents were painters. Nicholson attended the Slade School of Fine Art in London in 1910–11; between 1911 and 1914 he traveled in France, Italy, and Spain. He lived briefly in Pasadena, California, in 1917–18. His first solo show was held at the Adelphi Gallery in London in 1922. Shortly thereafter he began abstract paintings influenced by Synthetic Cubism. By 1927 he had initiated a primitive style inspired by Henri Rousseau and early English folk art.

From 1931 Nicholson lived in London; his association with Barbara Hepworth and Henry Moore dates from this period. In 1932 he and Hepworth visited Jean Arp, Constantin Brancusi, Georges Braque, and Pablo Picasso in France. Jean Hélion and Auguste Herbin encouraged them to join Abstraction-Création in 1933. Nicholson made his first wood relief in 1933; the following year he met Piet Mondrian and married Hepworth. In 1937 Nicholson edited *Circle: International Survey of Constructivist Art*, which he had conceived in 1935.

After moving to Cornwall in 1939 the artist resumed painting landscapes and added color to his abstract reliefs. In 1945–46 he turned from reliefs to linear, abstract paintings. Nicholson was commissioned to paint a mural for the Time-Life Building in London in 1952. He was given retrospectives at the Venice Biennale in 1954, and at the Tate Gallery, London, and the Stedelijk Museum, Amsterdam, in 1955. Nicholson moved to Castagnola, Ticino canton, Switzerland, in 1958 and began to concentrate once more on painted reliefs. In 1964 he made a concrete wall relief for the Documenta III exhibition in Kassel, Germany, and in 1968 was awarded the Order of Merit by Queen Elizabeth. The Albright-Knox Art Gallery, Buffalo, organized a retrospective of his work in 1978. Ben Nicholson died on February 6, 1982, in London.

AMÉDÉE OZENFANT

1886–1966

Amédée J. Ozenfant was born on April 15, 1886, in Saint-Quentin, Aisne, France. At age fourteen he began painting, and in 1904 he attended the Ecole Municipale de Dessin Quentin-La Tour in Saint-Quentin. The following year Ozenfant moved to Paris, where he entered an architecture studio. At this time he also studied painting with Charles Cottet at the Académie de la Palette, where he became a friend of Roger de La Fresnaye and André Dunoyer de Segonzac.

Ozenfant's first solo exhibition was held in 1908 at the Salon de la Nationale in Paris. In 1910 he contributed works to the Salon d'Automne and in 1911 he participated in the Salon des Indépendants. From about 1909 to 1913 he made trips to Russia, Italy, Belgium, and the Netherlands and attended lectures at the Collège de France in Paris. In 1915 Ozenfant founded the magazine L'Elan, which he edited until 1917, and began to formulate his theories of Purism. In 1917 the artist met the Swiss architect and painter Charles-Edouard Jeanneret (Le Corbusier); together they articulated the doctrines of Purism in their book Après le cubisme. Its publication coincided with the first Purist exhibition, held at the Galerie Thomas in Paris in 1917, in which Ozenfant was represented. Ozenfant and Le Corbusier collaborated on the journal L'Esprit nouveau, which appeared from 1920 to 1925.

Ozenfant participated in the second Purist exhibition at the Galerie Druet, Paris, in 1921. In 1924 he and Fernand Léger opened a free studio in Paris, where they taught with Alexandra Exter and Marie Laurencin. Ozenfant and Le Corbusier wrote La Peinture moderne in 1925. During that year Ozenfant exhibited at the controversial Pavillon de l'Esprit Nouveau at the Exposition des arts décoratifs in Paris. The artist was given a solo show at Galerie L. C. Hodebert, Paris, in 1928. His book Art was published in French in 1928; an English edition appeared as The Foundations of Modern Art in 1931. Ozenfant taught at the Académie Moderne in 1929 and founded the Académie Ozenfant in 1932. From 1935 to 1938 he operated the Ozenfant Academy in London, also teaching at the French Institute in that city. From 1939 to 1955 he taught at the Ozenfant School of Fine Arts in New York. His solo show at the Arts Club of Chicago was held in 1940. Ozenfant taught and lectured widely in the United States until 1955, when he returned to France. He remained there the rest of his life and died in Cannes on May 4, 1966.

ANTOINE PEVSNER

1884–1962

Antoine Pevsner was born on January 18, 1884, in Orel, Russia. After leaving the Academy of Fine Arts in St. Petersburg in 1911, he traveled to Paris where he saw the work of Robert Delaunay, Albert Gleizes, Fernand Léger, and Jean Metzinger. On a second visit to Paris in 1913 he met Amedeo Modigliani and Alexander Archipenko, who encouraged his interest in Cubism. Pevsner spent the war years 1915–17 in Oslo with his brother Naum Gabo. On his return to Russia in 1917 Pevsner began teaching at the Moscow Academy of Fine Arts with Vasily Kandinsky and Kazimir Malevich.

In 1920 he and Gabo published the Realistic Manifesto. Their work was included in the Erste russische Kunstausstellung at the Galerie van Diemen in Berlin in 1922, held under the auspices of the Soviet government. The following year Pevsner visited Berlin, where he met Marcel Duchamp and Katherine Dreier. He then traveled on to Paris, where he settled permanently; in 1930 he became a French citizen. His work was included in an exhibition at the Little Review Gallery in New York in 1926. He and Gabo designed sets for the ballet La Chatte, produced by Sergei Diaghilev in 1927. In Paris the two brothers were leaders of the Constructivist members of Abstraction-Création, an alliance of artists who embraced a variety of abstract styles.

During the 1930s Pevsner's work was shown in Amsterdam, Basel, London, New York, and Chicago. In 1946 he, Gleizes, Auguste Herbin, and others formed the group Réalités Nouvelles; their first exhibition was held at the Salon des Réalités Nouvelles in Paris in 1947. That same year Pevsner's first solo show opened at the Galerie René Drouin in Paris. The Museum of Modern Art in New York presented the exhibition Gabo-Pevsner in 1948, and in 1952 Pevsner participated in Chefs-d'oeuvre du XXe siècle at the Musée National d'Art Moderne in Paris. The same museum organized a solo exhibition of his work in 1957. In 1958 he was represented in the French Pavilion at the Venice Biennale. Pevsner died in Paris on April 12, 1962.

FRANCIS PICABIA

1879–1953

François Marie Martinez Picabia was born on or about January 22, 1879, in Paris, of a Spanish father and a French mother. He was enrolled at the Ecole des Arts Décoratifs in Paris from 1895 to 1897 and later studied with Fernand Cormon, Ferdinand Humbert, and Albert Charles Wallet. He began to paint in an Impressionist manner in the winter of 1902–03 and started to exhibit works in this style at the Salon d'Automne and the Salon des Indépendants of 1903. His first solo show was held at the Galerie Haussmann, Paris, in 1905. From 1908 elements of Fauvism and Neo-Impressionism as well as Cubism and other forms of abstraction appeared in his painting, and by 1912 he had evolved a personal amalgam of Cubism and Fauvism. Picabia worked in an abstract mode from this period until the early 1920s.

Picabia became a friend of Guillaume Apollinaire and Marcel Duchamp and associated with the Puteaux group in 1911 and 1912. He participated in the 1913 Armory Show, visiting New York on this occasion and frequenting avant-garde circles. Alfred Stieglitz gave him a solo exhibition at his gallery "291" that same year. In 1915, which marked the beginning of Picabia's machinist or mechanomorphic period, he and Duchamp, among others, instigated and participated in Dada manifestations in New York. Picabia lived in Barcelona in 1916 and 1917; in 1917 he published his first volume of poetry and the first issues of *391*, his magazine modeled after Stieglitz's periodical *291*. For the next few years Picabia remained involved with the Dadaists in Zurich and Paris, creating scandals at the Salon d'Automne, but finally denounced Dada in 1921 for no longer being "new." He moved to Tremblay-sur-Mauldre, outside of Paris, the following year and returned to figurative art. In 1924 he attacked André Breton and the Surrealists in *391*.

Picabia moved to Mougins in 1925. During the 1930s he became a close friend of Gertrude Stein. By the end of World War II Picabia returned to Paris. He resumed painting in an abstract style and writing poetry. In March 1949 a retrospective of his work was held at the Galerie René Drouin in Paris. Picabia died in Paris on November 30, 1953.

PABLO PICASSO

1881–1973

Pablo Ruiz y Picasso was born on October 25, 1881, in Málaga, Spain. The son of an academic painter, José Ruiz Blanco, he began to draw at an early age. In 1895 the family moved to Barcelona, and Picasso studied there at La Lonja, the academy of fine arts. His visit to Horta de Ebro from 1898 to 1899 and his association with the group at the café Els Quatre Gats about 1899 were crucial to his early artistic development. In 1900 Picasso's first exhibition took place in Barcelona, and that fall he went to Paris for the first of several stays during the early years of the century. Picasso settled in Paris in April 1904 and soon his circle of friends included Guillaume Apollinaire, Max Jacob, Gertrude and Leo Stein, as well as two dealers, Ambroise Vollard and Berthe Weill.

His style developed from the Blue Period (1901–04) to the Rose Period (1905) to the pivotal work *Les Demoiselles d'Avignon*, 1907, and the subsequent evolution of Cubism from 1909 into 1911. Picasso's collaboration on ballet and theatrical productions began in 1916. Soon thereafter his work was characterized by neoclassicism and a renewed interest in drawing and figural representation. In the 1920s the artist and his wife Olga (whom he had married in 1918) continued to live in Paris, to travel frequently, and to spend their summers at the beach. From 1925 into the 1930s Picasso was involved to a certain degree with the Surrealists and from the fall of 1931 he was especially interested in making sculpture. With large exhibitions at the Galeries Georges Petit in Paris and the Kunsthaus Zürich in 1932 and the publication of the first volume of Christian Zervos's catalogue raisonné the same year, Picasso's fame increased markedly.

By 1936 the Spanish Civil War had profoundly affected Picasso, the expression of which culminated in his painting *Guernica*, 1937. Picasso's association with the Communist party began in 1944. From the late 1940s he lived in the south of France. Among the enormous number of Picasso exhibitions that were held during the artist's lifetime, those at the Museum of Modern Art in New York in 1939 and the Musée des Arts Décoratifs in Paris in 1955 were most significant. In 1961 the artist married Jacqueline Roque, and they moved to Mougins. There Picasso continued his prolific work in painting, drawing, prints, ceramics, and sculpture until his death on April 8, 1973.

JACKSON POLLOCK

1912–1956

Paul Jackson Pollock was born January 28, 1912, in Cody, Wyoming. He grew up in Arizona and California and in 1928 began to study painting at the Manual Arts High School in Los Angeles. In the fall of 1930 Pollock came to New York and studied under Thomas Hart Benton at the Art Students League. Benton encouraged him throughout the succeeding decade. By the early 1930s Pollock knew and admired the murals of José Clemente Orozco and Diego Rivera. Although he traveled widely throughout the United States during the 1930s, much of Pollock's time was spent in New York, where he settled permanently in 1935 and worked on the WPA Federal Art Project from 1935 to 1942. In 1936 he worked in David Alfaro Siqueiros's experimental workshop in New York.

Pollock's first solo show was held at Peggy Guggenheim's Art of This Century gallery in New York in 1943. Guggenheim gave him a contract that lasted through 1947, permitting him to devote all his time to painting. Prior to 1947 Pollock's work reflected the influence of Picasso and Surrealism. During the early 1940s he contributed paintings to several exhibitions of Surrealist and abstract art, including *Natural, Insane, Surrealist Art* at Art of This Century in 1943, and *Abstract and Surrealist Art in America*, organized by Sidney Janis at the Mortimer Brandt Gallery in New York in 1944.

From the fall of 1945, when Lee Krasner and Pollock were married, they lived in the Springs, East Hampton. In 1952 Pollock's first solo show in Paris opened at the Studio Paul Facchetti and his first retrospective was organized by Clement Greenberg at Bennington College in Vermont. He was included in many group exhibitions, including the annuals at the Whitney Museum of American Art, New York, from 1946 and the Venice Biennale in 1950. Although his work was widely known and exhibited internationally, the artist never traveled outside the United States. He was killed in an automobile accident on August 11, 1956, in the Springs.

ARNALDO POMODORO

b. 1926

Arnaldo Pomodoro was born on June 23, 1926, in Morciano, Romagna, Italy. From the mid-1940s until 1957 he served as a consultant for the restoration of public buildings in Pesaro, while studying stage design and working as a goldsmith. In 1954 Pomodoro moved to Milan, where he met Enrico Baj, Sergio Dangelo, Prospero Fontana, and other artists. His work was first exhibited that year at the Galleria Numero in Florence and at the Galleria Montenapoleone in Milan. In 1955 his sculpture was shown for the first time at the Galleria del Naviglio in Milan.

Pomodoro visited New York in 1956 and traveled in Europe in 1958. In Paris in 1959 he met Alberto Giacometti and Georges Mathieu, before returning to the United States, where he organized exhibitions of contemporary Italian art at the Bolles Gallery in New York and San Francisco. In New York the following year Pomodoro met Louise Nevelson and David Smith. He helped found the Continuità group in Italy in 1961–62. The sculptor traveled to Brazil on the occasion of his participation in the 1963 São Paulo Bienal, where he was awarded the International Sculpture Prize. A solo show of his work was included in the Venice Biennale of 1964. In 1965 he was given the first of many solo exhibitions at the Marlborough galleries in New York and Rome.

The artist taught at Stanford University in California in 1966. In 1967 Pomodoro was represented in the Italian Pavilion at *Expo '67* in Montreal, and he received a prize at the Carnegie International in Pittsburgh. In 1968 he taught at the University of California at Berkeley; in 1970 he returned to Berkeley to attend the opening of an exhibition of his work that originated there and later traveled in the United States. During the late 1960s and early 1970s he executed commissions for outdoor sculpture in Darmstadt, New York, and Milan. In 1975 a Pomodoro retrospective was sponsored by the Municipality of Milan at the Rotonda della Besana. Pomodoro lives and works in Milan.

GERMAINE RICHIER

1902–1959

Germaine Richier was born in Grans, Bouches-du-Rhône, France, on September 16, 1902. After six years at the Ecole des Beaux-Arts in Montpellier, she moved to Paris in 1926, where she studied privately with Antoine Bourdelle from 1927 to 1929. Her first solo exhibition was held at the Galerie Max Kaganovitch in Paris in 1934. Richier was granted a sculpture prize in 1936 by the Blumenthal Foundation in New York and in 1937 took part in the Paris World's Fair, where she received an award. Also in 1937 she participated in an exhibition of European women artists at the Musée du Jeu de Paume in Paris. Richier showed with Pierre Bonnard, Georges Braque, Marc Chagall, Robert Delaunay, André Derain, Jacques Lipchitz, and others in the French Pavilion at the 1939 World's Fair in New York.

Richier lived primarily in Switzerland and Provence during World War II. In Switzerland she exhibited at the Kunstmuseum Winterthur in 1942 and shared an exhibition with Arnold d'Altri, Marino Marini, and Fritz Wotruba, at the Kunstmuseum Basel in 1944. After her return to Paris in 1946 she developed her metamorphic imagery. She became increasingly well-known after the war and during the late 1940s and the 1950s exhibited widely in the United States and Europe. Her work was represented at the Venice Biennale in 1948, 1952, and 1954. In 1948 she exhibited with Jean Arp and Henri Laurens at the Galerie d'Art Moderne in Basel and was given an important solo show at the Galerie Maeght in Paris. She executed a Crucifixion for the church of Assy in 1950. Richier was awarded a sculpture prize in 1951 at the São Paulo Bienal. Following an important retrospective at the Musée National d'Art Moderne in Paris in 1956, she settled again in Provence. The next year her first solo show in New York took place at the Martha Jackson Gallery. In 1958 Richier participated in group exhibitions at the Kunsthalle Bern and the Musée Rodin, Paris, and was given her first solo presentation in an American museum at the Walker Art Center in Minneapolis. She returned to Paris in 1959, visiting Antibes that summer on the occasion of her solo exhibition at the Musée Grimaldi, Château d'Antibes. Richier died in Montpellier on July 31, 1959.

MARK ROTHKO

1903–1970

Marcus Rothkowitz was born in Dvinsk, Russia, on September 25, 1903. In 1913 he left Russia and settled with the rest of his family in Portland, Oregon. Rothko attended Yale University in New Haven on a scholarship from 1921 to 1923. That year he left Yale without receiving a degree and moved to New York. In 1925 he studied under Max Weber at the Art Students League. He participated in his first group exhibition at the Opportunity Galleries in New York in 1928. During the early 1930s Rothko became a close friend of Milton Avery and Adolph Gottlieb. His first solo show took place at the Portland Art Museum in 1933.

Rothko's first solo exhibition in New York was held at the Contemporary Arts Gallery in 1933. In 1935 he was a founding member of the Ten, a group of artists sympathetic to abstraction and expressionism. He executed easel paintings for the WPA Federal Art Project from 1936 to 1937. By 1936 Rothko knew Barnett Newman. In the early forties he worked closely with Gottlieb, developing a painting style with mythological content, simple flat shapes, and imagery inspired by primitive art. By mid-decade his work incorporated Surrealist techniques and images. Peggy Guggenheim gave Rothko a solo show at Art of This Century in New York in 1945.

In 1947 and 1949 Rothko taught at the California School of Fine Arts, San Francisco, where Clyfford Still was a fellow instructor. With William Baziotes, David Hare, and Robert Motherwell, Rothko founded the short-lived the Subjects of the Artist school in New York in 1948. The late forties and early fifties saw the emergence of Rothko's mature style in which frontal, luminous rectangles seem to hover on the canvas surface. In 1958 the artist began his first commission, monumental paintings for the Four Seasons Restaurant in New York. The Museum of Modern Art, New York, gave Rothko an important solo exhibition in 1961. He completed murals for Harvard University in 1962 and in 1964 accepted a mural commission for an interdenominational chapel in Houston. Rothko took his own life in his New York studio on February 25, 1970. A year later the Rothko Chapel in Houston was dedicated.

GIUSEPPE SANTOMASO

b. 1907

Giuseppe Santomaso was born in Venice on September 26, 1907. He studied at the Accademia di Belle Arti there from 1932 to 1934. In 1938 he began his work in graphics, a medium that continues to interest him. In 1939 the artist traveled to Paris on the occasion of his first solo exhibition at the Galerie Rive Gauche. Santomaso participated in the Quadriennale of Rome in 1943 and executed illustrations for Paul Eluard's *Grand Air* in 1945. In 1946 he was a founding member of the antifascist artists' organization Nuova Secessione Artistica Italiana—Fronte Nuovo delle Arti in Venice.

Since 1948 Santomaso has participated often in the Venice Biennale, where he was awarded the Prize of the Municipality of Venice in 1948 and First Prize for Italian Painting in 1954. He received the Graziano Prize from the Galleria del Naviglio in Milan in 1956 and the Marzotto Prize at the *Mostra internazionale di pittura contemporanea* in Valdagno in 1958, among other awards. Santomaso taught at the Accademia di Belle Arti in Venice from 1957 to 1975. His first exhibition in the United States was held at the Grace Borgenicht Gallery in New York in 1957. The Stedelijk Museum in Amsterdam gave the artist a solo exhibition in 1960. In 1961 he participated in the São Paulo Bienal and he traveled to Brazil the following year. A Santomaso retrospective toured from the Kunstverein in Hamburg to the Haus am Lützowplatz in Berlin and the Museum am Ostwall in Dortmund in 1965–66. He contributed lithographs to *On Angle*, a book of Ezra Pound's poetry published in 1971. His work appeared in the International Engraving Biennial in Cracow in 1972 and 1978. Solo exhibitions of his work were presented in 1979 by the Fondacio Joan Miró in Barcelona and the Staatsgalerie Moderner Kunst in Munich. The Borgenicht Gallery organized a Santomaso show for the spring of 1983. The artist continues to live in Venice.

KURT SCHWITTERS

1887–1948

Herman Edward Karl Julius Schwitters was born in Hannover on June 20, 1887. He attended the Kunstgewerbeschule in Hannover from 1908 to 1909 and from 1909 to 1914 studied at the Kunstakademie Dresden. After serving as a draftsman in the military in 1917, Schwitters experimented with Cubist and Expressionist styles. In 1918 he made his first collages and in 1919 invented the term "Merz," which he was to apply to all his creative activities: poetry as well as collage and constructions. This year also marked the beginning of his friendships with Jean Arp and Raoul Hausmann. Schwitters's earliest *Merzbilder* date from 1919, the year of his first exhibition at Der Sturm gallery, Berlin, and the first publication of his writings in the periodical *Der Sturm*. Schwitters showed at the Société Anonyme in New York in 1920.

With Arp he attended the *Kongress der Konstructivisten* in Weimar in 1922. There Schwitters met Theo van Doesburg, whose De Stijl principles influenced his work. Schwitters's Dada activities included his *Merz-Matineen* and *Merz-Abende* at which he presented his poetry. From 1923 to 1932 he published the magazine *Merz*. About 1923 the artist started to make his first *Merzbau*, a fantastic structure he built over a number of years; the *Merzbau* grew to occupy much of his Hannover studio. During this period he also worked in typography. Schwitters was included in the exhibition *Abstrakte und surrealistische Malerei und Plastik* at the Kunsthaus Zürich in 1929. The artist contributed to the Parisian review *Cercle et Carré* in 1930; in 1932 he joined the Paris-based Abstraction-Création group and wrote for their organ of the same name. He participated in the *Cubism and Abstract Art* and *Fantastic Art, Dada, Surrealism* exhibitions of 1936 at the Museum of Modern Art, New York.

The Nazi regime banned Schwitters's work as "degenerate art" in 1937. This year the artist fled to Lysaker, Norway, where he constructed a second *Merzbau*. After the German invasion of Norway in 1940, Schwitters escaped to Great Britain, where he was interned for over a year. He settled in London following his release, but moved to Little Langdale in the Lake District in 1945. There, helped by a stipend from the Museum of Modern Art, he began work on a third *Merzbau* in 1947. The project was left unfinished when Schwitters died on January 8, 1948, in Kendal, England.

GINO SEVERINI

1883–1966

Gino Severini was born on April 7, 1883, in Cortona, Italy. He studied at the Scuola Tecnica in Cortona before moving to Rome in 1899. There he attended art classes at the Villa Medici and by 1901 met Umberto Boccioni, who had also recently arrived in Rome and later would be one of the theoreticians of Futurism. Together Severini and Boccioni visited the studio of Giacomo Balla where they were introduced to painting with "divided" rather than mixed color. After settling in Paris in November 1906, Severini studied Impressionist painting and met the Neo-Impressionist Paul Signac.

Severini soon came to know most of the Parisian avant-garde, including Georges Braque, Juan Gris, Amedeo Modigliani, and Pablo Picasso, Lugné-Poë and his theatrical circle, the poets Guillaume Apollinaire, Paul Fort, and Max Jacob, and author Jules Romains. After joining the Futurist movement at the invitation of Filippo Tommaso Marinetti and Boccioni, Severini signed the *Manifesto tecnico della pittura futurista* of April 1910, along with Balla, Boccioni, Carlo Carrà, and Luigi Russolo. However, Severini was less attracted to the subject of the machine than his fellow Futurists and frequently chose the form of the dancer to express Futurist theories of dynamism in art.

Severini helped organize the first Futurist exhibition at Bernheim-Jeune, Paris, in February 1912, and participated in subsequent Futurist shows in Europe and the United States. In 1913 he had solo exhibitions at the Marlborough Gallery, London, and Der Sturm, Berlin. During the Futurist period Severini acted as an important link between artists in France and Italy. After his last truly Futurist works—a series of paintings on war themes—Severini painted in a Synthetic Cubist mode, and by 1920 he was applying theories of classical balance based on the Golden Section to figurative subjects from the traditional commedia dell'arte. He divided his time between Paris and Rome after 1920. He explored fresco and mosaic techniques and executed murals in various mediums in Switzerland, France, and Italy during the 1920s. In the 1950s he returned to the subjects of his Futurist years: dancers, light, and movement. Throughout his career Severini published important theoretical essays and books on art. Severini died in Paris on February 26, 1966.

CLYFFORD STILL

1904–1980

Clyfford Still was born in Grandin, North Dakota, on November 30, 1904. He attended Spokane University in Washington for a year in 1926, and again from 1931 to 1933. After graduation he taught at Washington State College in Pullman until 1941. Still spent the summers of 1934 and 1935 at the Trask Foundation (now Yaddo) in Saratoga Springs, New York. From 1941 to 1943 he worked in defense factories in California. In 1943 his first solo show took place at the San Francisco Museum of Art, and he met Mark Rothko in Berkeley at this time. The same year Still moved to Richmond, Virginia, where he taught at the Richmond Professional Institute.

When Still was in New York in 1945, Rothko introduced him to Peggy Guggenheim, who gave him a solo exhibition at her Art of This Century gallery in early 1946. Later that year the artist returned to San Francisco, where he taught for the next four years at the California School of Fine Arts. Solo exhibitions of his work were held at the Betty Parsons Gallery in New York in 1947, 1950, and 1951 and at the California Palace of the Legion of Honor in San Francisco in 1947. In New York in 1948 Still worked with Rothko and others on developing the concept of the school that became known as the Subjects of the Artist. He resettled in San Francisco for two years before returning again to New York. A major Still retrospective took place at the Albright Art Gallery, Buffalo, in 1959. In 1961 he settled on his farm near Westminster, Maryland.

Solo exhibitions of Still's paintings were presented by the Institute of Contemporary Art of the University of Pennsylvania in Philadelphia in 1963 and at the Marlborough-Gerson Gallery in New York in 1969–70. He received the Award of Merit for Painting in 1972 from the American Academy of Arts and Letters, of which he became a member in 1978, and the Skowhegan Medal for Painting and Sculpture in Maine in 1975. Also in 1975 a permanent installation of a group of his works opened at the San Francisco Museum of Modern Art. The Metropolitan Museum of Art in New York gave him a major exhibition in 1980; Still died on June 23 of that same year in Baltimore.

RUFINO TAMAYO

1899–1991

Rufino Tamayo was born on August 26, 1899, in Oaxaca, Mexico. Orphaned by 1911, he moved to Mexico City to live with an aunt who sent him to commercial school. Tamayo began taking drawing lessons in 1915 and by 1917 had left school to devote himself entirely to the study of art. In 1921 he was appointed head of the Department of Ethnographic Drawing at the Museo Nacional de Arqueología, Mexico City, where his duties included drawing pre-Colombian objects in the museum's collection. Tamayo integrated the forms and slaty tones of pre-Columbian ceramics into his early still lifes and portraits of Mexican men and women.

The first exhibition of Tamayo's work in the United States was held at the Weyhe Gallery, New York, in 1926. The first of his many mural commissions was given to him by the Escuela Nacional de Música in Mexico City in 1932. In 1936 the artist moved to New York, and throughout the late thirties and early forties the Valentine Gallery, New York, gave him shows. He taught for nine years, beginning in 1938, at the Dalton School in New York. In 1948 Tamayo's first retrospective took place at the Instituto de Bellas Artes, Mexico City. Tamayo was influenced by European Modernism during his stay in New York and when he traveled in Europe in 1957. In that year he settled in Paris, where he executed a mural for the UNESCO Building in 1958. Tamayo returned to Mexico City in 1964, making it his permanent home. The French government named him Chevalier and Officier de la Légion d'Honneur in 1956 and 1969, respectively, and he was the recipient of numerous other honors and awards. His work was exhibited internationally in group and solo shows. Important Tamayo retrospectives took place at the São Paulo Bienal in 1977 and the Solomon R. Guggenheim Museum, New York, in 1979. He died in Mexico City on June 24, 1991.

TANCREDI

1927–1964

Tancredi Parmeggiani was born on September 25, 1927, in Feltre, Belluno, Italy. He became a friend of Emilio Vedova while studying at the Accademia di Belle Arti in Venice in 1946. The following year he visited Paris. From 1948 to 1949 he divided his time between Venice and Feltre. His first solo show took place at the Galleria Sandri in Venice in 1949. Tancredi moved in 1950 to Rome, where he associated with the Age d'Or group, which sponsored exhibitions and publications of the international avant-garde. He participated in an exhibition of abstract Italian art at the Galleria Nazionale d'Arte Moderna in Rome in 1951. That year the artist settled in Venice, where he met Peggy Guggenheim, who gave him studio space and exhibited his work in her palazzo in 1954. He was awarded the Graziano Prize for painting in Venice in 1952.

In 1952 Tancredi and others signed the manifesto of the Movimento Spaziale, a group founded by Lucio Fontana in Milan about 1947 advocating a new "spatial" art appropriate to the postwar era. He was given solo exhibitions at the Galleria del Cavallino in Venice in 1952, 1953, 1956, and 1959, and at the Galleria del Naviglio in Milan in 1953. In 1954 he participated in *Tendances actuelles* with Georges Mathieu, Jackson Pollock, Wols, and others at the Kunsthalle Bern. His work was included in a group show in 1955 at the Galerie Stadler in Paris, a city he visited that year. In 1958 Tancredi was given solo exhibitions at the Saidenberg Gallery in New York and the Hanover Gallery in London, and he took part in the Carnegie International in Pittsburgh. In 1959 he settled in Milan, where he showed several times at the Galleria dell'Ariete. That same year Tancredi traveled again to Paris and in 1960 he visited Norway. Also in 1960 the painter participated in the exhibition *Anti-Procès* at the Galleria del Canale in Venice; the gallery gave him solo shows this year and in 1962. He received the Marzotto Prize in Valdagno, Italy, in 1962 and exhibited at the Venice Biennale in 1964. Tancredi committed suicide in Rome on September 27, 1964.

YVES TANGUY

1900–1955

Raymond Georges Yves Tanguy was born on January 5, 1900, in Paris. While attending lycée during the 1910s, he met Pierre Matisse, his future dealer and lifelong friend. In 1918 he joined the Merchant Marine and traveled to Africa, South America, and England. During military service at Lunéville in 1920, Tanguy became a friend of the poet Jacques Prévert. He returned to Paris in 1922 after volunteer service in Tunis and began sketching café scenes that were praised by Maurice de Vlaminck. After Tanguy saw Giorgio de Chirico's work in 1923, he decided to become a painter. In 1924, he, Prévert, and Marcel Duhamel moved into a house that was to become a gathering place for the Surrealists. Tanguy became interested in Surrealism in 1924, when he saw the periodical *La Révolution surréaliste.* André Breton welcomed him into the Surrealist group the following year.

Despite his lack of formal training, Tanguy's art developed quickly and his mature style emerged by 1927. His first solo show was held in 1927 at the Galerie Surréaliste in Paris. In 1928 he participated with Jean Arp, Max Ernst, André Masson, Joan Miró, Pablo Picasso, and others in the Surrealist exhibition at the Galerie au Sacre du Printemps, Paris. Tanguy incorporated into his work the images of geological formations he had observed during a trip to Africa in 1930. He exhibited extensively during the 1930s in solo and Surrealist group shows in New York, Brussels, Paris, and London.

In 1939 Tanguy met the painter Kay Sage in Paris and later that year traveled with her to the American Southwest. They married in 1940 and settled in Woodbury, Connecticut. In 1942 Tanguy participated in the *Artists in Exile* show at the Pierre Matisse Gallery in New York, where he exhibited frequently until 1950. In 1947 his work was included in the exhibition *Le Surréalisme en 1947,* organized by Breton and Marcel Duchamp at the Galerie Maeght in Paris. He became a United States citizen in 1948. In 1953 he visited Rome, Milan, and Paris on the occasion of his solo shows in those cities. The following year he shared an exhibition with Kay Sage at the Wadsworth Atheneum in Hartford and appeared in Hans Richter's film *8 x 8.* A retrospective of Tanguy's work was held at the Museum of Modern Art in New York eight months after his death on January 15, 1955, in Woodbury.

THEO VAN DOESBURG

1883–1931

Christian Emil Marie Küpper, who adopted the pseudonym Theo van Doesburg, was born in Utrecht, the Netherlands, on August 30, 1883. His first exhibition of paintings was held in 1908 in the Hague. In the early 1910s he wrote poetry and established himself as an art critic. From 1914 to 1916 van Doesburg served in the Dutch army, after which time he settled in Leiden and began his collaboration with the architects J. J. P. Oud and Jan Wils. In 1917 they founded the group De Stijl and the periodical of the same name; other original members were Vilmos Huszár, Piet Mondrian, Bart van der Leck, and Georges Vantongerloo. Van Doesburg executed decorations for Oud's *De Vonk* project in Noordwijkerhout in 1917.

In 1920 he resumed his writing, using the pen name I. K. Bonset and later Aldo Camini. Van Doesburg visited Berlin and Weimar in 1921 and the following year taught at the Weimar Bauhaus, where he associated with Raoul Hausmann, Le Corbusier, Ludwig Mies van der Rohe, and Hans Richter. He was interested in Dada at this time and worked with Kurt Schwitters as well as Jean Arp, Tristan Tzara, and others on the review *Mécano* in 1922. Exhibitions of the architectural designs of Gerrit Rietveld, van Doesburg, and Cor van Eesteren were held in Paris in 1923 at Léonce Rosenberg's Galerie l'Effort Moderne and in 1924 at the Ecole Spéciale d'Architecture.

The Landesmuseum of Weimar presented a solo show of van Doesburg's work in 1924. That same year he lectured on modern literature in Prague, Vienna, and Hannover, and the Bauhaus published his *Grundbegriffe der neuen gestaltenden Kunst (Principles of Neo-Plastic Art).* A new phase of De Stijl was declared by van Doesburg in his manifesto of "Elementarism," published in 1926. During that year he collaborated with Arp and Sophie Taeuber-Arp on the decoration of the restaurant-cabaret L'Aubette in Strasbourg. Van Doesburg returned to Paris in 1929 and began working on a house at Meudon-Val-Fleury with van Eesteren. Also in that year he published the first issue of *Art concret,* the organ of the Paris-based group of the same name. Van Doesburg was the moving force behind the formation of the group Abstraction-Création in Paris. The artist died on March 7, 1931, in Davos, Switzerland.

GEORGES VANTONGERLOO

1886–1965

Georges Vantongerloo was born on November 24, 1886, in Antwerp. He studied about 1900 at the Académie des Beaux-Arts of Antwerp and of Brussels. He spent the years 1914–18 in the Netherlands, where his work attracted the attention of the queen. While working on architectural designs there, Vantongerloo met Piet Mondrian, Bart van der Leck, and Theo van Doesburg and collaborated with them on the magazine *De Stijl*, which was founded in 1917. Soon after his return to Brussels in 1918 he moved to Menton, France. In France he developed a close friendship with the artist and architect Max Bill, who was to organize many Vantongerloo exhibitions. In 1924 Vantongerloo published his pamphlet "L'Art et son avenir" in Antwerp.

In 1928 the artist-architect-theorist moved from Menton to Paris; there in 1931 he became vice-president of the artists' association Abstraction-Création, a position he held until 1937. His models of bridges and a proposed airport were exhibited at the Musée des Arts Décoratifs in Paris in 1930. In 1936 he participated in the exhibition *Cubism and Abstract Art* at the Museum of Modern Art in New York. His first solo show was held at the Galerie de Berri in Paris in 1943. Vantongerloo shared an exhibition with Max Bill and Antoine Pevsner in 1949 at the Kunsthaus Zürich. His seventy-fifth birthday was observed with a solo exhibition at the Galerie Suzanne Bollag in Zurich in 1961. The following year Bill organized a large Vantongerloo retrospective for the Marlborough New London Gallery in London. Vantongerloo died on October 5, 1965, in Paris.

EMILIO VEDOVA

b. 1919

Emilio Vedova was born on August 9, 1919, in Venice. He is essentially self-taught as an artist. About 1942 Vedova joined the Milanese anti-fascist artists' association Corrente, which also included Renato Birolli, Renato Guttuso, Ennio Morlotti, and Umberto Vittorini. Vedova participated in the Resistance movement throughout World War II. His first solo show took place at the Galleria la Spiga e Corrente in Milan in 1943. In 1946 he collaborated with Morlotti on the manifesto *Oltre Guernica* in Milan and was a founding member of the Nuova Secessione Artistica Italiana—Fronte Nuovo delle Arti in Venice. Solo exhibitions of Vedova's work took place at the Art Club of Rome in 1946 and the Galleria Cavallino in Venice in 1947.

In 1948 the artist participated in *Arte astratta in Italia* at the Galleria di Roma and in a presentation of the Fronte Nuovo group at the Venice Biennale. His first solo show in the United States was held at the Catherine Viviano Gallery in New York in 1951. In 1952 he participated in the *Gruppo degli otto pittori italiani*, organized by Lionello Venturi, and traveled to France. He visited Brazil in 1954 when his solo exhibition was presented at the Museu de Arte Moderna in Rio de Janeiro. Vedova was represented in the first Documenta in Kassel in 1955 and won a Guggenheim International Award in 1957. He executed his first lithographs in 1958, the year he went to Poland on the occasion of his retrospective at the Muzeum Narodowe in Poznań and the "Zachęta" in Warsaw. The artist traveled frequently during the 1960s and 1970s, visiting England, Scandinavia, Germany, Cuba, Yugoslavia, and the United States, where he has lectured extensively. In 1965 a Vedova retrospective took place at the Institute of Contemporary Art in Chicago. That summer he succeeded Oskar Kokoschka as head of the Internationale Sommerakademie für Bildende Kunst in Salzburg. In 1979 an exhibition of Vedova's graphics opened at the Art Gallery of Western Australia in Perth and toured Australia, and in 1982 he was given a solo show at the Stedelijk Van Abbemuseum in Eindhoven. Vedova lives and works in Venice, where he has taught at the Accademia di Belle Arti since 1975.

INDEX OF ARTISTS AND WORKS